W9-BMO-171

Roses
for
Michigan

Nancy Lindley
Laura Peters

Lone Pine Publishing

©2004 by Lone Pine Publishing
First printed in 2004   10 9 8 7 6 5 4 3 2 1

The Publisher: Lone Pine Publishing

10145 – 81 Avenue   1808 B Street NW, Suite 140
Edmonton, AB T6E 1W9   Auburn, WA
Canada   USA 98001

Website: http://www.lonepinepublishing.com

National Library of Canada Cataloguing in Publication
Lindley, Nancy, 1954–
    Roses for Michigan / Nancy Lindley, Laura Peters.

    Includes index.
    ISBN 1-55105-367-5

        1. Rose culture—Michigan. 2. Roses—Varieties—Michigan.
I. Peters, Laura, 1968– II. Title.

SB411.L55 2004   635.9'33734'09774   C2003-906013-6

Editorial Director: Nancy Foulds
Project Editor: Shelagh Kubish
Illustrations Coordinator: Carol Woo
Photo Editor: Don Williamson
Production Manager: Gene Longson
Book Design: Elliot Engley, Heather Markham
Cover Design: Gerry Dotto
Layout & Production: Curtis Pillipow
Illustrations: Ian Dawe
Hardiness Zones Map (based on USDA plant hardiness zones map): Curtis Pillipow

Photography: All photographs by Tamara Eder or Robert Ritchie except Agriculture Canada (Dr. Campbell G. Davidson) 140a&b, 166; Bailey Nursery Roses 22b, 132, 150, 234, 245a, 250; J.C. Bakker & Sons Nurseries 24b, 51a, 161a&b; Paul Barden 24c, 101a&b, 113, 121, 195, 208; Dee Choi 222; Conard-Pyle Roses 4, 48a, 53a, 114, 125, 127, 137, 159a&b, 177a, 185, 207, 238, 245; Saxon Holt 9a, 49b, 65, 94, 102, 110b, 116, 145, 190, 204a&b, 255; Jackson & Perkins 181, 183, 186, 259; Brad Jalbert 6a, 236a&b; Paul E. Jerabek 194a&b; Liz Klose 36, 58a&b, 59 (all), 67a&b, 68, 69, 70; Charles W. Lentz 23a, 97, 98; Norman R. Lightfoot/Eco Art Productions, Inc. 16b; George Mander 256; Jim Martin 235; Kim Patrick O'Leary 247a; Laura Peters 34a,b,c&d, 39, 40, 41 (all); Pickering Nurseries 30, 109, 117b, 217, 220; Poulsen Roser ApS 182; David Smith 100; Weeks Roses 1, 22a, 23c, 126, 142, 202, 233, 247b; Don Williamson 31, 87.

Front and back cover photographs by Tamara Eder and Robert Ritchie.

We acknowledge the financial support of the Government of Canada through the Book Publishing Industry Development Program (BPIDP) for our publishing activities.

PC: P1

CONTENTS

ACKNOWLEDGMENTS 4

INTRODUCTION 5

Hardiness Zones Map 8

ROSES IN HISTORY 10

ANATOMY & ROSE TERMINOLOGY 14

ROSES IN THE GARDEN 16

Landscape Uses 16

Rose Features 18

GETTING STARTED 27

Climate and Microclimate 27

Sun 28

Wind 28

Competition 28

Soil 29

BUYING ROSES 31

Grafted Plants 32

Own-root Plants 32

What to Look For 33

PLANTING ROSES 34

Preparing the Soil 34

When to Plant 35

Preparing the Rose 36

Preparing the Hole 38

Placing the Rose 38

Backfill 42

Protecting the Rose 43

Transplanting 43

Planting Methods for Different
Landscape Uses 44

CARING FOR ROSES 50

Watering 50

Mulching 53

Fertilizing 54

Pruning 58

Removing Rootstock Suckers 67

Deadheading 69

Winter Protection 70

PROPAGATION 73

PROBLEMS & PESTS 74

Glossary of Pests & Diseases 80

Other Problems 89

ABOUT THIS GUIDE 94

THE ROSES 95

RESOURCES 262

GLOSSARY 266

INDEX 268

Acknowledgments

We gratefully acknowledge all who were involved in this project. Thanks to local rose societies and gardening clubs for their sound advice and direction. We appreciate the work of our primary photographers, Tamara Eder and Robert Ritchie. Thanks to the people at the many beautiful public and private gardens and garden centers that provided the setting for photographs in this book. Special thanks are extended to the following individuals and organizations: American Rose Society, David Austin Roses, Ltd., Bailey Nursery, J.C. Bakker and Sons, Paul Barden, Dee Choi, Conard-Pyle Co., Campbell G. Davidson, Saxon Holt, Jackson and Perkins, Paul E. Jerabek, Liz Klose, Charles Lentz, George Mander, Jim Martin (Carolina Nurseries), Kim Patrick O'Leary, Pickering Nurseries, Poulsen Roses ApS and Weeks Roses.

I would like to thank my parents, Gary and Lucy Peters, for their love and support and my friends for their endless encouragement. It would have been impossible to begin this project without Don Williamson or complete it without Shelagh Kubish. Thanks to the entire Lone Pine team and to the growers and breeders, rosarians, gardeners and garden centers who shared their knowledge with me. I would like to thank Nancy Lindley for her contributions to this book. —*Laura Peters*

I would like to thank my husband, Roger, and the staff at Great Lakes Roses for their understanding and support. I would also like to thank my parents, Melvin E. and the late Helen E. Long, for teaching me the craft of writing. Thanks are due to numerous Michigan rosarians—Doug and Judy Bell, George Hartley, Jon and Lois Wier, Beverly and the late Morris Anderson, Marilyn Whittaker, Karen Schmidt, the late Dick Schmidt and the late Ruth Esler. Special thanks and appreciation, too, for the Michigan State University Department of Horticulture, MSU Extension and Master Gardeners throughout the state. —*Nancy Lindley*

INTRODUCTION

Among the most beautiful plants to grow, roses reward the gardener in many ways. Thought by many to be demanding and difficult, roses can in fact grow almost anywhere with the right combination of sun, water and care. This book showcases 144 of the best roses for Michigan gardens and contains all the information you need to get growing.

In most of Michigan, January is the coldest month and July the hottest. The average January temperature can range from 10°–15° F in Marquette and Sault Ste. Marie while the Lower Peninsula experiences an average 21° F. July temperatures average 64° F throughout the Upper Peninsula whereas Lower Peninsula temperatures are an average of 5–10 degrees higher, an increase most evident in Detroit, Grand Rapids, Lansing and throughout the Lower Peninsula. Cold winters allow a good period of dormancy, and an equally long and warm growing season allows the well-rested roses to grow and bloom prolifically. This general pattern, along with the good rainfall, makes Michigan a great place to grow a variety of roses.

Easy Going

There is a beautiful rose for every hardiness zone in Michigan.

Despite the overall similarities, conditions do vary within the state. Michigan has a population of roughly nine million; the coldest area, the Upper Peninsula, comprises a third of the state's total landmass but has only 300,000 residents. The Upper Peninsula generally receives 70 or fewer frost-free days per year and is in climatic zones 3a to 5b. In the colder areas of the Upper Peninsula and north-central parts of the Lower Peninsula, which are designated zone 3, winter temperatures can dip as low as –40° F. Northern Michigan gardeners frequently use very hardy roses to ensure successful results, but some gardeners bravely experiment with tender varieties as well, taking care to carefully mulch them in late fall.

The population and average annual temperatures increase as you travel south. The terrain changes as well, from the rocky, forested land of the north dominated by lakes to the occasional rolling hill, high bluff and sand dunes that border Lake Michigan.

Morden Ruby

The lakes can have a tempering influence on winter weather, giving the entire state warmer temperatures than other places at the same latitude. Although winter is cold across the state, the degree of snow cover varies. Snow cover is important because it provides excellent insulation for dormant woody plants, maintaining consistent soil temperatures and providing shelter from drying winds. Gardens near the lakes receive more snow than gardens farther inland. As well, northern gardeners are at an advantage because the consistently lower temperatures maintain the snow cover most winters. Gardens in southern Michigan are susceptible to freeze-thaw cycles and less consistent snow cover, killing more tender roses that might survive in a better insulated but colder garden. A thick layer of organic mulch will protect roses in gardens where snow cover is unreliable.

Madame Hardy

Spring is generally cool and moist. The last frost occurs between late April and late May, depending on where you are in Michigan. Spring weather is also affected by the lakes. In areas close to the lakes, the cool, wet spring weather may be drawn out. Newly planted roses can become well established during this cool spring weather, though initial bloom might be delayed. Farther inland the last frost may occur later, but warmer, drier weather may arrive at the same time or even sooner than it does for gardens closer to the lakes.

Summer tends to be hot and humid. Excessively hot days that may

Rosemary Harkness

Hardiness Zones Map

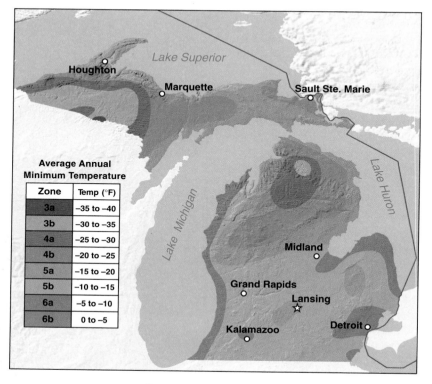

Zone	Temp (°F)
3a	−35 to −40
3b	−30 to −35
4a	−25 to −30
4b	−20 to −25
5a	−15 to −20
5b	−10 to −15
6a	−5 to −10
6b	0 to −5

Average Annual Minimum Temperature

stress roses can occur all over the state but are more common and frequent in the south. Both excessive rain and excessive drought can occur in summer, but vigilant gardeners can usually help their roses survive such summers. Good garden preparation will encourage a balance between moisture retention and drainage. Michigan does not receive enough rainfall, on average, for roses to really thrive. Mulch and other organic materials reduce evaporation and maintain moisture in the soil for longer periods as well, reducing the need to water. When planning a garden, gardeners should also consider how they will provide supplemental watering. Soaker hoses, snaked under the mulch, are a low-cost and effective way of augmenting rainfall.

Fall is a wonderful season for gardening in Michigan. Days are warm, nights are cool and rain is usually plentiful, providing ideal conditions for most roses. Though the first light frost can happen in September, some roses will continue to bloom up until the first hard frost. Gardens in southern Michigan may not see frost until well into October. It's not unheard-of to be enjoying roses well into November. Fall is an excellent time to plant roses; the warm soil and cool air temperatures encourage root development, not top growth.

Outstanding rose shows, public gardens, arboretums and show gardens in Detroit, Lansing, Ann Arbor, Grand Rapids and Midland attract gardeners from all over the world. The plants are usually labeled so you know what to buy if you want to try something in your own garden. Local rose societies are a wealth of information and inspiration for all rose gardeners, from the beginner to the enthusiast and the rosarian. Many Michigan gardeners have a detailed knowledge of planting and cultivation techniques, skill in identifying specific roses and plenty of passionate opinions on what is best for any little patch of ground. (For a list of rose societies and of gardens to visit, see Resources, p. 262.)

Open yourself to the possibilities, and you will be surprised by the diversity of roses that thrive in Michigan. Don't be afraid to try something different or new. Gardening with roses is fun and can be a great adventure. When the right rose is chosen for the right location and purpose, you should experience the fewest problems and the best success. Sometimes the rose world can be a little daunting, with all the potential disease and pest problems, but rarely will you ever experience more than one or two problems at one time. If your gardening efforts fail, try again, and remember that gardening is discovery, and without discovery there would be little beauty.

Jeanne Lajoie

Olympiad

Roses in History

Michigan rose gardeners today continue a long and venerable tradition of growing and enjoying these plants. Fossil evidence suggests roses flourished up to 32 million years ago; people have been cultivating roses for about 5000 years. Three roses—the gallica, alba and damask—are among the most ancient cultivated plants still grown today.

The ancient Romans used rose petals for medicine, perfume, garlands and wedding confetti. Roses were even consumed in puddings and desserts. Roman nobility sponsored large public rose gardens. Cleopatra covered the floors of her palace in a deep layer of fresh rose petals, and the sails of her barge were soaked in rose water. Rose water also flowed through the emperor's fountains, and pillows were stuffed with petals.

The use of rose oil—which can be found in cosmetics, perfumes and aromatherapy—began in ancient Persia. When it was discovered that rose water lasted indefinitely once bottled, people no longer had to surround themselves with bushels of roses for the wonderful fragrance; they merely had to open a bottle of rose water or the pure essential oil, also known as attar of roses.

Early Christians associated roses with pagan rites and the excesses of

William Lobb

the Romans. Any personal indulgence was considered sinful—including the ancient Roman practice of bathing in water scented with rose oil—and roses fell out of favor. Nevertheless, during the sixth century, St. Benedict planted a little rose garden, or Roseta, which became the model for monastic rose gardens through the Middle Ages. If not for the monastic gardens, some of the ancient roses might have died out.

In the 17th century, roses and rose water were in such demand that they could be used as legal tender to barter or pay for goods. In France, Napoleon transported gallons of violet and rose scents on his campaigns. It is said that during the Napoleonic Wars, ships carrying roses for Empress Josephine were given free and safe passage. Josephine's rose garden, created in the late 18th century at Malmaison, contained every rose known to exist at that time.

Rosa gallica versicolor

Emperor Nero had a party room with a painted ceiling resembling the heavens, which opened up, sprinkling perfume and flowers on the guests. At one such party, guests were said to have been smothered to death by the enormous quantity of rose petals that fell from the heavens.

Reine des Violettes

The ancient Greeks considered rose water more valuable than its weight in gold. The Roman Catholic Church used rose petals to make the beads for rosaries, hence the name.

The Victorians of the late 19th century were charmed by the rose, and roses began to appear in poetry and prose, representing virtue and innocence. The form of the modern rose garden, with its well-spaced plants and symmetry, arose in the 19th century.

The magnificent beauty of roses continues to inspire poetry, paintings and fragrances. Roses are still

Stanwell Perpetual

Roses decorated the crests of kings and princes in the 15th-century 'War of the Roses' between rivals for the English throne. The white rose symbolized the House of York, and the red rose symbolized the House of Lancaster.

A formal rose garden

bred at an astonishing rate, with over 20,000 cultivated varieties in existence. It's hard to imagine a day without roses, without their sweet fragrance and beauty, medicinal and practical uses and all these flowers represent. Roses are a wonderful part of our history and will no doubt always be a part of our future.

William Lobb

Hénri Martin

Tournament of Roses

A Greek legend attributes the creation of the rose to Flora, the goddess of spring and flowers. She found the lifeless body of one of her beautiful nymphs in the forest and asked the gods to give the creature new life by transforming her into a flower, one that surpassed all others in beauty. The request was granted, and the new flower was named Rose, Queen of Flowers.

Anatomy & Rose Terminology

Getting to know the parts and names associated with the rose is a good place for beginners to start. With a little practice you'll be speaking like a seasoned rosarian.

petal

bud

bract

hip (seedpod)

bud eye

sepals

true leaf (composed of five or more leaflets)

stem

lateral branch

stipule

leaflet

prickles (thorns)

Grafted Rose

Roses in the Garden

LANDSCAPE USES

Woody plants—trees and shrubs—are the foundation of your landscape. Roses are flowering shrubs and can be used in any situation that calls for a sun-loving shrub. Roses can even substitute for annuals and perennials in planting beds. Choose a rose that will work well in the situation you want to use it in. When choosing a rose for a certain purpose or location, consider its hardiness, disease resistance, height and spread, maintenance requirements, growth habit, flowering form and color. The following are landscape situations in which roses can be used to good effect.

Beds

Rose beds can be formal or informal. Formal rose beds are laid out in precise, geometric patterns that allow the maximum number of rose plants to fit in the beds. Roses with an upright growth habit and uniform height are chosen for beds. Variation in height is added by using standard, or tree, roses or by training small climbers on an obelisk. Formal rose beds are suitable for large gardens and cut-flower gardens. Roses may also be used as accents or features in formal gardens rather than devoting the entire beds to them.

Informal rose beds have no precise layout and often include other plants. The choice of which rose to use is limited only by your imagination. Informal style is good for border plantings. Planting roses, or any plants, in odd numbers will help create an informal, natural character.

Tournament of Roses

Niagara Parks Rose Garden

Hedges

Roses can be grown as informal (non-manicured) hedges using one or two rows of plants. Hedges using two rows usually have a staggered arrangement. Species and shrub roses, especially those that sucker, make good hedges. The suckers make the hedge thicker from the bottom up. Rose hedges make excellent barriers as they are nearly impenetrable once established. Do not plan to have a highly manicured rose hedge, as roses do not respond well to being sheared.

Groundcovers

If you have areas that need some color but are hard to plant or maintain, try low-growing or trailing roses. Trailing roses make the best groundcovers. They look good draping over retaining walls or steep slopes. Roses with dense growth can be effective for weed suppression. Begin with an area that is free of weeds for the best result.

Covering and Masking

Climbing, rambling and larger shrub roses can be used to cover structures such as pergolas, archways, fences, arbors, posts and buildings. Climbers and ramblers require a supporting structure solid enough to handle the weight of their flower-laden canes. It is best to choose a structure that won't require any maintenance, such as painting, over time because it can be tedious to unwind and detach the shoots from the support only to have to reattach the shoots again.

Informal planting in mixed bed

Hedge

Groundcover

Handel trained on a trellis

Lavaglut

Gourmet Popcorn

Accents

Beautiful roses, with their bright colors and wonderful fragrance, are useful accent plants, drawing attention to themselves and away from less attractive parts of your garden.

Containers

Roses grown in containers, such as planters and hanging baskets, can be used on a deck or balcony or in the garden. They bring the flowers and fragrance close to outdoor sitting areas where they can be enjoyed, and they are a good choice if space is limited. Miniature, polyantha and floribunda roses work well in containers. Standard roses are often grown in containers with shallow-rooted bedding plants. Containers can be used anywhere the growing conditions are right for good rose performance. Containers can be moved to a sunny position and then moved again for winter storage in an unheated shed, garage or cool greenhouse.

ROSE FEATURES

Before you go out rose buying, familiarize yourself with some of the different features and classes of roses. This book is divided into nine sections according to the classes of the roses. The sections are species, old garden, shrub, groundcover, climbers and ramblers, hybrid tea, floribunda, grandiflora and miniature. Each section begins with an explanation of the characteristics of the class.

Classification

Classifying roses is complex considering there are approximately 150 species and over 20,000 varieties and cultivars. Classification is becoming more difficult as rose hybridizing continues and hybridizers select breeding parents from a large number of possible candidates. Different groups of rosarians have tried to develop systems of classification that encompass all roses. The American Rose Society (ARS) recognizes 55 official classes, the British Association Representing Breeders recognizes 30 official classes and the World Federation of Rose Societies recognizes 39 official classes. In 1971, delegates to the World Rose Convention adopted a system dividing all roses into climbing and non-climbing classes and then further dividing them into recurrent and non-recurrent bloomers.

Adding to the complexity is that different groups classify roses for different purposes. Scientists classify roses according to the botanical characteristics of the flower and plant. The ARS classification system is most useful to those who exhibit roses in competitions. Nurseries and garden centers classify roses according to their growth habit and use in the landscape, a classification system most practical for the average rose gardener.

Rose societies around the world unite rose growers and disseminate information. Some of the most well-known include:
ARS   American Rose Society
RNRS   Royal National Rose Society
RHS   Royal Horticultural Society

The fragrant Double Delight

Abraham Darby

Fragrance

One of the most important features of roses is fragrance. The smell of a rose can reach you long before you see the plant. The fragrances can be sweet, spicy, fruity, musky or one of many other wonderful aromas. The petals usually produce the scent, but the leaves, stems and thorns may also be fragrant. For example, in the moss roses, fragrance comes from the hairs that cover the stems and bottoms of the flowers, as well as from the flowers themselves.

Many of the modern varieties, such as the hybrid teas and floribundas, have little or no scent at all. On the other hand, some of the most intense scents come from the modern varieties. Double Delight, for example, combines superb flower form and color with a strong fragrance. The English roses bred by David Austin Roses Ltd. (also known as Austin roses) combine rich, heady scents of the once-blooming antique and old garden roses with the repeat blooming of the modern varieties.

Double Delight petals can change to red over time.

Double flowers generally have more fragrance than single flowers, and the healthier the plant, the more intense the fragrance. The fragrance is strongest on bright, warm sunny days when the air is a little humid and the wind is light. The aroma is reduced on cloudy days and close to undetectable on rainy days. The best time to enjoy the aroma is when the blooms are just opening in the early morning, which is when roses are picked for the perfume industry.

Some of the older classes of roses such as damasks, gallicas, albas and bourbons have rich, complex aromas and are worth growing for this reason alone. If you want a fragrant rose, a good choice would be any of those listed at right and on the next page.

Evelyn

Blanc Double de Coubert

Martin Frobisher

Most Fragrant Roses
Abraham Darby
America
Blanc Double de Coubert
Constance Spry
Cuthbert Grant
Double Delight
Evelyn
Fantin-Latour
Folklore
Hénri Martin
Martin Frobisher
Rosa gallica versicolor
Rosarie de l'Haÿ
Rose de Rescht
Westerland

Gamble Fragrance Award Winners

- Crimson Glory
- Tiffany
- Chrysler Imperial
- Sutter's Gold
- Granada
- Fragrant Cloud
- Papa Meilland
- Sunsprite
- Double Delight
- Fragrant Hour
- Angel Face
- Secret

Betty Boop

The prestigious Gamble Fragrance Award is given to a rose that exhibits a good, strong fragrance but also has good vigor, good pest and disease resistance and good color and is a top seller for more than five years. To date there have been only 11 winners of this award, and these varieties are readily available.

Color

Flower color is the feature most people look for when buying and growing roses. Red, pink, yellow, orange, white, mauve, tan and apricot are a few of the colors available, and there is considerable range within each color. For example, pink roses range from light pastel pink to deep pink to vivid neon pink. Flowers can be blends of color including different shades of the same color or two different colors on the same flower—often referred to as a multi-colored flower. Rose petals can be almost every color except black, blue and green. There are roses that look black but are really very deep red. The green-flowered rose, *Rosa chinensis viridiflora*, has no true petals. The green petal-like sepals give the flower its color.

Flower color is affected by sunlight, temperature, soil and water. If your rose has the right environmental conditions and is healthy, you will almost be guaranteed gorgeous blooms.

The International Registration Authority for Roses, run by the ARS, authorizes 18 official colors for roses. Every new rose variety registered has to list one of the 18 official colors as its color. The color descriptions in

Hawkeye Belle

catalogs and some reference books (including this one) are generally more detailed than the official color listing. Breeders are also given latitude in color classification. For example, Dr. Griffith Buck registered his rose, Hawkeye Belle, as white although most people would consider it to be light pink.

Flower form

Roses have a variety of flower forms. One of the most familiar is the pointed hybrid tea flower, the classic rose shape we have come to expect when we give or receive florist roses. Other forms include the flat, single flowers of some species roses and the quartered rosette flowers of some old garden roses.

The terms *single, semi-double* and *double* refer to the number of petals and their arrangement on the flower. Single flowers have up to 12 petals arranged in a single row. Semi-double flowers have 13–20 petals arranged in two or three rows. Double flowers have 20 or more petals. Some sources list an additional category for flowers with 35 or more petals. These are called *very double* or *fully double* flowers.

The following are the different rose flower forms:

Flat: Open flowers that are single or semi-double with the petals perpendicular to the stem.

Cupped: Open flowers that are single or semi-double having petals that curve upward forming a shallow cup.

Flat form

Cupped form

Pointed form

Urn-shaped form

Rounded form

Rosette form

Quartered rosette form

Pompom form

Pointed: Semi-double to double flowers with high-pointed centers created by the tight wrap of petals before they fully unfurl. One of the most familiar forms.

Urn-shaped: Semi-double to double flowers with flat tops and slightly outward curving petals. Similar to the pointed shape but slightly looser and more open in the center.

Rounded: Double flowers with overlapping petals of even size, creating a rounded bowl silhouette.

Rosette: Double flowers with slightly overlapping, unevenly sized petals creating a flattish outline.

Quartered Rosette: Double flowers with petals of uneven size forming a quartered appearance and a flattish outline.

Pompom: Double flowers with many small petals forming a small, rounded outline.

Substance

Substance is the amount of moisture in the petals. It affects the texture, firmness, thickness, stability and durability of the petals. Roses have substance at different levels, and rose flowers with good substance have a long vase life.

Hips

Hips are the fruits of roses. They develop when flowers are pollinated, usually by bees. Hips can provide fall and winter interest. They ripen to shades of red, orange and yellow and come in a variety of shapes, from round and globe-like to football shaped to teardrop shaped.

The formation of hips and production of seeds in the hips signal the plant to stop flowering and to prepare for winter dormancy. Not all roses produce hips. In general, roses with lower petal counts are more likely to produce showy hips.

Hardiness

The hardiness of a plant is its ability to withstand climatic and other environmental conditions. Cold hardiness designates the plant's ability to survive the minimum average cold temperatures for an area. A rose's cold hardiness is a function of its genetics, not where it's grown. Some classes of roses, such as the rugosa roses, thrive with no winter protection in areas that get quite cold. Other roses are so tender that they are often grown as annuals and re-planted each year. Hardiness ratings are general, however. Other factors can affect what can and cannot successfully grow in a particular location based on exposure, winds and shelter. These areas are referred to as microclimates.

Rose hip (seedpod)

Standard rose (tree rose)

Plant form

Plant form is the shape and growth habit of the plant. The forms available today can be easily used in the garden and landscape. Growth can be upright, such as the hybrid teas with their straight, sturdy canes. Roses can also have graceful arching canes or they can be mounding shrubs that rival any of the flowering shrubs used in landscapes. Climbing and rambling roses produce long, supple canes that can be trained on trellises, fences and pillars or left alone to form large, spreading shrubs. Standards, also known as tree roses, have a lollipop look created by budding or grafting a rose plant onto a tall stem. Standards are also available in trailing or spreading forms, resulting in an umbrella-like appearance.

Foliage

Rose foliage can be delicate and fern-like with many leaflets per leaf, such as *Rosa pimpinellifolia,* or large and crinkled as in the rugosa roses. The leaves can be dull or shiny, and colors include dark green, light green or shades of blue-green and gray-green. Some roses have foliage with excellent fall color in shades of yellow, red and bronze-red. *Rosa glauca (Rosa rubrifolia)* is a rose with beautiful foliar color, bearing blue-green to purple foliage that dramatically contrasts with the pink flowers in season but is most stunning in fall.

Thorns

What we usually refer to as thorns are really prickles, defined botanically as small, thin, sharp outgrowths of the young bark, whereas thorns are sharp outgrowths from the wood of the stem. Rose prickles come in a variety of sizes and levels of nastiness. The prickles of *Rosa acicularis* (the Prickly Rose) are thin and sharp and cover the stems. The Wingthorn Rose, *Rosa sericea pteracantha,* has large, bright red, winged prickles, which provide color all year. Some roses, such as the climber New Dawn, have large, hooked barbs that make pruning a truly dangerous task. Regardless of the type of prickle, handling roses requires care and attention.

Rosa glauca

Rose foliage can vary in texture and color.

Thorns

Getting Started

Roses are not difficult to grow once you consider a few basics. Planning is essential, though. Good planning will allow you to plant the right rose in the right location for long-term success. Not all roses need the same conditions to perform well. Complete a site analysis, which can be as simple as walking around your garden and observing the conditions at different times of the day or season, to determine if you have the right environment for growing a given rose. You might find it helpful to make an overhead-view scale drawing of your property to plan the layout of your garden.

CLIMATE AND MICROCLIMATE

Climatic conditions to consider before selecting a rose include the temperature range of your area, the risk and timing of frost, prevailing winds and the amount of rainfall, humidity and sunshine available. It is far easier to select a rose that is adapted to your local climate than to battle against the climate. Most roses will grow in a range of hardiness zones, with minimum winter temperature being the most limiting factor. Zones should be used only as guidelines. Some tender roses may be grown in zones colder than they are rated for as long as adequate winter protection is provided. Check the hardiness zones map on page 8 for a general guide to hardiness zones in Michigan.

A microclimate is an area that has a slightly different climate than the surrounding area. The area near the south side of a building will be warmer than other areas of a yard. The area under the eaves of the house will be drier than other parts of a yard. The top of a hill or slope will be drier than the bottom. Cold air runs downhill, so the bottom of the slope will be cooler than the top. Part of your site analysis will be to determine the microclimates in your yard. Warm microclimates enable the gardener to successfully grow roses that are not completely hardy, with minimal to extra winter protection based on the initial zoning.

Prairie Joy

SUN

Roses require a minimum of six hours of sunlight per day for good flowering. Morning sun is best as it helps the foliage dry quickly, lessening the chance of fungal disease. Any rose grown in full shade will be weak and spindly with very few to no flowers. Some roses, such as the hybrid musks, are better adapted to growing in light to partial shade. (See the list of shade-tolerant roses on p. 92.)

In general, the lower the petal count of a rose, the more shade it will tolerate. All roses thrive in full sun, but if your garden gets intensely hot in summer, some light afternoon shade will help prevent sun damage to the flowers and foliage.

Blanc Double de Coubert

WIND

Wind can be the enemy of roses, increasing evaporation from the soil and drying a rose out quickly, especially when there has been little rain. A strong wind can dry and shred flowers. Winter wind can dry and destroy canes. Shelter your roses from the prevailing winds with fences, buildings and hedges. Consider the use of burlap screens and antidesiccant sprays in fall to help reduce moisture loss from the dormant canes.

Some wind, however, can help roses. A gentle breeze helps keep foliage dry, minimizing the incidence of disease. That breeze can also carry the fragrance of a rose a long way.

COMPETITION

Roses are heavy feeders and drinkers. They expend a great deal of energy producing their flowers and don't like to share root space with many other plants. Trees, turf, other garden plants and weeds may compete with roses for space and resources. In

Rotes Meer

particular, avoid planting roses near trees such as spruce, ash, poplar and elm, which have large, wide-spreading root systems. Plants with shallow, well-behaved root systems are good companions for roses.

SOIL

Soil provides support for the plant, holds and provides nutrients and water and makes oxygen available to the roots. Roses prefer a fertile, well-drained, moisture-holding loam with at least five percent organic matter, but they can grow in a wide range of soil types.

Soil is made up of particles of different sizes. Clay particles are very small or fine, silt particles are slightly larger but still considered fine, and sand particles are the largest of the three. Soils with a high percentage of clay particles are considered heavy, while soils with a high percentage of sand particles are considered light. Heavy soils hold water and nutrients but they do not drain well. Loams are soils with a balanced mix of clay, silt and sand particles. Roses like loams and clay-based soils as long as there is adequate drainage. Sandy soils require more frequent watering and fertilizing.

It is important to consider the pH level (the scale on which acidity or alkalinity is measured) of soil, which influences the availability of nutrients. An acid soil has a pH under 7.0 while an alkaline soil has a pH over 7.0. Roses perform best in slightly acidic soils, with pH between 6.0 and 7.0. Soil pH can be changed but it takes a

Testing a location's drainage

long time and routine applications of either sulfur or lime to maintain the desired level. It is a good idea to check the pH of your soil at least every two years.

Soil Testing

Complete soil testing kits are available from the MSU Extension office in your county. A soil test will tell you the soil pH; the percentage of sand, silt, clay and organic matter; the amount and type of nutrients available and provides recommendations for correcting soil deficiencies and fertilizing your garden. Be sure to request testing for organic content, which is an extra-cost option beyond the standard soil test but gives you a helpful breakdown of the percentage of the different organic matters in the soil. See Soil Testing in Resources, p. 262.

Garden centers sell simple test kits for pH and some major nutrients. Based on the results of the test, the garden center staff should be able to make some recommendations about which amendments to use and how to use them. Soil amendments are used to improve fertility, drainage and workability. Read about amendments in the Planting Roses section of this introduction.

It may also be a good idea to have your water tested, especially if you are using well water. Knowing the pH, mineral composition and salt content of your water source can help identify problems. Some nutrients can be rendered unavailable to plants depending on the mineral content of your water.

Drainage

Roses use a lot of water but do not like to have their roots sitting in water. The soil must drain well enough to allow air to reach the roots and hold enough water for the rose to use.

Heavy soils can have the drainage improved by adding organic matter or by installing perforated drainage tile under the roses or by double digging the soil (see p. 34). Sandy soils drain water quickly but do not retain nutrients for long. Organic matter helps sandy soils hold more water and nutrients.

If you are unsure that the spot you have chosen will drain well enough to prevent standing water, try this simple test. Dig a test hole that is 12" wide and deep. Fill the hole to the top with water and let it drain completely. Fill the hole with water again and note the time it takes for the water to completely drain from the hole. A drainage rate of $1/2$" or less per hour is considered poor and will require work to improve the drainage.

Harison's Yellow

Buying Roses

Roses can be purchased from nurseries, garden centers, mail-order suppliers, supermarkets and home-improvement stores. You will likely get the best quality plants and advice from nurseries, garden centers and mail-order suppliers that specialize in roses. Roses that are produced locally are good choices because they are already adapted to the climate. Ordering roses through the mail or over the Internet is very convenient and the roses come right to your door. (See Resources, p. 262)

Roses are available for sale in three forms: bare-root, packaged bare-root and containerized (in pots).

Some roses are shipped bare-root, especially from mail-order nurseries. These roses are dug up from the field when they are dormant. The soil is removed from the roots and the roots are wrapped in plastic, newspaper or wood wool before shipping. Ideally the roses should arrive in the dormant state with no new growth. The roses sometimes start growing during transport. Before planting, remove shoots longer than 2".

Packaged bare-root roses are often found in supermarkets and home-improvement stores. Each rose comes in a plastic or waxed cardboard container with the roots surrounded by moist sawdust, peat moss, wood chips or shredded paper. Buy packaged roses early in the season when the roses are still relatively

dormant. Even if you can't plant them right away, you can store them in a cool location. The canes of packaged roses are often waxed to prevent the canes from drying out during shipping and before planting. The wax will come off during the growing season. Plant packaged roses in April or very early May before they start to leaf out.

Container roses are grown in pots, not fields, though some stock sold in containers may have been bare-root plants potted by the nursery staff. Container roses are available throughout the growing season and can be planted any time. Often a container rose will be in flower and you can see exactly what you are purchasing.

GRAFTED PLANTS

Most roses available today are bud-grafted, a process in which a bud eye from a selected variety is grafted onto the rootstock of another variety. When the bud starts to grow, the top of the rootstock plant is removed. The energy that would have been used by the top is all directed towards the newly grafted bud. The area where the new bud is grafted onto the rootstock is called the bud union.

Budded plants mature more quickly than own-root plants that are propagated from cuttings. Some growers claim the flowers from a grafted plant are bigger and better than flowers from the same variety grown on its own roots. At one time it was believed that using a cold-hardy rootstock would increase the cold hardiness of the grafted variety, but in fact only the rootstock remains hardy and its hardiness does not transfer to the variety grafted on top of it.

Growers and hybridizers have many different rootstocks available and choose a rootstock that will provide the desired characteristics. Various rootstocks are often used in commercial rose production. Some of these rootstocks are not especially well-suited to Michigan because they can diminish the winter hardiness of a rose by failing to go dormant early in fall and by pushing on new growth too early in the spring. Always ask the supplier if the rootstock is appropriate for your area. For our area *Rosa multiflora* is the best rootstock. Be cautious when buying roses from the western and southern states, as they may be grafted onto Dr. Huey rootstock, which is not well-suited, in the long term, to Michigan.

Standard roses, often referred to as tree roses, have two grafts and an elongated main stem. The lower graft is between the rootstock and the stem. The other graft is between the stem and the variety at the top. Standard roses have special winterization needs since the top graft is difficult to protect and will not survive Michigan winters. Standard roses do not fit into any specific rose class, because the variety grafted to the top could be a miniature, floribunda or hybrid tea.

Own-root Plants

Own-root plants, as the name suggests, are grown on their own roots. They take longer to reach maturity than bud-grafted plants and are more expensive to produce, but they can be very long-lived and are hardier than grafted plants. Not having a bud union allows for a more natural plant form as the top growth does not all originate from one point. It also eliminates a weak point (the bud union) that is susceptible to attack by pests or damage from cold weather. Own-root roses are especially well-suited for Michigan, since they can sustain severe winterkill and still spring back true from their roots. Nearly all roses can be grown on their own roots, but own-root roses can be difficult to find in local stores. All root suckers of an own-root rose are the same variety as the top portion and do not need to be removed unless they are in an undesirable location.

What to Look For

When purchasing any rose, make sure the roots are moist. It is easy to check for moist soil if the rose is in a container. It is more difficult, but possible, to examine the roots of packaged roses. If the package is very light or you can see any dry soil or planting mix, the roots are probably dry.

Examine the root system. Bare-root roses should have a mass of long, fibrous roots. Avoid roses that have short spindly roots or that have had their roots pruned. Ensure that the roots of container roses have white tips and are not encircling the inside of the container or growing out the bottom of the container. Avoid plants with blackened or girdled roots. Roses with a weak root system will have a tough time establishing.

The canes of grafted bare-root and packaged roses should be supple and dark green, have small buds and be at least as thick as a pencil no matter the grade (see sidebar). Avoid plants with dry, shriveled canes. Any visible pith should be white or green. Roses with tan or brown piths may have sustained some damage.

On grafted roses examine the rootstock neck just below the bud union. It should be at least as big around as your thumb with no visible external damage. The neck should be no longer than about 3", because if it is any longer, planting could be awkward. Avoid bare-root roses with long, pale shoots.

Grafted, or budded, roses are sorted into three grades according to the size and number of main canes. More often than not, you'll come across only Grade 1 or Grade 1¹/₂ roses, indicating that the roses you've chosen is of excellent quality. It is best to invest a little more money when purchasing a rose, ensuring that it is of superior quality. Don't settle for cheap roses—the old cliché rings true: you get what you pay for.

Root-bound plant

Planting Roses

Preparing the proper planting site is an investment of time that will be rewarded when your rose blooms well. Proper care, placement and planting are critical to a rose's establishment and long-term success. Preparing the soil is the most important step, and it can begin long before planting.

PREPARING THE SOIL

Based on a soil test (see Soil Testing, p. 29), amend your soil as necessary with organic or inorganic amendments. Especially if you are planting a large area of roses, you should prepare the area the fall prior to spring planting so the soil has a chance to settle over winter before you plant your roses. If the soil settles too much, it is easy to top it up before planting.

You can prepare the soil just before planting, but be aware that your rose might settle more deeply than is recommended.

There are many possible methods for preparing an area to plant roses. The following method is referred to as **double digging**. Dig and set aside the topsoil from the planting area. Turn over the subsoil with a garden fork. To accommodate bush roses

Topsoil set aside

Adding amendments to subsoil

Mixing soil and amendments

Adding amendments to topsoil

such as hybrid teas, grandifloras and floribundas, the prepared area should be 18–24" deep and 24" wide for each rose. If you are planting miniatures, the depth and width can be 12". Robust climbers, ramblers and shrub roses may need an area up to 18–24" deep and 4' wide.

Sometimes it is impossible to dig the soil to the desired depth because of rock or hardpan. In such a case, you can use a raised bed to provide the necessary soil depth and drainage, you can try to break through the hardpan or you can choose a different location.

Add any amendments and mix them in well, then replace the topsoil. If possible, allow the area to sit for a few months to settle.

Organic soil amendments include compost, well-rotted manure (preferably cow or sheep manure), peat moss, leaf mold, bonemeal, alfalfa pellets and agricultural byproducts such as seed shells and husks, sawdust and composted wood or bark chips. Inorganic amendments include superphosphate, vermiculite and perlite. Each amendment has different properties and should be added to the soil only if deemed necessary, on the basis of a soil test.

Use only thoroughly composted materials. Amendments such as fresh manure may burn a rose's roots, and uncomposted organic materials, such as sawdust or woodchips, use the available nitrogen from the soil to aid their decomposition. Many municipalities in Michigan offer composted yard waste free for the hauling to their residents.

Double- or triple-shredded pine bark mulch is an excellent soil amendment, in addition to its common use as a top mulch. Unlike cedar or cypress mulch, pine bark decomposes within a year or two, improving the soil texture. Add a bit of extra nitrogen to your fertilizer program to compensate for the nitrogen that is used as the pine bark breaks down.

A common practice for rose growers is to add 25 to 33 percent of soil volume of compost or well-rotted manure—for example, adding 3–4" of compost or well-rotted manure to soil at a depth of 12".

WHEN TO PLANT

Dormant, bare-root roses establish best in cool, moist soil. Planting in early spring is best, from March to early May. Roses can be planted in fall but only if the plants become available at that time of year. If planting roses in fall, plant them immediately after purchase so they may become established before the ground freezes.

Container roses can be planted in spring, summer or fall. Container roses are the only roses that can be planted in summer because they already have an established root system. Diligent watering is mandatory for proper establishment of container roses and is even more important for those planted in summer. If planting in fall, plant no later than mid-November and at least three to four weeks before the ground is expected to freeze.

Soaking bare-root roses

PREPARING THE ROSE

Bare-root roses should be planted as soon as possible after purchase. Your new rose will require some preparation. If you buy a container rose, the preparation begins at the point of purchase. The rose must be thoroughly saturated before you take it home, so that the roots remain moist during transport. If you are transporting the rose home in a car, be aware of the temperature, as excess heat quickly dries plants out. If you are using an open truck for transport, lay the plant down or cover it to protect it from the wind, as even a short trip can be traumatic for a plant. Container roses can be planted days, weeks and even months after purchase provided that they are kept moist during the wait. Place container roses in the sun but away from drying winds. Container roses can dry out quickly, so daily watering may be necessary.

If you are going to plant bare-root roses within 24 hours, stand the roses in a bucket of muddy water, ensuring the roots are completely covered with water. Some rosarians soak the entire plant. The mud in the water will lightly coat the roots, helping to prevent desiccation during planting. Soak the plant for 12 to 24 hours but no longer.

If you have to store bare-root roses for a couple of days, do not remove

Heeling-in bare-root roses

the packaging but open it just enough to check that the roots are moist, adding water if necessary. Close the package and place it in a cool, dry, frost-free area such as a refrigerator or an unheated garage.

If your garden is still frozen or too muddy to work when your packaged or bare-root roses arrive, you will need longer storage. The usual method is called heeling-in, which involves digging a trench in a well-drained area, preferably with shade, such as an edge of a vegetable garden or under an eave. The trench should be 12" deep on one side with the bottom of the trench sloping up at a 45-degree angle. Lay the roses in the trench with the roots towards the bottom of the trench. Cover completely with soil except for the tips of the canes, and water the entire trench well. Keeping the tips uncovered helps you find the rose later, and the soil covering keeps the roses from drying out.

Dainty Bess

Heeling-in is a great method as long as the weather remains somewhat cool. If freezing weather is in the forecast, cover the heeled-in roses with mulch or burlap. Some sources say that heeled-in roses can be stored for a few months, but every effort should be made to plant as soon as possible. Use caution when digging up heeled-in roses to avoid damage to the roots and canes. Long-term storage is usually not necessary as mail-order suppliers time their shipments to coincide with the arrival of spring in your area.

Container roses will likely have to be hardened off before planting. Hardening off is the process of slowly acclimatizing a plant to its new surroundings. Sometimes this is done at the nursery; sometimes container roses have just come out of the greenhouse. When purchasing the rose, ask whether it's been hardened off and when it is safe to plant. If is still requires hardening off, begin by giving the plant sun and protecting it from stiff daily and nightly winds and freezing at night. Gradually increase the amount of time the rose is in the wind and evening cold. The process should take about a week.

Bonemeal is a slow-release fertilizer and gradually adds important nutrients, including phosphorous, which is essential for root development. It should be incorporated into the soil, near the rootzone, at the time of planting.

PREPARING THE HOLE

In your prepared rose area, you must dig a hole for each rose. Work about a half cup of bonemeal into the soil at the bottom of the hole (see sidebar).

For container stock, the depth in the center of the hole should be equal to the depth of the rootball, and one-and-a-half times the width of the container. All roses benefit from being planted deeply. If necessary, pull the leaves off the base of container roses. It is critical to plant grafted roses so that the bud union is 2–4" below the surface of the soil, even deeper in colder regions, to improve the winter survival of grafted roses. Own-root roses benefit, too, from deep planting, which helps them establish new roots and have sturdier canes.

For bare-root stock, the hole should be big enough to completely contain the expanded roots with a little extra room on the sides and a cone-shaped central mound (see diagram). The mound helps to evenly space the roots in the hole, prevents the rose from sinking as the soil settles and encourages excess water to drain away from the roots. Some rose growers form the mound in the center of the hole with amended backfill rather than soil alone.

It is a good idea to roughen the sides of the hole with a garden fork or trowel so that it's easier for roots to penetrate out of the hole.

PLACING THE ROSE

Plant your rose on an overcast or rainy day. If this is not possible, try to plant it during the early evening, when the temperatures are lower, rather than in the middle of the day.

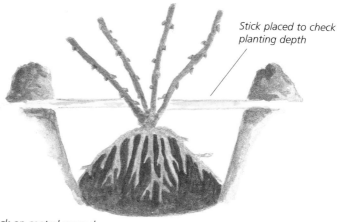

Stick placed to check planting depth

Bare-root stock on central mound

Bare-root roses

Remove the plastic and sawdust from the roots or retrieve the rose from your temporary storage. Prune out any broken, diseased or rotten roots or canes. Center the plant over the central mound and fan out the roots in the hole.

Cut the remaining canes to a height of 10–12". Some rosarians cut the canes to 5–8", which causes the new canes to form lower on the plant, giving a much bushier look. Other than to remove broken or diseased canes, fall-planted bare-root roses should not be cut back until all other roses are cut back in the spring.

If your rose is grafted, the depth of the bud union is important. Plant the union approximately 2" below the surface of the soil. In colder areas, plant it at a depth of 3–4". Some growers recommend that for tender grafted roses the bud union be planted at a depth of 6" in zone 3 or colder. Basically, the colder the zone, the deeper the bud union. If the rootstock neck is excessively long (3" or more) plant the rose at an angle, so the roots are not too deep but the bud union is at the correct depth.

Container roses

Container roses are very easy to plant. Containers are made of plastic or pressed fiber. Before planting, water the rootball thoroughly and gently remove the container to check the root mass. If the plant is girdled or root-bound (if the roots circle around the inside of the container between the container and the soil),

the roots must be loosened. Any large roots encircling the soil or growing into the center of the root mass instead of outward should be loosened before planting. Some roses might not have been in their containers long enough to develop enough roots to allow the container to be removed without soil falling away. If soil falls away from the roots, the new

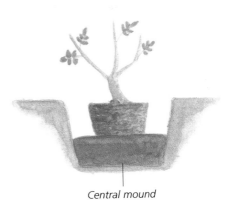

Central mound

Planting a container rose

Checking planting depth

feeder roots can be damaged, but do not be discouraged. Treat the rose as bare-root stock for planting.

All containers must be removed before planting well-established roses. Although some containers appear to be made of peat moss or natural fibers, they won't be able to decompose as fast as growing roots require. The roots may not be able to penetrate the pot sides, and the fiber will wick moisture away from the roots. The roots may never even leave the pot, resulting in girdled, constricted roots.

Place the rose, pot and all, on top of the central mound to check planting depth, adjusting if necessary. Remove the pot and place the rootball onto the central mound. Prune out any dead or diseased canes.

When planting container grafted roses, make sure that the bud union is the same depth as that required by bare-root roses.

Miniatures

Most miniature roses are sold as container roses and can be planted the same way as larger container roses. Most miniatures are grown in greenhouses and must be hardened off before planting.

Standard roses

Standard roses usually have two bud unions. When planting standard roses, ensure the lower bud union is at the proper depth (see p. 38). Standard roses need to be staked. Use a sturdy, rot-proof stake long enough that it can be set into undisturbed soil and reach up to just below the top bud union. The stake can be placed on the sunny side, which helps protect the main stem from sun scald, or to the side of the prevailing wind for extra support. Tie the main stem to the stake about halfway up the stake and near the top. Prune the top as for bare-root plantings. Standard roses are best grown in containers, so that

Backfilling hole

50% backfilled

Adding bonemeal to backfill

Settling backfill with water

Settling backfilled topsoil with water

Planting process complete

they can be moved and/or tipped and buried for winter protection.

Root pruning

We do not recommend root pruning when planting or transplanting, other than removing broken, diseased or dead roots for bare-root plantings. Scientific studies have confirmed that root pruning physiologically shocks the plant by throwing hormones out of balance. It increases water and nutrient stresses and makes the rose more susceptible to insect and disease attacks.

BACKFILL

With the rose in the hole it is time to replace the soil. Container stock will usually stay upright during backfilling while a bare-root rose will need to be held in position.

If you have not already amended the soil in your rose bed, amend the backfill soil. Leaf mold, well-rotted manure, compost, bonemeal and moist peat moss are all suitable amendments.

When backfilling, keep in mind that good root-to-soil contact is important to help the plant's stability

Planting tip

Steep willow twigs in water for a week and use the water when settling the backfill soil and when first watering the newly planted rose. The water contains a natural rooting hormone and salicylic acid, which both aid in root regeneration.

and establishment. Large air pockets remaining after backfilling could cause unwanted settling and increase the risk of desiccation. Tamping or stepping down on the backfilled soil used to be recommended, but the risk of injuring the roots and compacting the soil has made this practice fall out of favor. Use water to settle the soil gently around the roots and in the hole. Backfill in small amounts bit by bit rather than all at once. Add some soil then water it in, repeating until the hole is full.

Amending the backfill in heavy clay soils will provide a light soil medium for the root system to grow in until the roots reach the heavy clay. However, some of the roots will have difficulty penetrating through

Protecting newly planted rose with mounded soil

treewell

the clay, resulting in what is known as 'flower pot syndrome,' when the roots grow only in and around the amended soil, as if the rose were grown in a clay flowerpot. To prevent such a problem, remove the heavy subsoil and amend the entire bed before backfilling.

PROTECTING THE ROSE

Once the dormant bare-root rose is in the hole and properly backfilled, mound soil over it to a depth of 10–12", less if the canes are shorter. If you do not have enough soil, you can use mulch. Mounding the soil helps prevent desiccation of the canes while the rose rebuilds its feeder roots. Ensure the entire mound is moist and remains moist.

In three to four weeks, less if the weather is mild, the bud eyes will swell and produce new canes and foliage. When you see the new growth you can slowly remove the mound. Use either your hands or a tool, but be gentle. Choose overcast or rainy days for this task. Hot sunny days will scorch the newly exposed, delicate shoots. It should take about a week to remove the mound, enough time to allow the new, tender growth a chance to harden off. If there is a risk of frost, recover the rose with soil or mulch.

If the dormant rose fails to bud out, mound with moist peat and cover with plastic, creating a mini-greenhouse. Check daily to ensure the humidity under the plastic is not causing disease or rot to form and the peat remains moist but not soggy.

Some rosarians suggest that soil sickness does not exist. Regardless, adding fresh soil and amendments when replacing a diseased rose with a new one can only be a benefit.

Allow new growth to harden off. If the rose still doesn't break dormancy, cut the canes and look at the pith. If the pith is brown and no white tips are evident on the roots, it's time to dig up the rose and get a replacement.

TRANSPLANTING

The need to move a rose may arise. The younger the rose, the more likely it will be able to reestablish successfully when moved to a new location.

If you are moving a rose to a spot where another rose previously grew, add fresh soil or lots of compost, as the previous rose may have depleted the soil of nutrients. Also, if planting a new rose in a spot where a diseased rose was, it is very important to use fresh soil or lots of compost. There may be populations of organisms in the old soil, such as soil fungi, viruses and nematodes, that could use the rose as a host plant. This is sometimes referred to as **soil sickness**. The bad organisms attack the young feeder roots of new roses, limiting the rose's ability to absorb water and nutrients. Planting your rose with fresh soil will provide a new source of nutrients and aid in its establishment.

If you need to relocate an established rose, the best time to do so is in September. Prepare the new planting

Staggered double-row hedge

hole before digging up the rose. Prune back the top of the rose, or bind the canes together to make it easier to move. Dig through and around the roots to create a reasonably sized rootball. Have a tarp or piece of burlap ready next to the plant to wrap it in. Wrap the roots, taking care not to let them dry out, and immediately relocate the rose. Re-plant it as you would a bare-root rose, watering it daily during its first month in the ground.

PLANTING METHODS FOR DIFFERENT LANDSCAPE USES

Roses can be used for a variety of landscape uses. The following tips will help you as you think about planting roses in specific landscape situations.

Hedges

When planting hedges, staggering the rows allows the maximum number of roses for the size of the bed or hedge, gives a good mass effect and allows all the roses to be seen from one side. The modern bush roses are often planted in staggered rows, with a spacing of 30–36" from the center of one plant to the center of its neighbors. The more vigorous shrub roses are planted at 80 percent of the spread at maturity so the branches eventually intermingle to form the hedge. For taller hedges, the planting distance can be increased slightly. The best rose hedges are grown from own-root roses because any suckers developing from the roots will help thicken up the hedge and are from the rose variety you planted.

Climbers

Planting climbers requires some extra preparation. Have the support structure in place and a supply of rose ties. Special rose ties are available at your local garden center or from specialty rose nurseries, but rose ties can be any piece of non-abrasive material used to tie the rose to the supports. Support can consist of stiff wires strung horizontally along a wall or hooks attached to a wooden fence. Hooks make rose maintenance and training a little easier, because the canes merely have to be tied to the hooks. It really doesn't matter what the support is as long as it is sturdy enough to support the weight of the plant in full bloom.

Plant the rose about 18" from the wall, fence or whatever you have chosen to train the climber on. Angle the canes toward the lowest support and tie them in place. You will want the canes to form a fan shape as you attach them to the support. You can purchase ties to attach the canes to the support (as in our illustration) or tie the cane loosely to the support using yarn and a Figure 8 pattern, with one loop of the Figure 8 around the support and the other loop around the rose cane.

Plant your climbing rose far enough away from other trees and shrubs so that the rose doesn't have to compete for water and nutrients.

Groundcovers

When planting roses as a groundcover, you must first remove any weeds. An easy, non-chemical method is to pasteurize the soil:

- Remove any surface weeds and add appropriate soil amendments
- Rake the area smooth and cover it with a sheet of flexible black plastic
- Bury the edges of the plastic and leave it in place for a couple of months; the heat under the plastic will prevent annual weed seeds, soil diseases and insects from penetrating the soil
- Remove the plastic
- Plant, disturbing the soil as little as possible.

Single-row hedge

The way you space and plant groundcover roses will depend on what roses you are using. A rule of thumb is to space at two-thirds of the spread at maturity. For consistency and a good massing effect, all the roses should be the same variety. After planting the roses, cover the entire area with mulch, being careful not to mound the mulch directly around the crown of the rose.

Planting in containers

Planting roses in containers is different than planting container roses, which are often meant to be in their pots temporarily. Any rose can be planted in a container, but the larger the rose, the larger the container you will need and the heavier it will be once it is filled with soil. If the containers are too heavy to lift, casters on the bottom of the container can make them easy to move. Containers can be made of many different materials, including wood, plastic, metal or clay. Straight-sided containers offer more room for the roots than those with tapered sides. Ensure the bottom of the container has an adequate number of drainage holes. Choose a container that won't be so heavy that it's difficult to move, especially when full of moist soil. There are pots made of materials such as fiberglass and plastic resins that look like terra-cotta or ceramic but are light and last much longer than natural materials.

Smaller containers will require water and fertilizer more often.

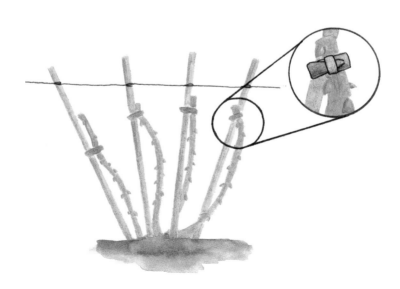

Attaching climber or rambler canes to support

Choose a container that will accommodate the rootball's growth over a long period of time.

Floribundas, polyanthas, miniatures and the smaller hybrid teas are excellent choices for containers. Miniatures can be in containers as small as 12" in diameter and 10–12" deep. Floribundas, polyanthas and hybrid teas should have pots with a minimum 16" diameter and depth. For standard roses, match the container size to what is

Rise 'n' Shine

Roses grown on their own roots do not have a bud union. The crown should be planted 1" below soil level, stripping off lower leaves if necessary.

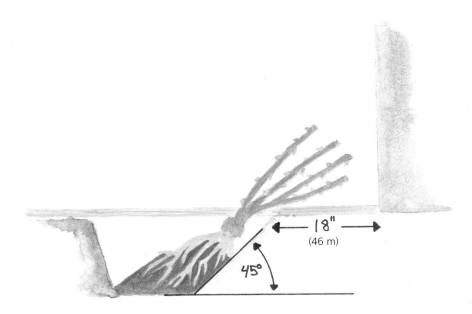

Proper planting distance and angle for climbers and ramblers

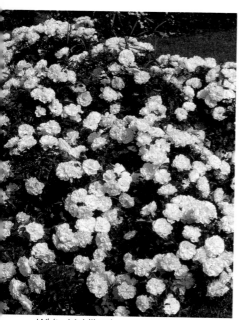

White Meidiland

Tabris

needed by the variety grafted to the top of the standard.

Don't use gravel at the bottom of your container. Studies have shown that the soil on top of the gravel must be completely saturated with water before it drains through the gravel beneath. A fiberglass or metal window screen is better for covering the drainage holes on the bottom of the container; water will drain out but soil will not.

The soil for containers must be non-compacting, moderately rich, moisture holding and well drained. Sterile planting mixes, some specifically designed for roses, are available from your local nursery or garden center. Sterile mixes won't provide any nutrients to the rose, however, so make sure to supplement with a regular fertilizing program. Once-a-year slow release fertilizers and moisture-retaining soil polymers are good additions to sterile planting mixes used for long-term container growing. After the rose is planted and the soil settled in the container, the soil should be 1–2" below the rim of the container so that water will soak through to the roots of the rose and not run over the edge.

Planting in a container is similar to planting in the ground. Place the rose in the container and backfill in the same way as if you were planting in the ground.

Plants in containers may need protection from extreme temperatures. Rot-resistant wood such as cedar makes an attractive container that offers protection from excessive heating and cooling. Containers made of other materials may need help keeping the roots cool. One method is to place one container into another with at least 1" between the containers for insulating material such as moistened vermiculite, sawdust or Styrofoam packing peanuts. Alternatively, the inside of a container may be lined with stiff foam insulation for straight-sided containers or a couple of layers of carpet underlay for curved-side containers.

Ingrid Bergman

With containers of beautiful roses, patios, decks and entryways can become colorful spaces.

Green Ice

Caring for Roses

WATERING

Watering is probably the most important maintenance practice for roses. Roses, especially repeat-blooming roses, need moisture for good blooming. If your soil has good drainage, it is difficult to overwater. The soil, wind, amount of sunlight, daylight temperature and amount of rainfall all must be considered when determining how much water to apply and when to apply it. Sandy soil will require more frequent watering than clay soil. It takes less time for water to get to the correct depth in sandy soil than in clay soil. Roses in windy locations will need more water than roses in sheltered locations. If the air temperature is particularly hot, the rose will need extra water. A rose needs twice as much water at 90° F than at 70° F.

Rainfall may not supply all a rose's water needs. A rain gauge indicates how much rain has fallen and will help you determine how much water you need to apply. Check your roses daily throughout the growing season. If the soil is dry several inches below the soil surface, it needs water. If you notice the bud, flowers or foliage beginning to wilt, water immediately.

Container roses should be watered daily—water until the water comes out the holes in the bottom of the container. Larger containers generally need water less often than smaller containers. Do not use a saucer or tray

Roseraie de l'Haÿ

underneath any outdoor container. The saucer will trap water, which can drown the roots.

A general guideline is to apply 1" of water per week or about 5 gallons per plant. You will have to determine what watering regime is right for your area and soil composition. When you apply water, it should penetrate through the rootzone to a depth of at least 18". Shallow watering promotes root growth near the surface rather than deep root growth. Shallow roots may be damaged by cultivation or weeding, may suffer fertilizer burn and are susceptible to drought conditions.

To determine if you are watering deeply enough, dig a small hole beside a rose you have just watered and see how far down the water has penetrated. Give the water at least half an hour or so to soak in before you check how far it has penetrated. If you watered for 15 minutes and your check shows that the water has gone down 9", you know you need to water for a total of 30 minutes to get water to a depth of 18".

Another method of measuring soil penetration is poking a stick into the watered soil. If the stick moves easily through the soil, the soil is wet enough; if the stick does not move easily, the soil is too dry. You can also use a soil probe, a hollow tube with a T-handle with the lower part of the hollow tube cut away on one side. Soil probes are available at irrigation supply businesses and some garden centers.

Watering in spring begins when the ground has almost completely

Eglantyne

Europeana

thawed. Your rose will not need as much water at the beginning of spring as it does in mid-summer, but you still must water deeply. In spring water any dry beds and any roses under house eaves. Ease back on watering in fall to help the rose prepare itself for winter.

There are different ways to water. Using a hose and watering wand with a flood nozzle allows you to observe each rose close up. It is a great method but time consuming. Using sprinklers takes less of your attention but the amount of water making it to the plant's rootzone is affected by wind and evaporation. If you are using a sprinkler, it is best to water in the morning to give the foliage a chance to dry in the morning sun. Wet foliage is an invitation to fungal diseases. Watering in the morning also reduces the amount of evaporation that can occur when watering in the hot afternoon sun. Soaker hoses are widely available. They are easy to use and apply water directly to the rootzone without wetting the foliage. Black plastic 'weeping' soaker hoses are almost invisible under mulch and do not need to be removed for winter.

Efficient watering techniques are especially important in areas with imposed water restrictions during hot and dry summers. You can reduce the amount of watering you need to do by adding mulch or by creating a treewell or watering basin.

A treewell is a low mound of soil 2–6" high built up in a ring around the outer edge of the planting hole. Treewells contain the water underneath the plant, preventing the water from flowing away before soaking in. When watering roses with treewells, fill the treewell to the top and leave it. Water your other roses and plants, then come back and fill the reservoir again. You might have to fill the treewell four to five times depending on the volume of the treewell. The treewell should be removed in fall, to prevent the roots from becoming waterlogged in winter.

Treewell

MULCHING

Mulching is placing a layer of organic or inorganic material on top of the soil. Mulching slows evaporation, keeps roots cool, protects roots from damage from cultivation, suppresses weed growth and prevents soil-borne diseases from splashing onto the foliage. Mulching allows feeder roots to grow near the surface, increasing the rose's ability to absorb nutrients and water. Mulching prevents soil from crusting over or becoming compacted. Organic mulch also improves the soil as it decomposes, releasing nutrients and maintaining an open structure that encourages root penetration. Mulching looks good, giving the bed a finished, natural appearance.

A Knock Out rose with mulch

Morden Ruby

Organic mulches include compost, well-rotted manure (fresh manure can burn roots), pine and spruce needles, shredded leaves, shredded bark, grass clippings and locally available agricultural byproducts, such as bedding from horse stables. Inorganic mulches include gravel, rocks, plastic and landscape fabric. Inorganic mulches can make winterizing and the subsequent spring cleanup very difficult. We recommend organic mulches for the benefit they provide to the soil.

If you choose to use grass clippings as mulch, ensure the grass was not treated with herbicide that can harm the rose. Do not add grass clippings after the end of August, because the grass could add nitrogen to the soil, stimulating growth that will likely suffer winterkill. Avoid

If you live in a big city, your roses may get covered in dust and pollutants, which inhibit photosynthesis. Wash roses once a week, in the morning so the foliage dries quickly. Washing roses also helps keep the spider mite and aphid populations down to a minimum.

using peat moss alone as a mulch. Alone it dries quickly, and when dry it repels moisture. It is very light and can blow away in the wind. Mixed with other materials, peat moss is a suitable organic mulch.

Mulch may rob some nitrogen from the soil as it decomposes throughout the season. Compensate by applying a small amount of nitrogen fertilizer, such as fish fertilizer, when laying down the mulch. Avoid sawdust, especially from pressure-treated lumber and softwood trees, because it may release oils that retard plant growth. Both walnut leaves and large leaves should be avoided. Walnut leaves are toxic to rose growth when they break down. Large leaves tend to mat together, restricting air and water movement; shred and compost large leaves before using as mulch. Bark mulches should also be shredded because larger chunks of bark leave spaces and allow weed seeds to fall in between and grow.

A good mulch allows air and water to penetrate into the soil. Apply mulch to a depth of 3", thick enough to suppress weeds and still allow air circulation into the soil. Keep the mulch 2–4" away from the base of the rose. Some rosarians keep mulch out of the treewells to make it easier to clean up fallen rose leaves.

FERTILIZING

Give your roses a good start by digging well-rotted manure or compost and any organic amendments prescribed by a soil test into the soil during preparation (see Preparing the Soil, p. 34). Even if you have amended the soil for your roses before planting, you still need an ongoing program of fertilizing throughout the growing season.

Roses are heavy feeders, so it is important to establish a routine fertilizer program. The fertility program for your roses depends on the type of roses you are growing and the nutrients available in your soil. Modern roses, such as hybrid teas and grandifloras, grow best in a rich, fertile soil. If you are growing species roses to naturalize an area, you will not fertilize to the same extent. If you have questions about fertilizing, contact your local MSU Extension office or rose society in your area, which can provide information or put you in touch with someone who can help

Cardinal de Richelieu

you develop a fertilizing program. A soil test will dictate what the soil needs. Don't add fertilizer just for the sake of adding it. You may end up feeding your roses to death; too much fertilizer will damage your rose, not benefit it, and may possibly pollute waterways.

The key to a successful fertility program is to feed the soil, not the plant. Healthy soils are dynamic ecosystems containing thousands of soil organisms that work in harmony with each other and the plants growing in them. Any practice that disrupts the balance of the soil ecosystem can mean problems for plants. Perhaps the chemical fertilizer you are using has changed the pH of the soil, making it difficult for the soil microorganisms to thrive. They can no longer break down the organic matter in the soil to provide the plant with nutrients, leaving your plant dependent on chemicals for nutrients. When the soil is out of ecological balance, insects and diseases can move in. If you take care of your soil, it will produce good quality roses.

A healthy City of York

When to fertilize

The first fertilization of the year is just after spring pruning or when winter protection is completely removed, usually in late April or early May. The last fertilization of the year should be four to six weeks before the first frost. Frost can damage late, lush growth, so you don't want to fertilize too close to first frost. In southern Michigan, discontinue feeding in the middle of August. A safe approach is to stop using nitrogen fertilizers in mid-July and fertilize after that time with fall fertilizer, which is high in potassium.

The label on the fertilizer container will tell you how often it needs to be applied. In general, natural organic fertilizers should be applied every four to six weeks from early May through August. Some slow-release chemical fertilizers need to be applied only once a year, in May. Newly planted roses should be fertilized lightly six weeks after planting. Only bonemeal should be applied when planted (see p. 38).

Electron

Love

What to use

The numbers on a package of chemical fertilizer, for example 24–14–14 or 20–24–14, represent nitrogen, phosphorous and potassium, respectively. The numbers are referred to as the 'fertilizer analysis.' The higher the number, the greater the amount of nutrient. A fertilizer with all three nutrients is called a complete fertilizer. A fertilizer specifically designed for roses contains the nutrients most needed by roses. Follow the directions on the package for proper application rates, methods and precautions.

Organic and chemical fertilizers are available in granular and liquid forms. Granular fertilizers are small, dry particles that can be easily spread by machine or hand. Granular chemical fertilizers have nitrogen available in either quick-release or slow-release formulations. Quick-release fertilizers provide a big shot of plant-available nitrogen in a short time. Too much nitrogen too quickly will favor foliage growth over flowers. It may burn the roots and the foliage. It may also create lush growth that is susceptible to insects and diseases. Slow-release fertilizers are a better choice because they release their nutrients over a long period, lowering the potential for burning, excessive vegetative growth and leaching of the fertilizer into the groundwater. Granular organic fertilizers are naturally slow releasing. Many rosarians supplement their slow-release fertility program with a small amount of quick-release nitrogen to ensure the rose is adequately fed, just after pruning or when the swollen flower buds have just begun to show color.

Liquid fertilizers come as liquid concentrate or powder that is mixed with water and applied to the soil or sprayed on the leaves. The most common soil-applied liquid fertilizer formulation is 20–20–20, but there are organic options available.

Organic fertilizers include compost, well-rotted manure, fish emulsion, fish meal, bloodmeal (high in nitrogen), alfalfa pellets, bonemeal (a good source of phosphorous), banana peels and seaweed extracts. You can create a balanced organic fertilizer mix for roses using coffee grounds, egg shells and banana peels. Compost tea (see recipe) can be used as a liquid feed.

Organic fertilizers are better for the health of the soil and its inhabitants. For example, seaweed extracts such as kelp not only supply micronutrients, they also contain a substance that releases micronutrients already in the soil. (Micronutrients are organic compounds essential in minute amounts to the health of the plant.) When applied as a foliar feed in spring and fall, the seaweed extracts also help improve roses' cold hardiness and drought resistance. Fish emulsion and fish meal stimulate budding, blooming and foliage green-up. Fish emulsion can be used as a liquid feed throughout the growing season, applied right over the mulch. Fish meal can be gently scratched into the soil. Consult your county's

Compost Tea Recipe

Mix a shovelful of compost in a 5 gallon bucket of water or a bucketful of compost in a 45-gallon barrel of water and let sit for a week. Dilute this mix, preferably with rainwater or filtered water, until it resembles weak tea. Best if used when watering or as a spray.

MSU Extension office before using Epsom salts (magnesium sulfate). This often-recommended soil amendment is actually undesirable in Michigan because most Michigan soils are very high in magnesium.

Spraying the leaves with fertilizer is called foliar feeding. It won't provide all the nutrition a rose needs but is good for supplementing a soil fertility program. Foliar feeding is good for applying micronutrients. If your soil test reveals a need for micronutrients, a good form to use is chelated micronutrients sprayed on the foliage and onto the soil. The best time to apply foliar fertilizer is in the early morning, when the air is cool and the leaves will dry quickly. Do not apply foliar feeds if temperatures are 85° F or higher.

How to fertilize

If you are unsure about how much fertilizer to use, it is better to apply a little less fertilizer and a little more water. Most importantly, never fertilize a dry plant! Water the plant very well the day before you plan to fertilize to reduce the potential of burning.

Follow the directions that came with the fertilizer. Always wear gloves when using granular fertilizers. If you are using granular fertilizers, measure the recommended amount and spread it out in a ring around the base of the rose and lightly scratch the fertilizer into the soil with a cultivator or rake. Leave a 6–8" diameter of unfertilized area directly around the base of the rose so the fertilizer can reach the feeder roots.

Liquid fertilizers are mixed with water and poured onto the rootzone or sprayed onto the foliage. Hose-end sprayers, available at garden centers, home-improvement stores and some nurseries, make applying liquid fertilizers easy. Many rosarians use both granular and liquid fertilizers in various combinations.

PRUNING

Pruning is very important for roses. It is far better to prune a rose at least once a year than to not prune it at all. To prune effectively, you need to know why you are pruning, when to prune, how and where to make proper cuts, how to prune the specific rose you are growing and how to clean up after you are done.

Pruning removes any dead, diseased, damaged, interfering, crossing or rubbing canes. Pruning shapes the rose and keeps the center open to allow good air circulation. Pruning also keeps large roses from growing out of bounds.

The natural growth habit for roses is to send suckers up from the base of the plant. These shoots are vigorous and productive for a few years and then they lose their vigor. The rose then channels its energy into producing new vigorous shoots. The older shoots still produce flowers, but they are small and of poor quality. Removing the older shoots allows the rose to channel all its energy into the new shoots and large, robust flowers.

Unhilling the rose with a hoe before spring pruning

Using a stick to aid in unhilling

Uncovered rose is ready to prune

The hybrid tea at the front of the bed has been pruned.

A bed of hybrid teas after pruning

When to prune

The best time to prune most roses is in early spring, when the rose breaks winter dormancy, or about 15 days before the last spring frost date. Your local garden center, rose society or county's MSU Extension office should be able to provide information on the last spring frost date for your area. If there is a chance of a late cold snap, it is better to delay your pruning so any new tender growth will not be damaged by frost. Never prune roses before the forsythia shrubs bloom; wait until they are in full bloom. Do not prune in late summer or fall because pruning stimulates new growth that can be winterkilled.

Uncover your roses and level the soil before you begin pruning.

Once-blooming roses, such as old garden roses or species roses, are not pruned heavily in early spring, but any winter-damaged canes are removed at that time. These roses are pruned heavily after flowering is finished. Because these roses bloom mostly or entirely on two-year-old wood, pruning them in spring would remove the wood that produces flowers. Repeat bloomers should be pruned after the last flush or in spring. Once-flowering climbers can have flowering canes removed completely after flowering.

The roses at the Michigan State University Horticultural Demonstration Gardens are pruned at bud break in spring, in late April to early May.

Fall pruning should be done with restraint and only to prepare the rose for winter. Any fall pruning should occur after several hard frosts but before winter sets in. Late November and December is the best time for fall pruning. In areas with high winter winds, some roses are pruned in fall to shorten the plant by one-third or down to waist height to help prevent wind rock, which occurs when the action of the wind moves the rose enough to loosen the roots from the rootzone. You can also prevent wind rock by bunching and tying the canes together with soft but strong ties.

Equipment for rose pruning

You will need the following tools to do a good pruning job:

Hand pruners (secateurs) are used for cutting canes up to $3/4$" diameter. Using hand pruners for cutting canes larger than $3/4$" diameter increases the risk of damaging the remaining branch or stem and is physically more difficult for the person doing the pruning.

Loppers are long-handled pruners used for large, old canes up to $1^1/_2$" diameter.

Pruning saws can also be used for removing large, old canes. The teeth are designed to cut through green wood. Select a saw that has a short blade, around 8", with a pointed tip and tapered blade for cutting in tight areas.

Puncture-proof leather gloves, preferably with leather extending up the forearm.

The cleaner and sharper the cut, the easier it is for the rose to heal the cut, so make sure your tools are sharp and clean before you begin any pruning task. If the cane you are cutting is diseased, you must sterilize the tool before it is used again. A solution of

Hand pruners (secateurs) and loppers must be properly oriented when making a cut. The blade of the pruners or loppers should be to the plant side of the cut, and the hook should be to the side being removed. A cut made with the hook on the plant side will be ragged and difficult to heal.

1 part bleach and 9 parts water is effective for cleaning and sterilizing.

Bypass (scissors-type) pruners and loppers provide a cleaner cut than non-bypass models. Anvil-type pruners, which are non-bypass, have a cutting action similar to a cleaver and cutting board. The cuts from anvil pruners tend to be ragged, especially if the blade is dull. Anvil pruners, including ratchet pruners, are not suitable for use on roses.

Identifying bud eyes

New shoots arise from the buds, or bud eyes, as well as from the base of the rose. Most pruning cuts will be made just above a bud. Buds are immediately above where a leaf was attached to the cane. At pruning time most buds are easily identified as little half-circle bulges on the cane. If the buds are a little hard to spot, especially on older canes, look for a horizontal, flat or crescent-shaped scar left by the leaf and assume a bud will develop just above it. New growth from buds occurs in the direction the bud is facing. When selecting a bud to cut back to, always select one that is on the side of the cane that faces away from the center of the plant. Your rose bush will have a nicer shape and you will keep the center of the rose bush open. Keeping the center of a rose clear allows air to flow through, which is a good defense against fungal diseases.

Latent buds, also known as dormant buds, are located on either side of a primary bud. They are stimulated when an actively growing cane

Penelope

Jens Munk

is removed either deliberately or accidentally. They are easy to remove with your thumb if you want to direct more of the plant's energy to the primary bud. You might want to leave them because latent buds may need to develop to replace old canes that are removed.

How to prune

In general, tender roses need more pruning and hardy roses need less. The following pruning is the minimum that all roses should have annually:

- Remove any dead, diseased, damaged or interfacing canes (canes crossing each other, rubbing together or growing into the center of the plant).
- If the rose is mature, remove two or more of the oldest, unproductive canes, but don't remove too many. Roses store a lot of energy in their canes in the form of unused nutrients and plant-produced sugars and proteins. If more of the canes remain after pruning, the rose will not have to rely so much on its roots to get going in spring. Canes become non-productive after five or six years, so it's important to remove a few of the oldest ones each year to keep the plant rejuvenated.

If a rose has not been pruned for a few years and is gnarly and overgrown, don't cut it back all at once. Complete the task over three or four years, by removing no more than one-third per year, to lessen the shock for the plant. After the first pruning, there will still be foliage producing energy and food for the plant. Successive hard pruning stresses the plant and limits the growth of the root system, which in turn limits the new growth above the ground.

Pruning different varieties

Roses that grow vigorously and bloom on new growth might benefit from additional pruning. A severe pruning every year is recommended for hybrid teas, grandifloras, floribundas and miniatures. Ensure the center is opened and a nice vase-shaped plant outline is created. **Hybrid teas** should be pruned to three to five buds on four to six well-spaced canes.

Pruning cuts for a hybrid tea

White and yellow hybrid teas are generally less vigorous, so they should be pruned like floribundas and grandifloras. **Floribundas** and **grandifloras** should be pruned to five to seven buds on five to seven well-spaced canes. Miniatures should be pruned down to a height of just a few inches in the spring, with some of the oldest canes totally removed.

Pruning for **shrub** and repeat-blooming **old garden roses** involves mostly thinning and shaping. Prune in spring; do not prune after flowering other than to deadhead. Once-blooming old garden roses should be pruned heavily after flowering. Choose the rose to fit the space rather than having to constantly prune to keep the rose within bounds. Generally you can prune, to the crown or base, up to one-quarter of the old, unproductive canes

Pruning a floribunda

annually on mature plants. Remove thin twiggy growth (less than 1/4" in diameter) and all shoots lying on the ground. Shortening extra long canes on once-blooming varieties will stimulate flowering laterals. Remove

Pruning an old garden rose

Pruning cuts for a climber

about one-third of the oldest canes of old garden roses, right from the base of the plant, immediately after they bloom. Their total height can be shortened at that time too, if needed.

Climbing roses should not be pruned for two to three years after planting, other than removing deadwood, to allow the rose to produce long canes from which the flowering lateral branches will develop. Canes should be trained into position as they grow and mature. There are two aims when pruning climbers: encouraging growth of flowering lateral branches and initiating new main canes to replace old, unproductive canes. Annually remove one or two of the oldest canes (older than three years) and trim lateral branches to retain two to three bud eyes per lateral. Long canes can be trimmed to keep them within bounds.

If a main cane is growing in the wrong direction, make every attempt to train it into place by bending it and tying it to the support. If it does not want to cooperate, then remove the whole cane at the base. Long lateral branches may be treated as main canes.

After blooming, once-blooming **rambling roses** produce many long, flexible canes from the base and long laterals from the canes that have just flowered. Next year's flowers arise from this new growth. Remove any canes that are not producing long, vigorous laterals after they have flowered and train the new canes from the base to take their place. Cut back laterals to 24–36" from the main stem.

For repeat-blooming climbers, remove the flowering laterals to two to three buds from the main stem and remove one to two of the oldest canes to rejuvenate the rose. Train new canes to fill the space left from the removal of the old, unproductive canes. Remove excess new growth from the base, but leave some growth to replace old canes. Pruning of climbers can be done in late April–early May when you prune your bush-type roses, or you can wait until after the first bloom cycle is complete in late June.

Prune **groundcover roses** to keep them in the available space. If the groundcover rose is a creeping, stem-rooting variety, cut it well back from the boundary to an upward-facing bud or thin it out back to a main branch. Many groundcovers, such as Flower Carpet (p. 184), should be cut down to 10–12" to rejuvenate.

The goal for pruning **standard roses** is to have a nice balanced head. Shorten shoots by one-third. Ensure that the head is not too large or heavy to be supported. For weeping standards, remove stems that have finished flowering and leave the current season's growth alone.

New Dawn

Proper Pruning Cuts

If pruning cuts are made correctly the plant heals quickly, preventing disease and insect attacks. Pruning cuts for roses include (1) shortening canes to a bud or a branch and (2) removing old canes at the base.

When shortening a cane to a bud, the cut should be made approximately 1/4" above a bud (see diagram below). If the cut is too far away from or too close to the bud, the wound will not heal properly.

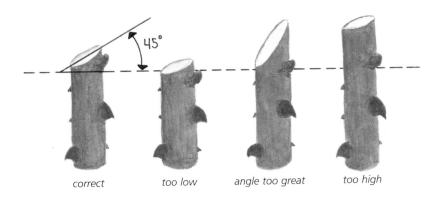

45°

correct   too low   angle too great   too high

Cutting back to a bud eye

Pegging down

When removing an old cane at the base, always cut as close as you can to the base (or bud union if it is exposed). Any deadwood or stubs left on the rose are potential homes for insect pests and disease. In areas where there are rose cane borer attacks, the ends of the cut canes may be sealed with a little dab of white wood glue or pruning paste. Ensure the sealant is spread over the entire cut end. Sealants are unnecessary if borers are not a problem.

Pegging down

Pegging down is the process of bending rose canes and pegging them to the ground near the tip of the cane. It is a way of controlling or training roses without actually cutting them. Roses are genetically programmed to grow to a certain height. Pegging the canes down tricks the rose into thinking it must send out new growth to attain that height. This is good for roses with long, flexible canes, especially hybrid perpetual and bourbon roses that tend to bloom only at the tips of their canes. Pegging down promotes flower production along the length of the cane.

In late summer or early fall, gently bend the canes over and peg the canes to the ground with long, stiff wire staples. You can use coat hangers bent in a U-shape or sod staples purchased from a landscape supply business. Another method is to tie the canes either to a low frame (no higher than 18") or to the lower canes of the rose itself (self-pegging). The shoots created by pegging down should be pruned to 4–6" annually, in spring for repeat-blooming roses and after flowering for once-blooming roses.

Spring pruning of tender varieties in cold winter areas

In cold winter areas, the canes of only the hardiest roses survive above their protective cover or snowline. Prune tender varieties in spring to remove winter-damaged wood back to healthy, outward-facing buds. Frost-damaged canes appear light brown to black with no green or reddish-brown color visible. Frost damage begins at the tip of the cane and works down, sometimes right to the base. The pith of frost-damaged wood is brown. Healthy wood has white or slightly green pith. In older canes healthy pith may be a little off-white.

Begin cutting at the top of the cane and work down until you encounter healthy wood. The correct way to proceed is little by little, to prevent the removal of too much healthy wood. If you are not sure whether the cane is alive, leave it alone until new growth begins so you can see exactly what is happening with the canes. Old canes of rugosa roses may look gray and frost damaged but are often still alive.

After-pruning care

After spring pruning, clean up around your roses. Remove any leaves remaining on the plant from the previous year. Clean up any debris and old leaves on the ground to remove insects and disease that may have overwintered there.

During spring cleanup, many rosarians spray their roses and the soil with a mixture of lime-sulfur or lime-sulfur and oil to destroy any insect eggs or disease spores that might still be there. Roses must still be dormant when applying this spray, which can burn unfurling leaves.

REMOVING ROOTSTOCK SUCKERS

A sucker is a shoot that arises from a plant's roots or underground stems. For grafted roses a sucker is unwanted growth that arises from the rootstock below the bud union. Watch for suckers throughout the growing season and remove them from grafted roses. They grow vigorously but flower just once a year, and they sap energy away from the variety above the graft union.

A floribunda rose before (left) and after (right) spring pruning

Unwanted rootstock suckers are growing to the left of this hybrid tea.

It's easy to spot suckers because the stem and foliage of the sucker will likely look different from the grafted variety. Remove a sucker and its latent buds by exposing the sucker where it attaches to the root and pulling it sharply away from the root. It's best to pull the suckers completely off the rootstock.

It is easiest to remove suckers when they are still small. If the sucker is too large to pull off without damaging the root, then prune it off the root if possible. Gouge the bud eyes out of the remaining root with a knife to prevent more suckers from being produced in the future. Standard roses tend to sucker along the stem. These suckers can be removed by hand.

Cut a sucker off the rootstock of a grafted rose.

DEADHEADING

Deadheading is the process of removing spent blooms. It helps to keep plants looking clean and tidy and, for repeat bloomers, it encourages more blooms. When a rose plant has finished flowering it naturally wants to produce seed-bearing hips, and when the rose is producing seed, it knows it doesn't need to produce any more flowers. Removing the old blooms encourages the formation of new flowers, as the energy that would have gone into seed production is redirected into new bloom production.

Remove spent blooms as quickly as possible after they droop and fade. For large-flowered roses such as hybrid teas, cut the stem just above the first strong outward true leaf (five or more leaflets). The shoot that will emerge from the bud will grow outward, allowing for an open form that will improve air circulation and light penetration. The thicker the cane is where you make your deadheading cut, the stronger the new cane will be, so it may be necessary to cut at the second or third true leaflet from the bloom, where the cane will be thicker.

For cluster-flowered roses such as floribundas, remove the entire cluster to just above the first strong outward true leaf.

Stop deadheading in late summer or early fall, four to six weeks before the first frost date, to allow for hip production, which signals the plant to prepare for winter dormancy.

It is better to not deadhead once-blooming roses. Removing the flowers means no hips will be produced. Many once-blooming roses have attractive hips that provide good fall and winter color as well as food for birds and other wildlife.

Deadheading

WINTER PROTECTION

Whether you need to provide winter protection depends on where you live, the type of roses you are growing and where you have planted them. Cold air accumulates in low spots, depressions or the bottom of slopes, and roses planted in those areas might need extra protection. Areas that are exposed to winter winds will need protection, such as a temporarily erected burlap screen. Tender roses such as hybrid teas, grandifloras or floribundas will require some form of protection. It is often not the winter cold that kills a rose but the freeze-and-thaw cycle that occurs when winter is ending and spring is beginning. It is said that roses with yellow and apricot-colored blooms suffer the most in winter and need extra protection.

Roses hilled for winter

Many beautiful roses, such as the Explorer series or rugosa roses, need no protection at all.

The best way to have a rose survive winter is to plant one that is hardy for your area. If you grow tender roses, the following methods are effective for winter protection.

Garden roses

Stop fertilizing with quick-release nitrogen fertilizer after the second flush of blooms (but no later than the end of July) for repeat-blooming roses and after blooming for once-bloomers.

Stop deadheading four to six weeks before the first frost date.

Allow hips to develop so the rose begins preparing itself for the winter dormant season.

Maintain your watering right to freeze-up to prevent the roots from drying out during winter. The plant does not stop growing over winter, it just slows down.

As soon as frost kills the foliage, remove any remaining foliage and clean up the ground around the rose to eliminate overwintering sites for insect pests and disease spores. Dormant oil and lime-sulfur spray can be applied to the canes and top portion of the soil around the rose to kill overwintering insects and disease spores.

Do not prune roses in fall, except if wind rock is a concern (see p. 60).

Mound soil or other suitable insulating mulch over the crown and canes of tender roses to a depth of 10–12". The mounding is to protect the crown or bud union. Give the mound a good soaking or tightly pack when hilling the soil with the back of a chop hoe or your hands. Some rosarians mound soil over the plant, surround the plant with a wire mesh screen and fill the remaining space with insulating material. This method takes extra work, but it works well in the coldest areas and for the most tender varieties.

If there is snow in your area, keep the roses covered with it. Often only the canes above the snowline are killed.

Plastic cones for covering roses are commercially available. They should not be used since the rose must be cut very short to fit under the cone. Also, the cones heat up the roses too early in spring, causing cane-rot diseases. It's much better to surround the rose with a wire or plastic collar that can be heaped with insulating mulch. Cold frames to protect tender roses can be built from plywood or rigid Styrofoam or polyfoam insulation. The cold frame should have a lid that can be opened on warm days.

Container roses

To protect container roses, use one of the following methods:

Move the container to an area that stays just around freezing but no colder than 23° F, such as an unheated shed or garage. Make sure the area does not get too warm or you might stimulate unwanted growth. Water the container thoroughly before you bring it indoors and check it monthly to ensure that it has not dried out.

OR

Bury the container upright with the bud union underground and the rose exposed and follow the method outlined above for protecting roses in the garden. The rose does not need to be in the sun, but it should be in a well-drained area. This method is often more successful than bringing container roses indoors.

Tree roses

Tree roses need to have two bud unions protected, and one of the unions is well off the ground. One method of protecting tree roses is to grow them in containers and take them into an unheated shed or garage in winter. Another method is to dig out the rose, dig a trench and bury the tree rose horizontally in the soil and mound with extra soil. Make sure to mark its location.

Climbers and ramblers

Protecting tender climbers and ramblers requires a fair amount of work. You can gently remove all the canes from their support and bury them in a trench, ensuring you also bury the crown of the plant. The trench can be long and narrow or just large enough to fit the coiled canes. Another method is to leave the canes where they are and wrap them in a couple of layers of burlap. The base of the rose will still need to be protected or hilled up with soil and mulch. In warmer areas of the state, hilling the roses is all that is necessary. There may be some dieback during severe winters, but new canes will shoot from the base. The easiest way to ensure that your roses survive the winter elements is to grow hardy roses such as the Explorer roses. Simply tie them securely to their supports in fall to prevent damage from winter winds.

All exposed rose canes benefit from a late-fall application of anti-desiccant spray, of the type used to protect hollies and azaleas. The anti-desiccant must be applied when the air temperature is above 40° F and it should be reapplied every 60 days from November through March.

Uncovering your roses

Different parts of your garden will heat up at different rates. Monitor your roses. As soon as you see new growth, start to remove the protection. You can remove the protection a little at a time, over several weeks.

Weak and spindly growth may occur if you wait too long before removing your winter protection. Many rosarians remove winter protection from their roses when they see the leaf buds of their local native trees beginning to break (swell and grow).

When uncovering roses, carefully use a chop hoe or your hands to remove the soil or mulch to avoid damaging any new growth. Do not graze the canes or knock off any shoots. If there is a risk of late frost, the rose can be covered with a sheet or blanket. Remove any dead leaves or debris from the area as part of your spring cleanup.

Hilled-up material can be dug back into the soil to help reduce compaction, the compressing of soil airpockets caused by heavy foot traffic, especially in wet weather. The airpockets, more commonly known by rosarians as soil micro or macro pores, are tributaries that carry water and nutrients throughout the soil. Rose roots, like all other roots, need air to breathe. Mulching the rose beds, reducing foot traffic during wet weather, digging in hilled amendments and encouraging a healthy earthworm population helps to reduce compaction. If leaves and straw were used to protect your roses, compost the material after uncovering the roses.

City of York

Propagation

If you have developed a passion for growing roses, you may want to move to the next level and begin propagating your own roses. There are many reasons to propagate your own roses, including developing new varieties and sharing roses with other gardeners. Following are brief discussions of some of the techniques used to propagate more plants. More information can be found in other print sources. See the Resources on page 262.

Roses are propagated by budding, seedings, taking cuttings, or, for some roses, ground layering. Budding is the most common means of commercially propagating roses. To simplify, budding is the process of inserting a leaf bud of one rosebush under the bark of a rootstock variety. It has to be done in a very particular manner and requires practice.

When creating a new variety, rose breeders pollinate one rose variety with pollen from another and grow hybrid plants from the resulting seeds. This is known as hybridizing.

The process of seeding roses is similar to seeding any perennial or woody ornamental, with the seeds of roses taken from the ripe hips. Seeding most often results in variable seedlings, with different colors, forms and so on, depending on what parentage was used.

Roses grown from cuttings are genetically identical to the plant the cuttings were taken from, so propagating by cuttings is used when you want more of a certain variety of rose. Patented roses are protected by plant patent laws and must not be reproduced by any means, even for personal use.

Ground layering allows future cuttings to form their own roots before they are removed from the parent plant. A section of a flexible branch is buried until it produces roots, at which time it is removed from the parent plant. This method works well with lax-stemmed roses such as groundcovers, albas, damasks, bourbons and some species roses.

With own-root roses, you can take advantage of the naturally occurring suckers. Let the sucker grow until it develops roots of its own. The sucker can then be removed and planted to a new location. It's kind of like automatic ground layering without all the work.

Handel

Problems & Pests

There is both good and bad when it comes to roses and pests and diseases. Many insects and diseases attack only one plant species while others, such as aphids, have a variety of hosts. Mixed plantings can make it more difficult for pests to find their preferred hosts and establish a population. At the same time, because roses are in the same spot for many years, problems can become permanent. The advantage is that beneficial insects, birds and other pest-devouring organisms can also develop permanent populations.

For many years pest control meant spraying or dusting, with the goal to eliminate every pest in the landscape. A more moderate approach advocated today is known as IPM (Integrated Pest Management or Integrated Plant Management). The goal of IPM is to reduce pest problems to levels at which only acceptable damage is done, by incorporating cultural, physical, biological and, lastly, chemical means of control. Of course, gardeners must determine what degree of damage is acceptable to them. Someone growing hybrid tea roses for exhibition will tolerate far less damage than someone growing species roses in a woodland garden. Consider whether a pest's damage is localized or covers the entire plant. Will the damage kill the plant or is it affecting only the outward appearance? Are there methods of controlling the pests without chemicals?

A good IPM program includes learning about your plants, the conditions they need for healthy growth, what pests might affect them, where and when to look for those pests and how to control them. Keep records of pest damage because your observations can reveal patterns useful in spotting recurring problems and in planning your maintenance regime.

Proper identification of what is affecting your rose will help you take appropriate corrective measures. Insects, disease or nutrient

Japanese Beetles

deficiencies can cause problems. If you are unsure what is happening to your rose, contact your local rose society, MSU Extension office or garden center for advice. The Internet is another good source of information.

Choose top quality roses that are resistant to the major diseases in your area. Many beautiful disease-resistant varieties are available. (See p. 93 for a list of disease-resistant roses.) Hybridizers are working at breeding back in the resistance that was being somewhat lost in the quest for the perfect flower form. If you want to grow roses that are susceptible to disease, you may need to tolerate a less-than-perfect rose or find a way to minimize the damage. A good way to determine which roses are the best for your garden is to contact a local rose society. Consulting rosarians are usually available to help you with your selection needs. You could also visit a local rose garden or walk through your neighborhood and see for yourself which roses are growing well.

There are four steps in effective and responsible pest management. Cultural controls are the most important. Physical controls should be attempted next, followed by biological controls. Resort to chemical controls only when the first three possibilities have been exhausted. It is important to properly identify the pest or disease so that the appropriate treatment is used. Consult our Glossary of Pests and Diseases beginning on p. 80.

Leaves afflicted with blackspot

Cultural controls are the gardening techniques you use in the daily care of your garden. Make sure your rose plants have adequate light, water and air circulation. Ensure the soil has adequate drainage, plenty of organic matter and nutrients and an ideal pH. Prevent the spread of disease and insects by keeping gardening tools clean. Thoroughly clean and remove fallen leaves and dead plant matter throughout the season, especially in fall. Providing the conditions roses need for healthy growth reduces plant stress. A stressed plant is vulnerable to pests and disease. Healthy plants can often fight off illness, although some diseases can infect plants regardless of their level of health. In that case, prevention is often the only hope. If a plant has been infected, remove the infected leaves and prune out infected branches immediately.

Physical controls are generally used to combat insect problems. An example of such a control is picking insects off plants by hand, which is not as daunting as it may seem if you catch the problem when it is just beginning. Simply squishing the insects is another method. Other physical controls include barriers that stop insects from getting to the plant, and traps that catch or confuse insects. Physical control of diseases often necessitates removing the infected plant part or parts to prevent the spread of the problem. Do not compost rose waste at home; instead, put it out for your municipal yard-waste pickup.

Biological controls make use of populations of predators that prey on pests. Birds, snakes, frogs, spiders, ladybird beetles (ladybugs) and certain bacteria can play an important role in keeping pest populations at a manageable level. Encourage these creatures to take up permanent residence in your garden. A birdbath and birdfeeder will encourage birds to enjoy your yard and feed on a variety of insect pests. Beneficial insects are probably already living in your landscape, and you can encourage them to stay by planting appropriate food sources. Many beneficial insects eat nectar from flowers such as perennial yarrow. Biological insects are available for purchase from various organic control suppliers as well.

Another form of biological control is the naturally occurring soil bacterium *Bacillus thuringiensis* var. *kurstaki*, or *B.t.* for short, which breaks down the gut lining of some insect pests. It is commonly available in garden centers.

Chemical controls should be used only as the last alternative for pest and disease management. These chemical pesticide products can be either organic or synthetic. If you have tried cultural, physical and biological methods and still wish to take

Frogs eat many insect pests.

further action, call your local county MSU Extension office to obtain a list of pesticides recommended for particular diseases or insects.

The main drawback to using any chemicals is that they may also kill the beneficial insects you have been trying to attract to your garden. Many people think that because a pesticide is organic, they can use however much they want, but an organic spray kills because it contains a lethal toxin.

Carefully follow the manufacturer's instructions regarding application rate and frequency, protective wear and storage and disposal. NEVER overuse any pesticide. Note that if a particular pest or disease is not listed on the package, it will not be controlled by that product. Proper and early identification is vital to finding a quick solution. When using any type of chemical pesticide, organic or synthetic, alternate different spray products so the pest won't build up a resistance to the chemical. Some common commercially available pesticides are listed on p. 79.

Biopesticides are made from plants, animals, bacteria and minerals. Microbial pesticides contain microbes such as bacteria, fungi, viruses and other microbes as the active ingredient. Plant pesticides are derived from naturally occurring plant compounds. Biochemical pesticides come from other naturally occurring substances that control pests by non-toxic means. They are much less harmful than conventional pesticides and for the most part target only the pest. They are effective in small quantities and they decompose quickly in the environment. These products should reduce the reliance on chemical pesticides.

You can apply fungicides as a preventive measure when conditions are right for disease growth or after you see the disease on your rose. You can choose between organic and chemical fungicides. If you choose to use chemical fungicides, check with the local garden center or rose society to acquire appropriate information about the fungicide. At all times follow the directions on the product label. And remember: more is not better.

The recipes on the next page incorporate commonly available ingredients. Many gardeners use these types of homemade mixtures as alternatives to commercially available pesticides. Please note that these homemade mixtures are not to be packaged, distributed or sold.

Not all experts recommend the use of homemade products to treat pests and diseases. Nancy Lindley advocates using only products that have been specifically developed, tested and labeled for use on plants. She reminds gardeners to read and follow the label instructions each time they use the product. She does not endorse homemade products for use on plants.

Apple cider vinegar

The following mixture can be used to treat leaf spot, mildew and blackspot.

In a spray bottle, mix:

3 tablespoons cider vinegar (5 percent acidity)

1 gallon water

Spray on the foliage, including undersides, every 2–3 days for a total of 3 applications.

Baking soda & horticultural oil

University testing has confirmed the effectiveness of this mixture against powdery mildew.

In a spray bottle, mix:

4 teaspoons baking soda

1 tablespoon horticultural oil

1 gallon water

Spray on the foliage, including undersides, every 3–4 days for a total of 3 applications. Do not pour or spray this mix directly into the soil.

Baking soda & citrus oil

The following mixture treats both blackspot and powdery mildew.

In a spray bottle, mix:

4 teaspoons baking soda

1 tablespoon citrus oil

1 gallon water

Spray on the foliage, including undersides, every 2–3 days for a total of 3 applications. Do not pour or spray this mix directly into the soil.

Garlic spray

This spray is an effective, organic means of controlling aphids, leafhoppers, whiteflies and some fungi and nematodes.

Soak:

6 tablespoons finely minced garlic in 2 teaspoons mineral oil for a minimum of 24 hours

Add:

1 pint of water and $1^1/_2$ teaspoons of liquid dish soap

Stir and strain into a glass container for storage. Combine 1–2 tablespoons of this concentrate with 2 cups water to make a spray. Test the spray on a couple of leaves and check after two days for any damage from the soap/garlic mixture. If there is no damage, then you can spray your rose thoroughly, ensuring good coverage of the foliage. One to two applications should be sufficient.

Milk spray

Milk spray helps prevent and control blackspot and mildew. It has been tested on roses and a variety of vegetables and has been moderately successful. Any kind of milk can be used, from high fat milk to skim and even powdered milk. Milk with a lower fat content is recommended as it will have less of an odor. Mix one part milk with nine parts water and apply in a spray every five to seven days for a total of three applications.

Fish emulsion/seaweed (kelp)

These products are usually used as foliar nutrient feeds but appear to also work against fungal diseases by either preventing the fungus from spreading to non-infected areas or by changing the growing conditions for the fungus.

Neem oil

Neem oil is derived from the neem tree (from India) and is used as an insecticide, miticide and fungicide. It is most effective when used as a preventive measure. Apply when conditions are favorable for disease development. Neem is virtually harmless to most beneficial insects and microorganisms.

Antitranspirants

These products were developed to reduce water transpiration, or loss of water, in plants. The waxy polymers also surround fungal spores, preventing the spread of spores to nearby leaves and stems. When applied according to label directions, antitranspirants are environmentally friendly.

Sulfur and lime-sulfur

These products work well as preventive measures. You can get ready-made products or wettable powders that you mix yourself. Do not spray when the temperature is expected to be 90° F or higher as doing so can damage the plant.

Bordo or Bordeaux Fungicides

These products can be used to treat fungal problems including blackspot, powdery mildew and rust. They are available in wettable powders and are easily applied either dry or wet. Follow the recommended rates and instructions to prevent the foliage from being burned.

Be careful if you are using copper mixtures, including Bordo or Bordeaux fungicides. They may effectively control fungal disease for the entire season but can be damaging to the soil and toxic to the user.

The foliage of this White Meidiland has blackspot.

GLOSSARY OF PESTS & DISEASES

The following glossary includes brief descriptions of some of the pests and diseases that may occur. You might want to further explore identification of pests and their lifecycles, their most damaging stage and the best methods of reducing damage. Check the list of resources on page 262, or contact your local library, rose society or county MSU Extension office for additional information.

Do not be discouraged after reading this section. You may never encounter any of these problems (blackspot, Japanese beetles and aphids are the most common). Remember that your best defense against any pest or disease is a healthy rose.

Aphids

Anthracnose and Leaf Spot Diseases

Leaf spots from anthracnose, alternaria and cercospora are fairly common; often confused with blackspot and downy mildew. Appear as irregular black, purple or reddish brown spots without the feathery edge of blackspot. Center of the spot may be white to gray and can even fall out, giving a shot hole appearance. Often occur in spring or fall. Not as virulent as blackspot and doesn't normally cause defoliation.

What to Do. Compost tea as a preventive measure is effective, as are Daconil and Mancozeb. Some have had good results after using diluted baking soda OR diluted apple cider vinegar as a treatment after a proper diagnosis.

Aphids

Tiny, pear-shaped insects, winged or wingless; black, brown, green, red or gray. Cluster along stems, buds and leaves but most often found on new, tender growth. Suck sap from plants; cause distorted or stunted growth. Aphids produce honeydew, a sticky, sugary fluid deposited on leaves and stems. Sticky honeydew forms on surfaces and encourages the growth of black sooty mold. Aphids are like 'plant lice' and are the most common of rose insect pests and likely the easiest to eradicate.

What to Do. Squish small colonies by hand; dislodge them with brisk water spray; spray serious infestations with insecticidal soap; many predatory insects and birds feed on them. Plant feverfew *(Tanacetum parthenium)* close by to repel the aphids. An application of dormant oil in November and again in March will kill overwintering eggs.

Armillaria Root Rot (Shoestring Fungus, Oak Root Fungus)

Soil-borne, parasitic fungus; causes decay of roots and crown by breaking down tissue. May kill the plant quickly or slowly. Plants exhibit stunted growth. Leaves turn yellow or brown; plant wilts, then dies, often one stem or branch at a time. White fungal strands appear under the bark near the crown and on the roots. Honey-colored mushrooms appear around the base of the plant during wet weather. Attacks are most frequent in heavy, clay soils with poor drainage. It is most harmful and prevalent in oaks. Weakened or stressed plants are also vulnerable.

What to Do. Avoid planting susceptible varieties where the fungus is known to exist. Ensure good surface and sub-surface drainage. When preparing a planting area, remove all old tree and shrub roots and mix in a large amount of rich compost. Remove and destroy infected plants; re-plant only resistant plants.

Bacterial Canker

Enters the rose through wounded stem tissue and can attack any part of the rose. Weakened roses more susceptible. Red or yellow spots on the stem progress to form brown patches and lesions that shrivel and

Japanese Beetles destroy leaves and blooms.

die. If the disease is severe enough it will girdle the stem, killing all growth above the infected area.

What to Do. Maintain plant vigor. Avoid wounds on plants. Control borers. Prune out and destroy diseased branches (see Pruning, p. 58). Sterilize your pruning equipment after each cut. Remove rubbing or crossing branches.

Beetles

Many types and sizes; usually round with hard, shell-like outer wings covering membranous inner wings. Some types are beneficial, e.g., ladybird beetles ('ladybugs'); others are not. Both the adult insects and the larvae may feed on roses and other plants. Japanese Beetles skeletonize leaves and occasionally feed on the inside of the blooms, which makes them difficult to control. Rose Chafer destroys buds. Rose Curculio, sometimes known as Rose Weevil, drills holes in the buds. Cucumber Beetle feeds on the petals. Larvae feed on roots and other organic materials in the soil. June Beetle larvae can cause root damage. All of these overwinter in the soil as grubs.

What to Do. Remove by hand and drop in a container of soapy water daily to discourage mass quantities of beetles, which emit attractant hormones. Spray insecticidal soap or pyrethrin (plant-based insecticides) on visible insects. Treat soil with parasitic nematodes, spray roses with beneficial insect sprays, repellents such as garlic water, neem oil and other registered pesticides or beneficial bacteria. Milky spore can be effective on Japanese Beetle larvae and Rose Chafer larvae but may take up to three years of applications for complete control. Prune out infected portions and destroy. Use traps to catch Japanese Beetles, placing the traps at least 40' from desirable plantings.

Blackspot

The most prevalent fungal disease for roses. The fungus overwinters in the top portion of the soil, infected leaves and canes, so plant sanitation is important. Most problematic when warm, humid weather (70°–80° F) is sustained for over a week. Can cause weak growth and stems to die back. An infestation by a single spore can produce visible colonies in as little as 15 days. First appears on the lower foliage as black or brown blotches; yellow rings form to outline the blotches. Severely infected foliage drops; severe cases can defoliate a rose.

What to Do. Water early in the day so that leaves dry quickly. Keep the area free of fallen infected leaves. Remove all the leaves before winterizing to prevent overwintering spores. Use a preventive fungicide when the environmental conditions

Rose heavily afflicted with blackspot

are favorable for fungal infection. The spores are too small to see before they infect the leaf. Take extra care to spray the undersides of the leaves. Mancozeb and Daconil are common and effective chemical controls and must be used regularly. Apply lime-sulfur spray in November and again in March to kill overwintering fungus spores.

Botrytis

Fungal disease that occurs in high humidity. Affects the stems and flowers of mature roses and the bare roots of poorly stored or shipped plants. Grayish-brown fuzzy mold on stems and flower buds; grayish-brown lesion runs down one side of the bud and onto the stem. Flower buds may not open or if they open partially, the petal edges may appear soft and brown.

What to Do. Plant the rose where the morning sun can dry the plant; remove and destroy any infected plant parts. Improve the air circulation around and through the plant. Do not mulch over the crown. Water the base of the plant, taking care not to get the blooms wet.

Cane Borers

Larvae of different insects. White to yellow and worm-like. Burrow into new and freshly cut canes. Destroy vascular tissue (plant veins and arteries) and structural strength. The stems die back from the tips. Look for small hole in the tip of the cane and a swollen band of tissue circling the cane at the bottom of the

Disinfecting Tools

Dip pruning tools into denatured alcohol or a solution of 1 part liquid chlorine bleach and 9 parts water. Disinfect tools between each plant when pruning non-infected plants; between each cut when pruning infected plants. When you have finished your pruning task, disinfect the tools, scrub any discolored areas with steel wool, sharpen the cutting edges and oil metal surfaces.

dieback. Split canes lengthwise with a knife to expose the borer.

What to Do. Handpick visible larvae and drop into a bucket of soapy water. Cut out and destroy infected canes. Do not put cut canes in the compost. Seal the ends of pruned canes with a drop of white glue or a plant wound–sealing product. Avoid planting raspberries near roses, since raspberry cane borers can attack roses.

Caterpillars

Larvae of butterflies and moths. Include budworms, cutworms, leaf rollers, corn earworms and webworms. Chew foliage and buds. Severe infestation can completely defoliate a plant.

What to Do. Use high-pressure water and soap or pick caterpillars off by hand. Cut off and burn large tents or webs of larvae. Control biologically using the naturally occurring soil bacterium *Bacillus*

Insecticidal soap recipe

You can make your own insecticidal soap. Mix 1 teaspoon mild dish soap, with little to no fragrance or color, or pure soap (biodegradable options are available) with 1 quart water in a clean spray bottle. Spray the surface areas of your plants. Rinse them well within one hour of spraying.

thuringiensis var. *kurstaki*, or *B.t.* for short (commercially available), which breaks down gut lining of caterpillars. Insecticidal soap is effective. Apply dormant oil in fall and in spring. Plants such as cornflower, purple coneflower or passion vine will attract the caterpillars away from roses; use neem oil or organic and synthetic pesticides; release parasitic wasps; encourage predatory insects with nectar plants such as yarrow.

Crown Gall

Unusual wart-like swellings of plant tissues caused by bacteria; more prevalent on grafted roses; disease begins at the base of the plant or on the bud union. Bacteria in the soil enter through wounds in the root and crown. Makes tissue green and pliable before forming into dark, crusty growths on roots or crown. Stunts growth, restricts water and nutrient uptake and reduces foliage and bloom production. Easily spread by infected tools and composted garden waste. **What to Do.** Remove any plants that have galls. Replace contaminated soil. Disinfect tools. While some report success with pruning away galls and spraying the infected area with antibacterial solutions or copper compounds, use this solution only if the rose is highly valuable or irreplaceable. Consider, instead, propagating the rose from cuttings and removing the infected plant.

Deer, rabbits, groundhogs

Eat roses and can cause significant damage, especially in rural areas. **What to Do.** Place soap on stakes or in suspended bags throughout your garden and mist the bags early in the evening. Fill mesh bags or old nylon stockings with human hair and place in the affected areas. Natural spray repellents include egg and water mixed with an antidesiccant; bloodmeal solution; garlic oil solution. Most scent deterrents work for just a short time and scents must be reapplied. Fences to keep rabbits out must be buried deep into the ground to prevent the rabbits from burrowing underneath. A sprinkler activated by a motion sensor scares most wildlife away. A pesky dog can help, too.

Leaf Cutter Bee

Cuts neat, smooth circles from the edges of leaves for nesting material. **What to Do.** Nothing. It is a beneficial insect as a pollinator. Damage is only aesthetic.

Leafhoppers

Small, wedge-shaped insects, often green, but can be brown, gray or multi-colored. Jump around frantically when disturbed. Suck juice from plant leaves and cause distorted growth. Can transmit diseases from plant to plant as they feed.

What to Do. Encourage predators by planting nectar-producing plants. Wash insects off with strong spray of water; spray with insecticidal soap.

Mildew

Two types, both caused by fungus, but with slightly different symptoms. *Downy mildew:* may be confused with blackspot. One of the most feared rose diseases, although rare; isolated occurrences in some areas in southeastern Michigan. More commonly found on greenhouse-grown roses; rarely seen on garden roses. Prefers cool, moist or humid conditions with splashing water and wind to carry its spores to the next host. Two days of dry, hot weather (90° F or higher) will stop the disease, but spores remain for future infections. Purple-red irregular blotches on the new leaf and stem growth are systemic; lesions are a sign that the disease has spread throughout the plant. Infected plants drop their leaves quickly. Gray fuzz appears on undersides of the foliage. *Powdery mildew:* attacks many rose varieties in all climates but prefers warm, moist, cloudy days and cool, humid nights. Much less destructive and much more common than downy mildew. Appears on young leaves, stems and thorns. Begins as pinkish lesions and changes into a white or gray powdery coating. Canes can become distorted and flower petals appear dry and become discolored on the edges.

Severe infestations may lead to new growth being distorted and dying.

What to Do. Choose roses that are not susceptible to mildew. Fall cleanup is essential to prevent mildew overwintering on canes and fallen leaves. Provide good air circulation. Remove and destroy any infected foliage. Apply fungicides such as lime-sulfur or dormant oil while the rose is dormant in November and again in March or April. Spray the soil as well to decrease overwintering active spores.

Mossy Rose Gall

Golf ball–sized, spiny balls on leaves or stems. Caused by *Diplolepis spinosa*, a cynipid gall wasp. Insect larvae develop inside the gall; adult wasps emerge the following spring. The galls are unsightly, alter the plant's shape and stress the host plant by taking nutrients away from the plant. Large numbers of galls on a plant can kill the plant.

Powdery mildew

What to Do. After the leaves drop in fall, prune the infested branches, cutting below the gall and above a bud, and destroy. For leaf galls, pick up fallen leaves in fall.

Root Rot

Fungus that can cause weak, stunted growth. Leaves yellow and plant wilts and dies. Digging up plant will show rotted roots.

What to Do. Keep soil well drained. Do not overwater. Don't damage plant if you are digging around it; keep mulches away from plant base. Destroy plant if whole plant infected.

Rose Midge

Small, nearly invisible adult insects; hatch at the growing tips and use their rasping mouth parts to feed on tender new tissue, especially flower buds. Rose shrivels or bears no flowers but the rest of the plant is healthy. Other evidence is scorched or blackened newer growth, blind shoots and no buds. The symptoms are most evident in May and early June. Rose midge overwinters in soil.

What to Do. Difficult to control. Prune out and destroy blackened buds and canes; make sure to prune back hard to get rid of larvae that may have traveled down the cane. Add predatory nematodes to the soil to destroy the pupating larvae. Mist just the buds and blooms with an insecticide such as Orthene or Bayer Rose and Flower Spray. Place a sheet of black plastic around the base of the rose to stop the larvae from reaching the soil to pupate. Keep the area around the plant free of weeds and litter. Consult a local rosarian, garden center or nursery or rose society for other solutions.

Rose Mosaic

Viral disease. Often confused with a nutrient deficiency causing interveinal yellowing. Yellow, irregular rings, line or netting patterns appear on leaf. Weakens plant, making it vulnerable to other pests and winterkill. Blooms may be distorted or undersized; may be early leaf drop. Not transmitted by insects or pruning tools but by propagation practices.

What to Do. Remove the rose. Inform the people who sold you the plant that the plant had a virus. Contact the regional office of the Michigan Department of Agriculture because it is illegal to sell virus-infected roses in Michigan.

Leaves with rose mosaic virus

Rose Rosette

Viral disease; rare in Michigan. No known cure; 100 percent fatal. Can be transmitted through infected rootstock. Mites may carry the disease; visible in the top few inches of new growth, usually near the bud eyes. Unusually dense prickles form on overly large, deep red or purple canes. New foliage appears distorted and crinkled and deep red or purple. Leaf stems are often flattened. Weak, chlorotic stems grow.

What to Do. Remove the cane to which any infected stem is attached. If other canes on the same plant become infected, remove the entire plant. The disease does not spread rapidly. Pruning will not transmit the disease. The use of predatory mites and neem oil may be effective. Contact your county's MSU Extension office to report this rare disease.

Rose Sawfly Larvae

Also called rose slugs; ¹/₂" long green worms that coil into tight circle. Caterpillar-like larvae that skeletonize foliage; especially destructive early in the growing season; remain on the underside of the leaves. Rose slugs are exactly the same color as the underside of a rose leaf and are difficult to see. Normally there are just one or two generations of rose slugs each year and the damage isn't noticed until after they're gone. When the larvae are seen, treat as follows.

What to Do. Remove by hand (wear gloves—handling these pests can severely irritate skin); shake the larvae from the shrub and step on

Rose hips and leaves covered in rust

them. Spray with insecticidal soap or dust with pyrethrin to control severe infestations.

Rust

Bright orange spots on leaf undersides; brown spots on upper leaf surfaces. Severe infestations appear as lesions and attack stems, and new growth becomes distorted. Can cause complete defoliation if left unchecked. More common in mild, wet weather (65°–70° F) including humid and foggy days and heavy morning dew. Spores are transmitted by wind and water and will overwinter.

What to Do. Pick off and destroy infected leaves. Where the disease is common, spray weekly with sulfur in early spring. Prune at least 1" beyond the infected tissue.

Spider Mites

Tiny; eight-legged relatives of spiders; do not eat insects but may spin webs. Almost invisible to the naked eye; red, yellow or green; usually found on underside of leaves. May see fine webbing on leaves and stems; may see mites moving on leaf undersides. Suck juice out of leaves. Leaves become discolored and speckled; then turn brown and shrivel up. Spider mites prefer hot, dry weather; roses next to walls and pavement and those under drought stress are vulnerable to attack. Severe infestations can completely defoliate the plant.

What to Do. Wash off with strong water spray daily, especially targeting the underside of leaves, until all signs of infestation are gone; predatory mites are available through garden centers; spray plants with insecticidal soap, light horticultural oil or neem oil; ensure roses receive a deep and thorough watering as water-stressed plants are inviting to these creatures; special miticides (pesticides specific to mites) are available.

Thrips

Tiny, flying insects. Scrape the flower surfaces and suck the juice from the open wounds. Damage is mainly on buds and open blooms. Petals appear bruised and discolored with light brown, translucent spots especially around the petal edges. Flowers can be deformed and buds can fail to open. Thrips seem to prefer tight, full buds of large-flowered yellow, pink or white roses. They thrive in hot and dry weather.

What to Do. Remove and destroy infected plant parts; encourage native predatory insects; spray serious infestations with insecticidal soap. Spunbound polyester covers can be effective.

Whiteflies

Tiny, white insects that flutter up into the air when the plant is disturbed. May appear as white dust

Ladybird beetle (ladybug), a gardener's best friend

above the foliage; tend to live near the top of the plant. Pierce the tissue and suck plant juices, causing yellowed leaves and weakened plants; produce honeydew. Damage may also include loss of foliage and stunted growth.

What to Do. Destroy weeds where insects may live. Encourage predatory insects and parasitic wasps. Spray severe infestations with insecticidal soap. Can use sticky traps, pheromone traps or light traps. Organic pesticides such as neem oil, horticultural oil and garlic water may be used.

OTHER PROBLEMS
Balling

Flowers open only partially; petal edges turn brown and rot. Triggered by weather; occurs in high humidity and when watering from above. Some roses more susceptible than others, especially roses in shade or those with large blooms with thin petals. Balling blooms feel slimy and smell like decomposing organic matter. May also be caused by aphids, so keep aphid populations to a minimum.

What to Do. Caused by wet conditions. Water early in the day; water just the base of the plant. Prune out as if you were deadheading; i.e., down to the first outward-facing true leaf.

Blind Shoots

Sometimes shoots will arise that have no terminal flower buds. These are known as blind shoots. They take energy away from flower production.

What to Do. Cut any blind shoots back to the first true leaf that has an outward-facing bud and hope it produces a flowering shoot. If you prefer, you can leave the blind shoots alone to retain more foliage.

Heat stress

Major cause of yellowing leaves. Most noticeable during sudden temperature changes, especially on young plants and new growth. Very common with newly planted roses. Leaf margins may scorch. Blooms may have darkened petal edges.

What to Do. Increase watering frequency and duration during hot periods; screen new plants from the sun; plant roses out of the afternoon sun; apply mulch to keep roots cool.

Mechanical problems

Cultivating too close to roots can damage them, and if roots are damaged, water and nutrient uptake is reduced and suckers are encouraged. A sign of damaged roots is yellowing foliage. If any roots are visible after cultivating, cover them.

What to Do. Take care when cultivating, going no deeper than 1–2"; prune freshly exposed roots and re-plant; water deeply so roots penetrate below normal cultivation depths.

Salt stress

Accumulated salts compete with rose roots for moisture and can make required nutrients unavailable to plants (nutrient fixation), even though the nutrient is in the soil. The result is yellowed leaves, reduced plant growth, scorched leaf margins and eventually plant death. Container roses are most susceptible. The regular use of water-soluble fertilizers may lead to salt buildup, especially where soils are heavy or where irrigation or rainfall fails to wash these salts past the rootzone. Water high in phosphates may also cause salt buildup.

What to Do. Irrigate deeply; improve drainage; get soil tests done regularly; change soil in containers every three to four years.

Water stress

Excess water: veins in the leaves begin to turn yellow; then the entire leaf yellows and droops; blooms fail to open completely; pith becomes soft and brown. *Inadequate water:* leaf margins wilt and scorch; lower leaves turn yellow.

What to Do. Improve drainage; increase or decrease water as needed.

Nutrient Deficiencies

Nutrient deficiencies aren't a common problem with garden roses grown in organically rich, well-drained soil with an appropriate fertilizer program. Nutrient deficiencies are more common with container roses. But what may look like pest or disease damage may be a nutrient deficiency or toxicity. A soil test or a plant tissue test is the only way to tell for sure if there is a nutrient deficiency or toxicity. Check the Soil Testing resources (p. 264) for locations.

Boron is responsible for water movement within the plant. A deficiency manifests itself as mottled, yellow, misshapen new leaves and buds that are growing too close to each other at the top of the plant.

Calcium is a nutrient in liming materials used to increase soil pH. Calcium deficiency occurs in younger or upper leaves. Leaves brown, curl, shrivel and die. If there is an excess of calcium, phosphorus and iron aren't available to the plant.

Iron deficiency, or iron chlorosis, is seen as interveinal yellowing of younger leaves at the top of the plant and the new growth. Iron contributes to the production of chlorophyll, essential for photosynthesis. Iron chlorosis is often a sign that the soil pH is too high and the plant is unable to utilize the iron in the soil.

Magnesium deficiency looks like iron deficiency, but the yellow leaves with dark veins occur on the older, lower leaves first. Magnesium is a common nutrient in some liming materials used to increase soil pH.

Manganese is responsible for metabolic processes. Without enough manganese, the smaller leaf veins stay green but the younger leaves appear webbed or net-like. The new leaves may be spotted and older leaves mottled. Excess manganese reduces iron uptake.

Nitrogen encourages vegetative growth. It is responsible for a plant's lush green growth and overall size. It is the nutrient most commonly deficient because of leaching, especially from sandy soils. Nitrogen deficiency appears as undersized, pale green to yellow leaves, affecting the older leaves first. Stems may be weak and thin and blooms may be small. Overall plant growth is slow and stunted. Excess nitrogen causes overly lush dark green growth and weak stems susceptible to disease, winterkill and attack by insects.

Phosphorus encourages root development and is very rarely deficient. A phosphorus deficiency begins as dark green to purplish coloration in the older, lower leaves. Plant growth is stunted and spindly. Phosphorus toxicity appears as yellowing of the leaves between the veins. The leaves may be thicker, stems may be shorter and buds may be malformed or curled. Phosphorus accumulates in the soil, especially heavy soils.

Potassium promotes flowering, plant strength and structure so improves resistance to potential problems. It contributes to chlorophyll production. Potassium deficiency is seen first on the older, lower leaves. The leaves begin to yellow between the veins from the leaf tips and margins (leaf edge), and the edges begin to brown. Potassium toxicity is similar to phosphorus toxicity, but potassium toxicity results in

root loss, therefore affecting a plant's ability to take up water and nutrients.

Sulfur is commonly added to the soil (a different formulation of sulfur is used as a fungicide) to lower pH over time. It encourages the production of chlorophyll (responsible for the green color in leaves). Sulfur deficiency occurs on new growth. The leaves and leaf veins turn yellow and the roses become stunted. Excessive sulfur causes the leaf veins to turn yellow, followed by rapid loss of the lower leaves.

Zinc promotes water uptake. A deficiency appears as an interveinal chlorosis (yellowing between the veins), stunted growth, smaller foliage, thick stems, rosetting of new shoots and a whitish appearance. An excess of zinc reduces the uptake of manganese.

Ladybird beetle (ladybug) larva

Bonica

John Davis

Rosa glauca

Easy-to-grow Roses

groundcover roses
species roses
Ballerina
Bonica
Carefree Wonder
City of York
Earth Song
Gourmet Popcorn
Hope for Humanity
Ingrid Bergman
Jeanne LaJoie
Jens Munk
John Davis
Madame Hardy
New Dawn
Prairie Joy
Queen Elizabeth
Tournament of Roses
William Baffin

Shade-tolerant Roses

Ballerina
Betty Prior
Blanc Double de Coubert
Bonica
Carefree Delight
Clair Matin
Charles de Mills
Fru Dagmar Hastrup
Golden Wings
Hénri Martin
New Dawn
Rosa glauca
The Fairy

Drought-tolerant Roses

groundcover roses
species roses
Constance Spry
Europeana
Mister Lincoln
Roseraie de l'Haÿ
Stanwell Perpetual

Disease-resistant Roses

groundcover roses
species roses
Alexander Mackenzie
Betty Prior
Blanc Double de Coubert
Bonica
Carefree Wonder
City of York
Dainty Bess
Elina
Fantin-Latour
Fourth of July
Fru Dagmar Hastrup
Hébé's Lip
Hénri Martin
Honor
Iceberg
Jens Munk
Königin von Dänemark
Knock Out
Morden Snowbeauty
Polka
Prairie Joy
The Fairy
White Meidiland
Winnipeg Parks

Constance Spry

Elina

Honor

About This Guide

This book showcases 144 roses ideal for Michigan, divided into nine sections: species, old garden, modern shrub, groundcover, climbers and ramblers, hybrid tea, floribunda, grandiflora and miniature. Each section begins with an explanation of the characteristics of the class. The roses are arranged alphabetically according to the name they are most commonly known by. Alternative names are given below the main heading.

Clearly displayed in each entry are the features of the rose: the flowers' color, size and scent; height and spread ranges; bloom seasons and hardiness zones (see map, p. 8). Each entry contains information pertinent to growing and enjoying the rose.

The introduction to the book has tips for buying, planting, growing and caring for roses. The Glossary of Pests & Diseases beginning on p. 80 provides information on detecting and solving common problems.

Because our region is so climatically diverse, we refer to seasons only in a general sense. Keep in mind the timing and duration of seasons in your area when planning your rose garden. Hardiness zones, too, can vary within a region; consult a local rose society, garden center or your county's MSU Extension office for specific information. The Resources section beginning on p. 262 lists gardens, suppliers, MSU Extension offices for soil testing and additional information and rose societies in Michigan as well as books and websites about roses.

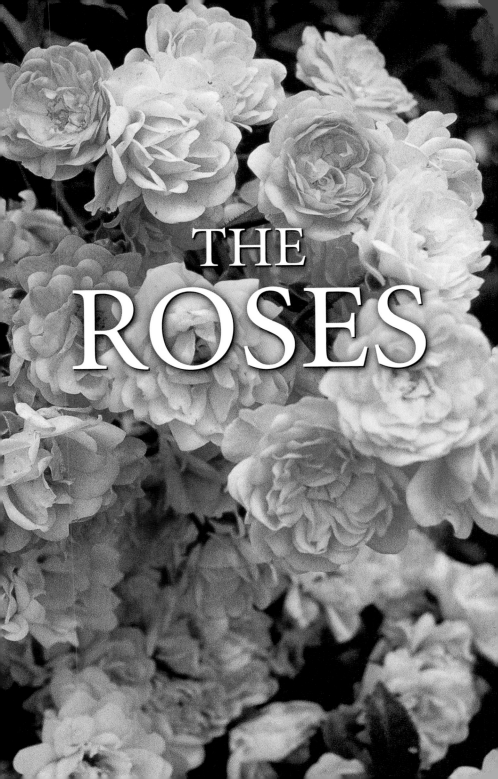

THE
ROSES

SPECIES ROSES

S pecies roses are roses that, when self-fertilized, produce seedlings that are identical to the parents. These roses have not been cultivated but have grown naturally throughout the northern hemisphere, likely since before man existed. Species roses are very cold hardy and come in a variety of growth habits, from vigorous climbers to compact shrubs. Species roses have low petal counts and can tolerate partial shade. Use species roses in informal borders, woodland gardens or hedges.

Species roses usually flower once a year and produce attractive hips. Some species roses have excellent fall color. This group of roses tends to be more resistant to drought and disease compared to modern roses. Unfortunately, species roses are not widely available, but the results are well worth the search.

Rosa eglanteria

Other names: Eglantine, *R. rubiginosa, R. suavifolia, R. walpoleana,* Sweet Briar Rose, Sweetbriar, Shakespeare's Rose, Shakespeare's Eglantine

Flower color: light pink

Flower size: 1½–2"

Scent: true rose

Height: 8–10'

Spread: 5–6'

Blooms: late spring to summer; no repeat blooming

Hardiness zones: 4–10

Rich red, oval hips, often covered in fine bristles, form after the flowers and remain on the plant well into fall.

Carolus Linnaeus, the 18th-century botanist regarded as the 'Father of Taxonomy,' introduced *Rosa eglanteria* over 450 years ago, and during the 19th century, it was the preferred rootstock for grafting rose standards. Today it stands on its own and is still sought after. Those who know it love it—including Shakespeare, who perfectly described this rose in 1594: '...a bank whereon the wild thyme blows, Where oxlips and the nodding violet grows/Quite over-canopied with luscious woodbine/With sweet musk-roses, and with eglantine.'

❀ With its single, flat flowers, this species rose looks simple and wild. Glands located on the underside of the leaves produce a remarkable scent reminiscent of apples.

❀ This rose would blend beautifully in a number of locations including a woodland garden. It would be a beautiful specimen or a dense hedge, where it could be kept in bounds with regular clipping. Clipping may reduce the overall quantity of flowers, but would encourage new young aromatic shoots.

❀ Plant *Rosa eglanteria* away from areas with high traffic, as the canes are tremendously thorny.

Rosa glauca

This rose thrives where most plants could not survive. It is used by municipalities in open planting areas because it looks good and needs little care. The starry, pink blossoms make a striking contrast to the young violet-tinted foliage that matures to a striking blue-gray. The flowers are followed by clusters of small, rounded, dark red hips that remain on the shrub well into the following spring.

Other names:
R. rubrifolia, R. ferruginea, Red-leafed Rose

Flower color:
mauve pink; white centers

Flower size: 1½"

Scent: slight

Height: 6–10'

Spread: 5–6'

Blooms: late spring; no repeat blooming

Hardiness zones: 2–9

✿ This species is sought after by floral designers for the colorful, dainty foliage that is perfect for floral arrangements. It is equally beautiful in the garden. *Rosa glauca* is ideal as a hedge because of its vigorous nature and arching, thorny, purple stems. It lends color to a stark winter landscape with its burgundy hips and maroon stems. It also makes a splendid specimen. This rose has both looks and strength.

✿ *Rosa glauca* tolerates shade but prefers full sun, which improves the depth of the foliage color.

✿ Keep this species under control with regular pruning, which will encourage new and colorful shoots. It is susceptible to mossy rose gall, which can be controlled with pruning.

✿ *Rosa glauca* was introduced into cultivation in Britain before 1830. Bushes can still be found on the terrace at the Crathes Castle in Aberdeen, Scotland.

This rose received the Royal Horticultural Society Award of Garden Merit, an official stamp of approval from the experts. It is extremely popular among rosarians and novice gardeners alike because it is so hardy and disease resistant.

Rosa palustris

Other names:
Swamp Rose

Flower color:
medium pink

Flower size: 2½"

Scent: very sweet

Height: 6–10'

Spread: 6–8'

Blooms: mid- to late summer; no repeat blooming

Hardiness zones: 4–8

I ts alternate name, Swamp Rose, is appropriate for this water-loving rose that is great for a moist location where little else will grow. Known to sucker, this upright shrub bears single flowers of five petals each that appear intermittently throughout summer. Amidst pale, matte foliage the pink petals open flat and surround bright yellow stamens.

✿ This rose produces hips covered with glandular bristles at the tips of reddish stems. The hips are very attractive to birds, which can spread the seed around after consuming the hips in wetlands and areas with large bodies of water.

✿ *Rosa palustris* is not considered invasive but is native to the eastern and central U.S., from Florida north to Canada and west to the Great Plains.

✿ This rose rarely experiences any problems with disease and requires little maintenance.

✿ *Rosa palustris* often grows in road-side drainage ditches and is easy to identify, as it comes into bloom later than most other species roses.

Rosa sericea pteracantha

This species rose is unique because of its wing-like thorns. The thorns are bright red to burgundy in color, rather ominous in size and translucent. Once mature, the thorns change into a muddy brown color. Fine-textured foliage sparsely covers the thorny canes, tipped with single white flowers. The flowers sometimes have four petals each rather than five, which is more common for a species rose. The flowers emerge in loose clusters. Later in the season orange-red, small, plump hips begin to form and remain on the plant well into winter.

- Plant this species rose in a row to create an impenetrable barrier or hedge. It grows into a narrow, vase-like form that is ideal for specimen plantings or mixed borders or as a vertical accent.
- Hard pruning in the spring encourages a new flush of growth and brightly colored, translucent thorns.
- This unusual rose never fails to attract notice. It is sometimes difficult to find but well worth the search.
- *Rosa sericea pteracantha* was discovered in an Asian garden setting by a French missionary, Abbé Delavay. He later introduced it to the world, sometime after 1824.

Other names:
Pteracantha, Wingthorn Rose, *R. omeiensis pteracantha*
Flower color: white
Flower size: 1½–2"
Scent: little
Height: 6–8'
Spread: 5–6'
Blooms: summer; no repeat blooming
Hardiness zones: 5–9

OLD GARDEN

O ld garden roses are members of rose classes discovered or hybridized before 1867. Many of the oldest varieties bloom once during the growing season, producing a large quantity of fragrant flowers for a short time. Hybridizing in this class continued after 1867, but hybrids are still classified as old garden roses. This large and diverse class includes the following groups.

Gallica

Gallica roses are forms of *Rosa gallica*, often called the French Rose. It was the dominant rose in Europe from the 12th to the early 19th centuries but was in cultivation even earlier. Gallicas reached their peak in the early 19th century, when over 1000 varieties were created by French rose breeders. These roses have upright, tidy to free-branching growth and intensely fragrant flowers that bloom once a year. The stems are moderately prickly, and fall foliage and hips are red. These hardy roses do not mind a little shade. Their fragrance increases when the petals are dried, making them ideal for potpourri. Use gallicas in beds or borders, as hedges or specimens.

William Lobb

Damask

Hybrids of *Rosa damascena*, damask roses are prickly, open, sprawling shrubs with intensely fragrant flowers. They have been cultivated for centuries for attar of roses, an expensive perfume and cosmetic base. Like the gallicas, damask roses played a role in the heredity of modern roses. There are two groups of damasks. Summer damasks, derived from crosses of *Rosa gallica* with *Rosa phoenicea*, bloom once a year. Autumn damasks, derived from crosses of *Rosa gallica* and *Rosa moschata*, bloom twice a year. Use damask roses in a border or train on a support, such as a large peony hoop. This group is hardier than most other old garden roses, suitable for all regions within the state.

Alba

Alba roses are upright, graceful, free-branching shrubs with excellent pest and disease resistance, very good cold hardiness and excellent longevity. They have clean blue-gray foliage and can tolerate light shade better than other classes of roses. They are very low maintenance and bloom once a year with small clusters of small, intensely sweet flowers. Alba roses derive from a cross of *Rosa canina*, the dog rose, and *Rosa damascena*, the damask rose. They have been in cultivation since at least the time of the Roman Empire and were described by Pliny the Elder in his work *Historia Naturalis*. Alba roses are in the ancestry of many early hybrids. They are suitable for borders and beds, planted en masse or as specimens.

Centifolia

Centifolias were thought to be introduced around 1600. These roses are featured in the paintings of the Dutch and Flemish Masters of the 17th and 18th centuries. Centifolias, also known as cabbage roses, are very hardy, open shrubs with good pest and disease resistance and prickly stems. They are taller and more robust than gallicas. They bloom profusely with large, full, intensely fragrant flowers once a season. 'Centifolia' means '100-leaved,' referring here to the large number of tightly packed petals. Centifolias are derived from *Rosa centifolia*, likely a cross of an autumn damask and an alba cultivar. Use centifolia varieties in large borders or as specimens.

Moss

Moss roses began as sports of centifolia and damask roses. Balsam-scented, moss-like growth is produced on the unopened flower buds, stems and sometimes on the foliage. The feel of the moss indicates a moss rose's origin—if a rose has supple, fern-like moss, it has been derived from a centifolia, while stiff, prickle-like moss means a rose has been derived from a damask. Moss roses are generally hardy to zone 5. They perform just as beautifully in colder regions and thrive from year to year with adequate winter protection and the right care and attention.

Tuscany Superb

Portland roses are small, rounded, prickly shrubs with reasonable cold hardiness and a dislike of hot, humid climates. They are reliable repeat bloomers. Sometimes referred to as damask perpetuals, portlands derived from autumn damasks, gallicas and China roses. Their outstanding characteristics include a repeat flowering cycle and compact shrub form, making them attractive for modern gardens. Hybridizers crossed the portlands with the everblooming China roses to produce the forerunners of the hybrid perpetuals. Use portland roses in the bed or border, or try them in a hedge.

Bourbon

The first bourbon rose, *Rosa* x *borboniana*, was discovered in 1819 on the Isle of Bourbon (now Reunion Isle, a small island in the Indian Ocean) as a naturally occurring hybrid of China and autumn damask roses. Nearly all 19th-century hybridizers used this hybrid, and hundreds of cultivars were produced, with many of the best still widely available in commerce today. Bourbon roses are open, upright, vigorous shrubs with large, often quartered flowers. They are mildly prone to blackspot and powdery mildew and possess a variable level of cold hardiness. Use them in a border or bed, or train them on a fence, pillar, veranda railing or obelisk.

Hybrid Perpetual

Beloved by the Victorians for their fragrance, robust constitution, long stems and refined, lush flower form, hybrid perpetuals ruled the rose world in the late 19th century. Over 3000 varieties were bred to meet the demands of rose show exhibitors. The best of these remain in commerce and are sometimes confused with hybrid tea roses. While more winter hardy than modern hybrid teas, the hybrid perpetuals do not bloom as freely. The term 'perpetual' is not really accurate but was Victorian marketing hype; these roses have excellent spring bloom and a good fall repeat in Michigan, with some summer blooms. This class is the product of crosses between bourbons, portlands, chinas and tea roses. They range in color from white to the deepest maroon and some have interesting stripes, speckles or picotee edging. Grow these varieties in much the same way as hybrid teas: offer winter protection in harsh climates and be vigilant for fungal diseases in humid areas.

Charles de Mills

Hybrid Spinosissima
These roses derived from *Rosa spinosissima*, the Scotch Briar rose, and are low-growing, suckering shrubs with fern-like foliage. They are very hardy and long-lived, flowering profusely once a year in spring. The flowers are primarily single blooms in white, yellow or pink tones. The canes are heavily prickled although some varieties have few prickles. Many natural variations and hybrids have been introduced, but few remain in commerce. This group has been extensively used in the landscape for hundreds of years. Occasionally new cultivars are introduced.

Hybrid Eglanteria
Also known as sweetbriar roses, eglantine roses were originally crossed with hybrid perpetual, bourbon or other roses. These large, arching shrubs can reach 10–12' in height. They bear spicy, apple-scented foliage, and the blooms are borne singly or in clusters. The fragrant blooms are followed by bright red hips in fall. Most eglantine roses are once-blooming, but a few varieties do repeat bloom.

Hybrid Foetida
Hybrids of *Rosa foetida*, also known as Austrian Yellow or Austrian Briar, brought yellow, previously unseen in roses, into European rose breeding. *Rosa foetida* is often combined with other species to produce a brilliant yellow modern hybrid. The term *foetida* (origin of the word 'fetid') refers to an offensive scent found in the species.

Cardinal de Richelieu

Other names: Cardinal Richelieu, Rose van Sian

Flower color: dark reddish purple

Flower size: 2½–3"

Scent: moderate, sweet, peppery

Height: 3–6'

Spread: 4–6'

Blooms: mid-summer; no repeat blooming

Hardiness zones: 4–9

Cardinal de Richelieu is easy to grow and bears an abundance of flowers on smooth, arching, burnished dark green stems. It has a lax, bushy and tidy growth habit and is extremely hardy. It bears fully double, dark red flowers that fade to royal purple and reveal a green button eye. The flower color is reminiscent of dark red grapes in a vineyard, at their peak and ready for harvest. The central petals are folded inward, showing off a lighter tone on the reverse. The flowers fade to slate gray as they age and complement any mixed border or showy hedge.

✿ Cardinal de Richelieu is not a true gallica but is considered a triploid gallica-China hybrid. It produces the best flowers on the newest growth, and the flower color appears to change according to the light and time of day.

✿ Long-lasting, colorful flowers with long, smooth stems make Cardinal de Richelieu a wonderful rose for cutting. Cut the stems while still in bud to extend their vase life.

✿ Removing old and unproductive wood, feeding generously, providing fertile soil and practicing good cultivation will only increase the benefits offered by this shrub. Failing to prune moderately hard after flowering will cause the blooming to become more sporadic.

This rose was developed in 1840 by Laffay in France. Its namesake, Cardinal de Richelieu, was the chief minister to Louis XIII.

Charles de Mills

Charles de Mills bears the largest blooms in the family of gallica roses. It is often in garden books as the perfect example of an old garden rose. The unusually large, purply pink blooms pack 200 petals or more into each flower. The flower color can be violet, crimson, wine, purple or maroon. The flat-topped buds that open to flat blossoms, exposing a green button eye in the center, prove this to be a true gallica rose.

Other names: Bizarre Triomphant, Charles Mills

Flower color: rich purple with touch of crimson

Flower size: 3½–5"

Scent: moderate to strong

Height: 4–5'

Spread: 3–5'

Blooms: spring to early summer; no repeat blooming

Hardiness zones: 4–9

✿ The quartered blossoms are so full that the inner petals cluster and fold in towards the center. The petals look like they have been clipped at the tips, resulting in puckered blooms, a very unusual form.

✿ Under ideal conditions this variety will become larger and bloom profusely. Its tolerance of poor soils and partial shade, however, makes it useful in just about any landscape setting, including mixed beds and hedging and as an exhibition rose. It is also suitable for wild gardens, alongside meadows or in larger gardens.

✿ The best location would be where the fragrance can be fully enjoyed, near a bench or under a window.

✿ Very little maintenance is required to keep this rose looking great. Remove old and unproductive wood once flowering is complete to encourage dense, lush growth and heavier flowering.

This rose is a little prone to blackspot and powdery mildew, so provide a location with adequate air circulation.

Fantin-Latour

Fantin-Latour, considered one of the most fragrant old garden roses, is officially classified as a centifolia but displays characteristics of other classes. It shares qualities with gallica and China roses, but not the repeat blooming. The flowers are produced in large clusters of fully double, pale pink flowers, packed with 200 or more petals each. Each flower has a typical old rose button eye.

Other names: none
Flower color: pale pink
Flower size: 3–3½"
Scent: fresh, delicate and sweet
Height: 5–6'
Spread: 5–6'
Blooms: mid-summer; no repeat blooming
Hardiness zones: 5–9

✿ This rose bears smooth, matte foliage that doesn't seem to mind hot and dry weather.

✿ This fragrant and showy rose is used frequently as a large spreading shrub and can be trained to ramble on a fence. Once established, Fantin-Latour blends well into mixed beds and borders where space allows, and it is not troubled by large tree roots. It grows even larger in cooler settings but can be pruned once the blooming is complete. When Fantin-Latour is supported and left unpruned, it can reach heights of 10'.

✿ Though centifolias are reputed to be prone to blackspot and to have unsightly flowers after rain, Fantin-Latour does not have these tendencies. This rose is moderately disease resistant but a little prone to mildew. It tolerates poorer soils and needs to be pruned after flowering so it will bloom prolifically the following year.

Introduced around 1900, this rose was named after the celebrated French painter Henri Fantin-Latour (1836–1904), known for his many still-life and old garden rose paintings.

Harison's Yellow

This rose first appeared in 1830, in an area that is now downtown Manhattan, in the garden of attorney and amateur hybridist George F. Harison. It was carried by a number of pioneers on their journeys west and remains as popular today. Harison's Yellow is one of the hardiest hybrid foetida roses. It bears bright yellow, double flowers in a cupped form. Each flower is made up of 20 to 24 petals surrounding showy gold stamens. The sweetly scented flowers are known to hold their color until they fall away to the ground. It puts on a brief but spectacular show early in the season and is often the first rose to bloom in spring. After the rose blooms the ferny foliage remains attractive while black bristly oval hips form and last well into fall.

Other names: Harisonii, *R. foetida harisonii*, *R. lutea hoggii*, *R. x harisonii*, Pioneer Rose, *R. x harisonii* 'Harison's Yellow,' *R. x harisonii* 'Yellow Rose of Texas'

Flower color: bright yellow

Flower size: 2–2½"

Scent: sweet and fruity

Height: 6–8'

Spread: 5–7'

Blooms: spring to summer; no repeat blooming

Hardiness zones: 4–9

✿ The blossoms occur along mahogany arching canes with many prickles. Those canes form into an open but bushy shrub.

✿ Harison's Yellow tolerates drought, light shade and poor soils. It may bloom more heavily in dry, cool locations.

✿ Known to spread quickly by suckers, this rose is easily propagated by planting the suckers separately as new plants. It can also be divided in the same way as a perennial, with a shovel and a hatchet, and shared with friends.

This rose received the Royal Horticultural Society (RHS) Award of Merit in 1993.

Hébé's Lip

Other names:
R. damascene rubrotincta,
Rubrotincta, Reine Blanche,
Margined Hip

Flower color: white;
pink edges

Flower size: 3"

Scent: strong, musky

Height: 3–5'

Spread: 4–5'

Blooms: spring to
early summer; no repeat
blooming

Hardiness zones: 4–9

*This variety was
discovered before
1846 in the U.K. by
Lee and reintroduced
in 1912 by William
Paul of the U.K.*

Hébé's Lip is regarded as a damask and sweetbriar (eglantine) cross. It produces fat, creamy white pointy buds covered in pinky red. The buds open into clusters of semi-double, white blossoms with showy gold stamens and a pinkish 'lip' or edge. Upright, stiff, prickly canes support heavily textured, dull, dark green foliage. The foliage has a strong apple fragrance that is most noticeable after a rainfall and in humid conditions.

❀ Do not prune until the flowering cycle is complete. Pruning at this time will not diminish any future flowering cycles because Hébé's Lip blooms best on old wood.

❀ This rose rarely experiences disease. It tolerates poor conditions and neglect so is ideal for those who have little time to tend their roses.

❀ This tidy, compact and vigorous shrub was named after Hébé, the Greek goddess of youth and cup bearer for the gods. The pink-edged petals of this rose evoke her wine-stained lip.

Hénri Martin

This rose was introduced in France by Jean Laffay (1794–1852), who created and introduced nearly 40 roses and also created the hybrid perpetual class. This rose is widely known for its moss-covered stems and sepals that emit a subtle balsam scent. It bears clusters of rich crimson, fragrant blossoms that darken with age. The camellia-like, rounded blossoms are semi-double to double and open flat. Profuse flowering happens only once in the summer. It bears plentiful, disease-free, roughly textured foliage that looks fresh all season long.

Other names:
Red Moss, Old Red Moss
Flower color:
rich purply red
Flower size: 3"
Scent: strong, sweet
Height: 3–5'
Spread: 4'
Blooms: mid-summer; no repeat blooming
Hardiness zones: 4–9

- Support is required to prevent the arching, flexible canes from collapsing. Hénri Martin grows well on an obelisk, trellis, tripod or pergola.
- Once the flowers have finished, attractive orangy red hips begin to emerge, remaining on the shrub well into winter.
- This rose is considered very healthy and tolerates light shade, hot and dry summers and poor soil. It may suffer a little winter dieback in colder regions. Prune out any deadwood in spring.
- This moss rose is thought to have a damask rose as a parent. It was named after Hénri Martin (1810–83), a famous French historian and writer.

Jacques Cartier

Other names: Marchesa Boccella, Marquise Boçella, Marquise Boccella

Flower color: soft pink

Flower size: 4½–5"

Scent: rich and heady

Height: 3–4'

Spread: 24–36"

Blooms: summer to fall; repeat blooming

Hardiness zones: 5–9

Because there is no proof as to the breeder or location and date of origin for this rose, there is some debate that Jacques Cartier and Marchesa Boccella are the same rose. At rose shows, this variety is required to be known as Marchesa Boccella, but it is typically known throughout North America as Jacques Cartier. Classification varies as well, as it is regarded as a hybrid perpetual, a damask or a portland.

❧ The blooms display a green button eye surrounded by soft pink, double, quartered rosettes. The flowers emerge among leathery, light green foliage that changes over time to blue-green. Typical of portland roses, the small flower clusters of this variety huddle on the shorter stems. The flowers are slightly obscured within the foliage, a tendency that gives the plant a neat and tidy appearance but reduces the overall impact of the blooms.

❧ It may be necessary to prune this rose heavily or train it horizontally to stimulate new, lush growth. Without pruning, the growth habit can be quite sparse.

❧ Jacques Cartier is highly disease resistant and easy to grow in containers, in mixed beds and in borders and as hedging. It prefers fertile, well-mulched soil.

It was named after the 16th-century French master navigator who explored the St. Lawrence River and searched for a Northwest Passage.

Königin von Dänemark

This easygoing alba rose always exceeds expectations. It bears very double flowers that open from tight stubby buds. Each flower consists of up to 200 petals that form into an exquisitely scented, quartered blossom. Resembling a button, the center of each flower is slightly deeper in tone and tightly packed. The bluish green foliage is an attraction in itself. Even though it flowers only once, this rose flowers so heavily for five to six weeks that the branches often bow down to the ground from the weight. Large, scarlet hips form after the flowers have finished for summer and remain on the plant well into winter.

Other names: Belle Courtisanne, Queen of Denmark, Königin von Dänemarck, Reine du Dänemark

Flower color: medium pink

Flower size: 3–3½"

Scent: intense

Height: 3–5'

Spread: 4'

Blooms: mid-summer; no repeat blooming

Hardiness zones: 4–10

✿ Once the flowering cycle is complete, a little tidying up and pruning may be in order because this rose can become leggy over time.

✿ Compact for an alba rose, Königin von Dänemark is well suited to smaller modern gardens.

✿ Königin von Dänemark tolerates poor weather and poor soil and, like all alba roses, has highly disease-resistant foliage.

Louise Odier

Other names:
Mme. de Stella

Flower color:
medium pink with
a hint of lavender

Flower size: 3½–4½"

Scent: rich and sweet

Height: 4–5'

Spread: 4'

Blooms: mid-summer
to fall; repeat blooming

Hardiness zones: 5–10

*Raised by Margottin
in 1851, this rose is
the parent of many
popular French roses.*

L ouise Odier is one of the most floriferous old garden roses available in commerce. It is considered to be a first-rate cut flower and has long been popular with those who love roses. It grows into a bushy, upright but arching framework that supports camellia-like blossoms held on long stems. Soft olive green leaves and maroon prickles cover the stems. Each well-formed, fully double flower is the perfect shape for a bourbon rose, cupped at first, then opening flat and round, sometimes quartered, with central petals touched with lavender. The flowers are produced continuously, without fail, from the middle of summer to fall frost.

✿ Louise Odier is best grown with support and tolerates dappled shade. With winter protection it can withstand zone 4.

✿ If left unpruned, this rose can be trained as a climber, but it is usually used as a valuable addition to a mixed border.

✿ The rather slender, upright growth habit of this rose is not typical of the big, flowing bourbon roses. The blossoms are very full, fuller than might be expected for a rose that has only 35 to 45 petals (low for a bourbon rose) in each blossom.

Madame Hardy

Give it everything it requires, and Madame Hardy will produce the most perfect white flowers you could imagine. This rose bears hundreds of large, flat, double, green-eyed, white blossoms. The emerging flowers sometimes display a hint of pale pink when they first open, and the blooms are set against densely packed, lush, matte green foliage. Each flower is made up of 150 to 200 petals that almost totally obscure the stamens.

✿ Once Madame Hardy is established, it is very easy to grow in mixed borders, beds, cut-flower gardens or as a specimen.

✿ To keep the plant young and productive, every year remove some of the oldest canes from the base of the plant immediately after flowering.

✿ Madame Hardy tolerates poor soil conditions and light shade but tends to be less prolific under these conditions. It is best in full sun so the profuse flowering will be maintained for three to four weeks.

Other names: Mme. Hardy
Flower color: white
Flower size: 3–3½"
Scent: fresh and sweet with a hint of citrus
Height: 4–5'
Spread: 3–5'
Blooms: early spring; no repeat blooming
Hardiness zones: 4–9

Alexandre Hardy, who apprenticed at Empress Josephine's Malmaison and went on to become chief horticulturist of Paris' Luxembourg Castle, created this and many other rose varieties; he named this one after his beloved wife.

Mme. Isaac Pereire

Other names: Le Bienheureaux de la Salle

Flower color: deep pink with purple tones

Flower size: 3½–4"

Scent: intense, raspberry

Height: 4–6'

Spread: 4–5'

Blooms: spring to fall; repeat blooming

Hardiness zones: 5–9

This bourbon rose was raised by Garçon of France in 1881. Its parentage is unknown. After 120 years it still receives praise, and it was honored with the 1993 RHS Award of Garden Merit. Big and billowy, Mme. Isaac Pereire is famous for its fragrance and large, double pink flowers. Each flower is made up of 45 to 55 petals, forming into a fully cupped and unusually quartered blossom with a muddled center. Earlier blooms are sometimes malformed but the later blooms are usually perfect.

✿ This rose is often grown with its canes pegged down horizontally to the soil to promote a greater quantity of flowering side stems. It is also easily trained on a pillar, arch or obelisk where it produces a number of lateral canes, resulting in more blooms.

✿ This generally healthy plant is a little prone to powdery mildew and blackspot. Take all the necessary precautions (see the Problems & Pests section beginning on p. 74) to prevent any fungal problems.

✿ Mme. Isaac Pereire tolerates poor soils and cool shade where summers are warm.

✿ This rose was named after a member of a banking family during the reign of Napoleon III.

Reine des Violettes

The blooms of Reine des Violettes open carmine purple and later turn violet mauve. The color is most striking later in the season, as the days become cooler and shorter. The abundant gray-green, smooth, pepper-scented foliage blends well with the color of the flowers. The flowers are reminiscent of gallica blooms in shape and color, and some say it more closely resembles a bourbon rose, but it is classified as a hybrid perpetual.

Other names:
Queen of the Violets

Flower color: magenta with touch of lavender

Flower size: 3–4"

Scent: sweet, heady, peppery

Height: 3–5'

Spread: 3–5'

Blooms: early summer to fall; repeat blooming

Hardiness zones: 5–9

* Reine des Violettes can withstand winters in zone 4 with adequate protection.
* This rose is a heavy feeder. Regular but careful pruning diminishes a leggy and sparse growth habit, and a hard pruning every spring will encourage a more solid form.
* This rose is somewhat susceptible to blackspot but is more disease resistant than most other hybrid perpetuals. Fungal problems are easily alleviated by proper watering practices (see Watering in the book's introduction).
* Full sun, rich, well-drained soil and good air circulation are the only essentials for the success of this variety, cherished since its 1860 introduction by Millet-Malet of France.

Rosa gallica officinalis

One of the oldest cultivated roses, *Rosa gallica officinalis* was brought from Damascus to France in the 13th century by Thibaut le Chansonnier. A painting of it from 1430 is on an altarpiece in the Ghent Cathedral. Preserves, syrups and powders that included traces of the rose were said to cure several ailments. Today this rose is notable for its culinary and medicinal value, its use in crafts and its ability to control erosion on steep sites.

Other names:
Apothecary's Rose,
The Apothecary's Rose
of Provins, Double French
Rose, Officinalis, *R. gallica
maxima, R. gallica plena,
R. officinalis, R. provincialis,
R. x centifolia provincialis,*
Red Rose of Lancaster

Flower color:
crimson purple

Flower size: 3–3½"

Scent: fresh and intense

Height: 3–4'

Spread: 3–4'

Blooms: mid- to late
summer; no repeat
blooming

Hardiness zones: 4–10

✿ This species rose is a neat and bushy shrub with more bristles than thorns. It suckers freely— prune out unwanted suckers after the flowering cycle is complete. It blooms very early in the season and does not repeat. Small, rounded hips that turn a reddish brown in fall follow the flat, semi-double flowers on rough, dark foliage.

✿ The hips are high in vitamin C and have been used for centuries in medical preparations. The British revived this use during World War II.

✿ This rose is highly disease resistant and able to fight off any potential problems.

✿ Most descendants from the seven to eight species of wild European roses derive from the group Gallicanae, which comprises *Rosa gallica* and its near relatives.

A candied form of the hips was used hundreds of years ago and is still considered a delicacy in Turkey.

Rosa gallica versicolor

A sport of *Rosa gallica officinalis*, this rose discovered in the 16th century bears semi-double, striped, fragrant blossoms. The flowers are borne on upright stems with rough-textured, medium green foliage. It is sometimes confused with *Rosa damascena* but is superior to that species. It is a compact, rambling, rounded shrub that boasts the most striking and earliest blooms of all the striped species roses. The blooms will often revert to a non-stripe, creating a blend of striped and solid flowers. No two flowers have the same striping pattern or degree of coloration. Roundish dark red hips appear after the flowers have finished on canes with more bristles than thorns.

❀ Profuse flowering may cause the stems to become weighed down. Provide support or prune just after blooming so the shrub doesn't grow any taller than 3–3½ feet. Prune out the old wood and cut the new shoots down by one-third after flowering to maintain good air circulation and vigor. This rose can suffer dieback if temperatures drop below –13° F.

❀ This species rose prefers well-mulched soil in an open site. It bears an abundance of healthy foliage impervious to most diseases. It is very popular for its striking color and wonderful display of blossoms.

❀ An alternate name, Rosamund's Rose, refers to Henry II's unfortunate mistress, Fair Rosamond, Jane Gifford.

Other names:
Rosa Mundi
Flower color: white striped with pink and red
Flower size: 3–3½"
Scent: very fragrant
Height: 3–4'
Spread: 3–4'
Blooms: early summer; no repeat blooming
Hardiness zones: 4–9

This rose is known by many names including R. gallica 'Variegata,' R. gallica 'Versicolor,' Rosamund's Rose, Rose of the World, R. x rosa mundi, R. gallica rosa mundi 'Weston,' R. gallica variegata 'Thory' and R. gallica versicolor 'Linnaeus.'

Rose de Rescht

A number of theories have arisen over the years as to where this rose came from and when and how it was discovered. Some experts have stated that it originated in Iran while others think that it was simply found in a garden in France. The most popular explanation is that an English gardener named Nancy Lindsay brought Rose de Rescht from Persia to England in the 1940s. Whatever its origins, this rose produces intensely fragrant, deep purple roses with a vibrant hue in just about any climate. Each double blossom has at least 100 petals in a camellia-like form. The flowers sometimes appear a little ragged, but the rich aroma is reason enough to plant this rose.

Other names: Rose De Rescht, Gul e Rescht
Flower color: deep vibrant purple
Flower size: 2–2½"
Scent: sweet, heady
Height: 2½–3½'
Spread: 24–36"
Blooms: summer to fall; repeat blooming
Hardiness zones: 4–9

✿ Easy to grow and responding well to a hard pruning, this rose has great garden value. It is ideal for planting en masse or within a mixed border.
✿ Some damask roses, including this one, repeat bloom and are often called autumn damask roses.
✿ The colorful flowers are known to pale in the hot sun but last for long periods. The flowers repeat in six-week intervals from summer to fall.
✿ Rose de Rescht is healthy and durable, tolerates poor conditions and requires little care.

Rescht is an ancient caravan town in what is now Iran.

Souvenir de la Malmaison

T his may be the most famous bourbon rose available today. It was introduced in 1843 and bred by Jean Béluze in France. It was named for Empress Josephine's famous château near Paris. It was said that this rose created such a stir that Béluze and his wife watched during the night for thieves who might try to steal cuttings. History aside, this rose is simply beautiful, displaying large, quartered blooms made up of 65 to 75 petals each. The intensely scented flowers first open into a cupped form but later open flat. They pale with age to almost white. The autumn blooms are sometimes better than the summer ones with a sparse bloom period throughout mid-season. Though this rose is a little difficult to get established, the rewards far outweigh any difficulties.

Other names: Queen of Beauty and Fragrance, Souv. de la Malmaison
Flower color: pale pink
Flower size: 4½–5"
Scent: intense, spicy
Height: 3–4'
Spread: 3–4'
Blooms: summer to fall; repeat blooming
Hardiness zones: 5–9

✿ The blooms are vulnerable to wet weather and are known to ball. (See the Glossary of Pests & Diseases in the Introduction.) Otherwise this rose is moderately resistant to disease and requires no more care than any other old garden rose.

✿ A climbing Souvenir de la Malmaison was created by English hybridizer Henry Bennett in 1843. Sadly, it's too tender for Michigan.

✿ After her divorce from Napoleon, Empress Josephine retired to Malmaison where she collected every rose then in cultivation. She opened her garden to French rose breeders, who used her roses to create thousands of new varieties.

Stanwell Perpetual

S tanwell Perpetual has an uncertain history. Some say that it was developed by one of the two—Lee and Kennedy—who marketed the rose in 1838. It was happened upon in a garden at Stanwell in England. When it was released, it was classified as a hybrid spinosissima. It is also known as a burnet cross. Regardless of the controversy and mystery, it can bear 100 or more blooms in one flush, completely obscuring the grayish green foliage. The quartered flowers have an average of 45 to 55 petals each. The color intensifies as the temperatures cool in late summer. The double flowers have frilled edges and muddled centers. The fragrant flowers are followed by only an occasional red hip. Each cane is well clothed in long, reddish bristles and light green foliage touched with purple.

Other names: none
Flower color: pale pink, almost white
Flower size: 3–3½"
Scent: classic tea
Height: 3–5'
Spread: 4–6'
Blooms: late spring to fall; repeat blooming
Hardiness zones: 3–9

✿ Pruning is unnecessary, but the floriferous growth is encouraged by removing some of the oldest canes to the ground yearly, and it is a good idea to prune out unruly growth. Don't be surprised to see this rose sucker.

✿ This beauty tolerates just about anything, including poor soil, drought, drenching rain, intense summers and hard winters. It is resistant to disease but mildly prone to blackspot.

✿ Ideally suited to mass plantings in exposed areas and slopes, it is also stunning as a flowering border or impenetrable hedge.

✿ The foliage emits a subtle but sweet aroma when wet with rain or morning dew.

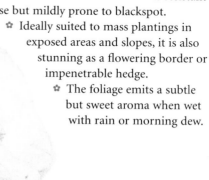

Tuscany Superb

L ike other old garden roses, Tuscany Superb is not very particular about what it needs to grow well. It is happy in just about any location, is impervious to disease and requires little to no pruning. Plant it where the fragrance can be enjoyed—near a bench, doorway or window.

Other names: Double Velvet, Superb Tuscany, Superb Tuscan, Double Tuscany, Tuscany Supreme

Flower color: blackish mauve purple

Flower size: 3–4"

Scent: mild, sweet

Height: 4–5'

Spread: 3–4'

Blooms: mid-summer; no repeat blooming

Hardiness zones: 4–9

❀ Rounded and compact, upright, neat and vigorous, Tuscany Superb is considered one of the most distinctive gallicas ever created.

❀ Long bristly stems bear large, rough, dark green foliage and large clusters of blackish purple double flowers that obscure bright yellow stamens.

❀ Prune out old and unproductive canes to encourage more compact growth and heavier flowering. It will sucker if the bud union is planted below soil level and even more profusely if grown on its own roots.

❀ This rose is resistant to blackspot but somewhat prone to powdery mildew in the appropriate conditions once the flowering cycle is complete. It prefers an open site and grows very successfully in poor soil.

Known since 1837, Tuscany Superb is thought to be a sport of Tuscany, with larger foliage and bigger blooms.

William Lobb

Other names: Duchesse d'Istrie, Old Velvet Moss

Flower color: dark crimson purple

Flower size: 3"

Scent: very sweet

Height: 6–8'

Spread: 5–7'

Blooms: mid-summer; no repeat blooming

Hardiness zones: 4–9

William Lobb is very popular and the most vigorous of all moss roses. The buds and sepals at the base of the flower clusters are covered in moss and smell of pine, especially when touched. Upright, arching, bristly canes form an open growth habit with coarse, large, dark gray-green foliage.

✿ The base is sparsely leafed, so plant another flowering shrub or perennial in front to disguise this characteristic.

✿ Hard pruning after flowering will create a more stout form while still showcasing the unique grayish brown moss and thorns. It can grow very large in zones 5 through 7. The long stems require support such as a climbing pillar, tripod, pergola, wall, trellis, arbor or arch.

✿ This rose, bred by Laffay in France in 1855, was named after the plant huntsman who brought the Monkey Puzzle Tree from Chile and popularized it in England.

Zéphirine Drouhin

Zéphirine Drouhin is a cherished vintage bourbon rose that was introduced in 1868 in Dijon, France, by Bizot. Prized for generations, this climber is most often recommended for locations near walkways because of its intense fragrance and its lack of thorns. The large, double flowers are borne mostly singly but sometimes in clusters. Each of the 25 to 30 pink petals has a ruffled edge and white base.

✿ This rose is generally resistant to disease but slightly prone to powdery mildew and blackspot.

✿ Zéphirine Drouhin requires a protected location and full sun to repeat bloom well.

✿ Naturally vigorous, this rose can be trained as a climber or pruned as a shrub or large hedge with average sunlight. In sunnier sites, it will grow higher. Grow it on a trellis, arch, pillar or obelisk to support the plant and to ensure good air circulation.

✿ Recipient of the RHS Award of Garden Merit in 1993, this rose was named after the wife of an amateur gardener living at Semur on the Cotê d'Or in France.

Other names: Belle Dijonnaise, Charles Bonnet, Ingegnoli Prediletta, Mme. Gustave Bonnet

Flower color: cerise pink with a white base

Flower size: 3–3½"

Scent: damask, raspberry

Height: 8–10'

Spread: 6–8'

Blooms: summer to fall; repeat blooming

Hardiness zones: 5–9

MODERN SHRUB

The category of modern shrub roses comprises a variety of rose groups that don't neatly fit into any of the other rose categories. Modern shrub roses are easy to grow and generally very hardy. They can be compact or quite large and often have prickly stems. The newer varieties bloom continuously and have good pest and disease resistance. The following groups fall into this category.

English Roses

Roses in this small but expanding group were bred by David Austin Roses Ltd. and first came to prominence in the 1970s. Although the flowers display the classic form of old garden roses, they are modern roses and have the positive qualities of a newer generation, including improved disease resistance. The foliage is moderately prone to blackspot. They are specifically chosen

for their flower form, reliable growth habit, foliage and fragrance. They are ideal for cutting and arranging. The canes of English roses are not as robust as those of the hybrid teas, and often the large, beautiful flowers nod at the top of the canes. They are somewhat tender in Michigan and require winter protection similar to that needed for hybrid tea roses. In Michigan they also require a regular fungicide program to reduce the potential for disease.

Explorer Roses

The roses in this group are some of the toughest on the planet. Explorer roses were developed with hardiness in mind by crossing *Rosa rugosa* or *Rosa kordesii* for their strongest characteristics. Bred in L'Assomption, Quebec, and in Ottawa by Agriculture Canada, these roses can withstand temperatures as low as –40° F, thriving from year to year without any winter protection. They are moderately to highly disease resistant and bear wonderful blooms. Explorer roses are repeat blooming. They are available in a range of colors and sizes, including climbers, and are most often found growing on their own roots. Although they were specifically bred for cold climates, they perform as beautifully in warmer regions.

Parkland Roses

This series is similar to the Explorer Series in that both series were bred from hardy, reliable rose stock. Parkland roses derive from *Rosa arkansana* crossed with floribundas and hybrid teas. They were bred specifically for the prairies at Agriculture Canada's Research Station in Morden, Manitoba. The result was a mix of hardy roses in beautiful colors, shapes and sizes. Generally the growth habit is compact and the blossoms are double to semi-double. Most roses in this series bloom repeatedly after the large flush of blooms in early summer and continue blooming until a hard fall frost. They primarily bloom on new wood and are grown on their own roots and should be pruned down low in spring to encourage new growth. If left unpruned, they often become leggy and non-productive. Most of them produce hips.

The Fairy

Sally Holmes

Rugosas

Native to cold regions of Asia, rugosas have naturalized in the U.S. and are known as 'Wild Beach Roses' in the northeast. This group contains a large number of varieties and hybrids of *Rosa rugosa*, a widespread, very hardy rose with disease-resistant, wrinkled foliage and blooms in shades of white, pink and purple. It is easy to identify hybrids that have *Rosa rugosa* as a parent. Rugosas are good, tough roses for the landscape, providing interest all year. They bloom in spring and fall and have large orange-red hips that provide color through late fall and winter. They should not be sprayed with any type of pesticide, liquid fertilizer or soap, as the foliage is easily burned. They are suitable for beds, borders and hedges and as specimens. Because they tolerate salt, rugosas can be used near roads, sidewalks, pathways and driveways. Some rugosa hybrids have smooth leaves and yellow or red blooms, the result of crosses with floribunda, hybrid tea and miniature roses. These smooth-leaved rugosas can sometimes get blackspot.

Shrub Roses

Shrub roses exhibit an elegant form unlike other rose bushes. Whereas most modern bushes are bred for their ability to repeat flower, shrubs are suitable for just about any garden setting. Not only are shrub roses easy to grow, but many varieties also grow into a naturally graceful form. Although the majority of shrub roses in commerce bloom throughout summer, some blossom only once.

Abraham Darby

Other names:
Abraham, Country Darby
Flower color: apricot yellow tinted with pink
Flower size: 4–5"
Scent: strong, fruity spice
Height: 4–7'
Spread: 3½–5'
Blooms: early summer to late fall; repeat blooming
Hardiness zones: 6–9

When cut in bud, the long-lasting flowers are wonderful for arrangements. Add a few foliage cuttings for contrast.

Abraham Darby is one of the most widely grown roses developed by David Austin Roses Ltd., and justifiably so. It has a strong growth habit, fruity fragrance, reliable re-bloom and old-fashioned flowers. It is moderately disease resistant and extremely vigorous. It can tolerate winters in zones 4 and 5 with protection.

✿ This rose, named after one of the prominent figures of the Industrial Revolution, bears small clusters of large, double blooms on well-armed, arching stems with waxy, dark green leaves.

✿ With its flexible canes, this rose can be trained as a climber. It is also ideal for borders or as a specimen when left in its natural form. Place it where the fragrance can be fully appreciated.

✿ Pruning is necessary only to remove dead or diseased wood and to help shape the bush into a well-formed, bushy, mounded shrub.

✿ Abraham Darby is not very resilient in a rainstorm because its weight makes it prone to collapse. It thrives in good weather and is only slightly prone to blackspot and rust.

Alexander Mackenzie

Alexander Mackenzie is known not only for its beauty and scent but also for its outstanding disease resistance. It bears fragrant double flowers in clusters of 6 to 12 on a tall, upright form. The glossy, light green foliage is lightly serrated, with hints of reddish purple on the stems. The long-lasting flowers resemble the blossoms of a grandiflora rather than those of an Explorer rose.

✿ This rose is extremely hardy and vigorous and is highly resistant to powdery mildew and blackspot. It requires very little maintenance; removing deadwood in spring and thinning out woody canes is the only pruning necessary.

✿ Deadheading regularly will encourage a longer, more prolific bloom cycle.

✿ Alexander Mackenzie is very hardy and can survive to zone 2b with some dieback, depending on the depth of the snow. It is one of the hardiest of the Explorer roses. It deserves to be seen more often in varied climates and zones other than just cold winter climates.

Other names:
A. Mackenzie,
Alex Mackenzie

Flower color: deep red with hot pink

Flower size: 2½–3"

Scent: mild, raspberry

Height: 5–7'

Spread: 5–7'

Blooms: spring to fall; repeat blooming

Hardiness zones: 3–9

Sir Alexander Mackenzie was a noted explorer and fur trader and the first person to cross the North American continent and reach the Pacific Ocean.

Aunt Honey

Other names: none
Flower color:
medium pink
Flower size: 4–5"
Scent: intense, damask
Height: 4–5'
Spread: 3–4'
Blooms: summer to fall;
repeat blooming
Hardiness zones: 4–9

Aunt Honey was bred by Dr. Griffith Buck and introduced into commerce in 1984. Buck roses are experiencing a resurgence of interest and availability. This magnificent rose bears large carmine pink buds that open into cotton candy pink, double flowers in clusters of 5 to 10. Each flower is made up of 38 petals that form into a high-centered flower. Short but sturdy stems are covered in awl-like, tan prickles and olive green, semi-glossy foliage. Dr. Buck was said to name this rose after Helen, the wife of the man who inspired him to begin breeding roses. As the story goes, Helen's nieces couldn't pronounce Aunt Helen and called her Aunt Honey instead, and that's how this rose got its name.

✿ Aunt Honey is relatively disease free. Regularly monitor it for signs of disease, and treat as necessary.

✿ The petals have excellent substance, and the long-lasting blooms are ideal for cut flowers.

✿ Aunt Honey works beautifully in a formal garden setting alongside hybrid tea roses. This rose is suitable for planting en masse, throughout borders or as a small specimen.

Ballerina

allerina was bred by Ann Bentall, the widow of Reverend Joseph Pemberton's gardener, and introduced in 1937. Reverend Pemberton was a distinguished English rosarian, breeder, exhibitor, president of the Royal National Rose Society and originator of the hybrid musk rose. After the reverend died, John and Ann Bentall bred their own hybrid musk creations. This hybrid musk bears large cascading clusters of single, dainty flowers. The lightly speckled flowers emerge a soft pink with a pale reverse and well-defined pink edges. The pink fades to a pinkish white eye at the base of the petals surrounding the golden stamens.

Other names: none
Flower color: pinkish white; darker pink edges
Flower size: 1–1½"
Scent: light musk or sweet pea
Height: 3–4'
Spread: 4'
Blooms: mid-season; repeat blooming
Hardiness zones: 6–9

❀ The flowers are supported by a dense mass of small, semi-glossy leaves on almost thornless stems. Tiny orange-red hips follow the flowers in fall.

❀ Ballerina is relatively trouble free and resistant to most diseases. It tolerates light shade and poor soil. The flowers may need deadheading after the first flush to keep the plant productive.

❀ With its arching growth habit, this rose is suitable for hedging, mixed borders, containers and mass groupings. It can also be trained as a short climber on a trellis or fence.

❀ This rose can withstand winters in zones 4 and 5 with adequate protection.

The flowers have been compared to apple blossoms, but this rose was given its name because the blooms resemble a ballerina's skirt.

Blanc Double de Coubert

Every rose garden should include one of these magnificent rugosas. Along with its dazzling white blooms, this 110-year-old rose has an interesting history and outstanding reputation as well. It was introduced in 1892 in France; Coubert is the French village where its creator lived. It bears leathery, wrinkled, dark green leaves. Loose-petaled, semi-double clusters of white, fragrant flowers are borne from buds occasionally flushed with a hint of pink. Each flower is made up of an average of 15 to 25 petals.

Other names:
Blanche Double de Coubert,
Blanc de Coubert
Flower color: white
Flower size: 3"
Scent: strong, sweet
Height: 4–7'
Spread: 4–7'
Blooms: early summer to fall; repeat blooming
Hardiness zones: 3–9

❀ Moderately vigorous, this arching, dense shrub tolerates light shade and most soils. It is highly resistant to disease.

❀ The soft-textured petals are easily marked and affected by rain, so they might appear spent not long after opening.

❀ Deadheading after the first flush will encourage more blooms. Stop deadheading closer to fall so that hips will develop. The hips transform into reddish orange spheres that stand out among the stunning fall foliage.

❀ Blanc Double de Coubert is excellent for hedging, borders or specimens. The blossoms are ideal for cutting as well, but cut the stems when they are still partially closed to extend the flowers' vase life.

Bonica

A Meilland introduction in 1982, Bonica was the first modern shrub rose to be named an All-America Rose Selections winner when it received the honor in 1987. It is durable and highly recommended for mixed beds, containers, hedges or as a groundcover or specimen. It bears an abundance of semi-glossy, rich foliage, beautiful enough to stand on its own. The blooms are lightly scented. Bright orange hips follow the double pink rosettes and remain on the shrub through winter.

Other names: Bonica '82, Demon, Bonica Meidiland
Flower color: light pink
Flower size: 1½–2"
Scent: delicate, sweet
Height: 3–5'
Spread: 4½–5'
Blooms: summer to fall; repeat blooming
Hardiness zones: 4–9

✿ Easy to maintain, this rose tolerates most conditions including partial shade and poor soil and is disease resistant and hardy.

✿ Bonica is a tidy, sprawling rose of modest size that blooms profusely through most of the growing season. It is suitable for just about any location.

✿ It's not surprising that this beautiful rose has been popular throughout the world since its introduction.

Buffalo Gal

Other names:
Foxi Pavement, Foxi,
Foxy Pavement

Flower color:
deep purple pink

Flower size: 3"

Scent: spicy and
very strong

Height: 30–36"

Spread: 30–42"

Blooms: summer to fall;
repeat blooming

Hardiness zones: 3–9

*Buffalo Gal looks
similar to Fru Dagmar
Hastrup (p.146), but
its blooms are more
double and are a
richer shade of pink.*

Buffalo Gal has award-winning fragrance, colorful flowers and disease-resistant foliage. This hybrid rugosa has large, semi-double flowers and deeply textured, medium green foliage. Dark hips follow the flowers and remain on the plant, providing winter forage for birds.

✿ This rose has a compact, mounded form, and the spreading, low branches can extend farther than normal in very rich soil. Its tolerance of pruning makes it suitable for low hedging and borders. It has a tidy habit and is more compact than other rugosas. It also has an excellent repeat bloom cycle.

✿ Buffalo Gal tolerates tough conditions and extreme temperatures.

✿ Deadheading isn't required for further blooming, and the hips will begin to form while the flowers are still being produced, resulting in an interesting visual contrast.

Carefree Delight

The name of this shrub rose is perfectly appropriate. Part of a series of Meidiland landscape roses, Carefree Delight is just that—carefree. It requires very little care and produces a delightful display of single, carmine pink blossoms amid dark, glossy foliage. It is an ideal landscape rose and almost always in bloom. The flowers emerge in large clusters and continue to bloom in waves throughout summer.

❀ Carefree Delight is consistent in all climates, making it suitable for just about any setting or region. It is almost evergreen in areas with warmer winter temperatures, and in areas with colder winters, the foliage changes to bronzy red in fall.

❀ This rose doesn't require much deadheading. It produces vast quantities of showy rose hips in fall and, like all roses with a low petal count, it tolerates some shade.

❀ Carefree Delight is used most often along borders but is also useful for hedging and mass planting.

Other names:
Bingo Meidiland, Bingo Meillandecor, Evermore

Flower color: carmine pink with a white eye

Flower size: 1½–2½"

Scent: none

Height: 3½–4'

Spread: 3½–4'

Blooms: summer to fall; repeat blooming

Hardiness zones: 4–9

Carefree Delight won the AARS designation in 1996, one of only a few shrub roses to receive this honor.

Carefree Wonder

Other names:
Dynastie, Carefully Wonder

Flower color:
bright pink blend

Flower size: 3½–4"

Scent: subtle

Height: 3–5'

Spread: 3–5'

Blooms: summer to fall; repeat blooming

Hardiness zones: 4–9

Few cluster-flowered roses exhibit all their positive qualities as beautifully or as long as Carefree Wonder. As its name implies, it is low maintenance and resistant to disease, a highly recommended rose.

Carefree Wonder, a 1991 AARS winner, lives up to its name and is an outstanding, all-around landscape rose. Municipalities throughout North America use this variety in public areas. It is considered an everblooming variety, bearing flowers continuously throughout summer and fall with a reliable repeat bloom. Each bloom has 25 to 30 bright pink petals with a silver reverse. The cupped form exposes a touch of white surrounding vivid yellow stamens. The bright pink tones deepen in cooler weather. As the blooms age and respond to different temperatures, they create a mosaic of pink hues, ranging from hot pink to soft pink.

✿ This rose is easily distinguished by its deeply serrated foliage and reddish bristles. Bright orange hips begin to form in fall, an indication that winter is just around the corner.

✿ Carefree Wonder is great for foundation plantings, informal hedging or as a self-contained shrub. It is very effective when planted en masse or as an accent.

✿ Deadheading after the first flush will encourage a faster repeat of flowers.

Champlain

Champlain was bred by Felicitas Svejda in 1982 as part of a series Agriculture Canada developed to tolerate northern winters. It was a great success and remains one of the exceedingly popular Explorer Series roses available today. This moderately vigorous shrub is compact, bushy and slightly spreading with a prolific blooming habit. Semi-double flowers of up of 30 petals each are borne in large, abundant clusters. The cup-shaped flowers are produced freely almost all season long. As the new reddish foliage expands, each small leaflet forms a dense collection of shiny foliage, unappealing to most insects, especially aphids.

❀ This rose is reasonably resistant to blackspot and powdery mildew. If subjected to extreme cold for two to three consecutive winters, it will experience dieback. It will begin to re-shoot within the same year but with a shorter blooming period. Winter protection will help reduce dieback.

❀ The floribunda-like flowers are made up of velvety red petals that become darker towards the tips. It always seems to have more flowers than foliage.

❀ Champlain may require thorough pruning in spring to remove any deadwood. It will readily bush back out from the lower branches as summer wears on.

Other names: none
Flower color: velvety red
Flower size: 2½–3"
Scent: slight
Height: 3–4'
Spread: 3–4'
Blooms: summer to fall; repeat blooming
Hardiness zones: 2b–9

This rose was named after Samuel de Champlain, a 17th-century cartographer and explorer who was known as the 'Father of New France.' He was credited as the first person in North America to cultivate roses, which he brought from France to plant in his Quebec garden.

Charles Albanel

Other names: none
Flower color:
medium pinky red
Flower size: 2¾–3½"
Scent: intense
Height: 24–36"
Spread: 3–4'
Blooms: early summer
to fall; repeat blooming
Hardiness zones: 2–9

This hybrid rugosa rose was bred by Felicitas Svedja in Canada, so you know it has to be tough enough for colder climates. This rose grows into a low, spreading groundcover. It begins to freely bloom from early summer and then only sporadically throughout the rest of the season. The blooms are semi-double and made up of an average of 20 petals each. The flowers hold their color well until they fall freely from the plant. Large attractive hips begin to form after the flowers are spent and remain on the plant well into fall, adding to the rose's beauty and character.

❀ The coarsely textured foliage is highly resistant to disease including blackspot and powdery mildew.
❀ Introduced in 1982, Charles Albanel has been tested in various locations throughout Canada and the northern U.S. since 1980 with very little to no evidence of winter damage.
❀ This rose was named after a French missionary, explorer and Jesuit priest who lived from 1616–96.

Cuthbert Grant

Cuthbert Grant is a member of the Parkland Series of roses, and it deserves to be used more often. It is cold hardy but displays the same great characteristics in warmer zones, too. It offers so much—prolific blooming, excellent disease resistance and a vigorous nature. Oval buds open into large, velvety, semi-double clusters of cupped flowers, which hold up well as cut flowers.

❀ The rich-looking flowers are intensely fragrant and worthy of any garden setting. The blooms are accompanied by glossy, disease-resistant foliage produced on upright, vigorous stems.

❀ The process of deadheading is slightly different for this rose. Remove the entire cluster of flowers as they fade, rather than a single flower at a time. Remove any deadwood in spring, and cut back the entire plant by at least half. New vigorous shoots will emerge.

❀ Cuthbert Grant led his people to victory at Seven Oaks in Manitoba, Canada, in 1816.

❀ Three years after its introduction, Cuthbert Grant received the Award of Merit from the Western Canadian Society for Horticulture. It was also chosen as the centennial rose for Manitoba in 1970.

Other names:
Manitoba Centennial Rose
Flower color: crimson red
Flower size: 4–5"
Scent: strong
Height: 3–4'
Spread: 3–4'
Blooms: early summer to fall; repeat blooming
Hardiness zones: 3–9

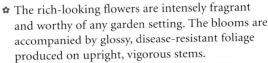
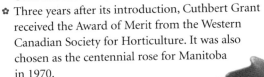

Distant Drums

Other names: none
Flower color:
peachy tan; mauve edges
Flower size: 4–4½"
Scent: intense, myrrh
Height: 3–4'
Spread: 3–4'
Blooms: summer to fall; repeat blooming
Hardiness zones: 4–9

Distant Drums has a unique name and unique coloration. It bears medium to dark mauve buds that open into pale mauve blossoms with peachy tan centers. This modern shrub has a floribunda-like growth habit and could easily be mistaken for a hybrid tea with its high-centered flowers. Dr. Griffith Buck developed this variety and introduced it into commerce in 1985 as another striking addition to his collection. Each flower is made up of 35 to 40 petals layering into a double form. The blooms are borne both singly and in clusters of up to 10 blooms. The fragrance of myrrh is intoxicating, especially during cool summer mornings.

✿ Distant Drums blooms a little later in the season. It has an excellent repeat bloom cycle, however, and will continue to produce flowers until fall.
✿ This rose's disease resistance is very reliable; it is resistant to any of the standard problems, including blackspot and powdery mildew.
✿ Distant Drums vigorously grows into an erect and bushy form. The stems are covered in awl-like, brown prickles and dark, leathery foliage.

Eglantyne

Eglantyne is reminiscent of roses depicted in classic oil paintings created hundreds of years ago. Though it looks old fashioned, it was introduced in 1994 by David Austin Roses Ltd. With its exquisite form, it is considered by its creator to be one of his most beautiful hybrids. It bears fully double pale pink rosettes, and the blossoms are very large and cupped. Most of the petals have gently ruffled petals that turn up at the edges, forming a shallow saucer that is filled with an abundance of tiny petals. Attractive and healthy foliage clothes the tall upright stems.

Other names: Eglantine, Eglantyne Jebb
Flower color: light pink
Flower size: 4–5"
Scent: strong, sweet, classic rose
Height: 3½–5'
Spread: 3–3½'
Blooms: late spring to early fall; repeat blooming
Hardiness zones: 6–9

* Eglantyne's bushy and perfect growth habit makes it ideal among lower-growing material, whether woody or herbaceous. It is exquisite when flowering, but when not blooming it can sometimes be lost among too many plants. Place it where adjacent plant material will not overwhelm the subdued nature of this rose when not in bloom. It is very effective in group plantings.

* Considered a very healthy rose, Eglantyne is only mildly prone to blackspot and tolerates drought. It tolerates winters in zone 5 with protection.

* In warmer climates, long shoots that seem out of place could emerge. These shoots need to be pruned out to encourage balanced growth.

* Eglantyne is a wonderful cut flower—the blooms are long lasting both on the plant and in a vase.

* Eglantyne Jebb, the namesake of this rose, founded the Save the Children charity fund during World War I.

Though their names are similar, Eglantyne should not be confused with the species rose Rosa eglanteria *(p. 98).*

Evelyn

Other names:
Apricot Parfait

Flower color: soft blend of apricot, pink and yellow

Flower size: 3–4"

Scent: sweet and fruity

Height: 3–4'

Spread: 30–36"

Blooms: summer to fall; repeat blooming

Hardiness zones: 6–9

Crabtree and Evelyn, a famous English company known for a range of rose-scented products, chose Evelyn to represent its perfumes in advertising and packaging.

When Evelyn was released in 1992, its breeder, David Austin, stated that it had the strongest, most delicious scent of all the Austin roses. In a poll of members of the Canadian Rose Society, Evelyn was voted the sixth most popular fragrant rose. The complex scent of this rose contains up to 84 different chemicals. Evelyn has other special characteristics as well. It bears huge, fully double, shallow-cupped rosettes in shades of pale apricot. The blooms are muddled in the centers, showcasing the yellow base of each petal. The satiny textured petals intertwine within, creating a beautiful form unlike that of any other rose. The apricot shades can change in hotter weather, a characteristic inherited from one of its ancestors. Evelyn gets its vigor and yellow color from Graham Thomas (p. 148) and its apricot pink color from Tamora.

✿ Evelyn forms into a strong, upright, bushy shrub. It blooms profusely and continuously through the season. It is ideal for mixed shrub and perennial borders. In warm climates it can grow taller and may require support.

✿ The foliage is healthy but a little prone to blackspot. Try to avoid wetting the foliage. Water only at the base of the shrub, early in the morning. This rose can survive winters in zone 5 with protection.

✿ Evelyn is a fantastic rose for cutting. The fragrance of one cluster can fill an entire room. Its vase life is longer than that of most roses.

✿ It may not be the most vigorous of the Austin roses, but its profusion of flowers is reason enough to integrate this rose into any garden setting.

F.J. Grootendorst

What F.J. Grootendorst lacks in scent it makes up for in health, hardiness and numerous high-quality blossoms. It bears tiny, double red blooms in clusters of up to 20. It's no wonder that the flowers resemble carnations because each flower is made up of 25 lightly fringed or serrated petals. The delicate but showy flowers are perfectly complemented by the large, wrinkled leaves on an upright, mounded form.

❀ This thorny shrub could be used as an impenetrable hedge, suitable as a means of security. It could also be used as a specimen to showcase its unique blossoms.

❀ Requiring little care, F.J. Grootendorst is generally resistant to disease but is a little prone to blackspot towards the end of the season.

❀ This rose is not inclined to set hips, which is why it flowers so readily and continuously throughout most of the growing season.

❀ F.J. Grootendorst produced several sports, including Pink Grootendorst, White Grootendorst and the deep red Grootendorst Supreme.

❀ Although classified as rugosas, the Grootendorst roses are half rugosa and half multiflora, which explains why they bear little fragrance and few hips.

Other names: Grootendorst, Grootendorst Red, Nelkenrose

Flower color: medium crimson red

Flower size: 2"

Scent: little to none

Height: 4–5'

Spread: 4–5'

Blooms: summer to fall; repeat blooming

Hardiness zones: 3–9

This rose was named after a Dutch nurseryman and bred by De Goey of Holland in 1918.

Fru Dagmar Hastrup

Other names:
Frau Dagmar Hastrup,
Frau Dagmar Hartopp

Flower color:
light silvery pink

Flower size: 3½"

Scent: cinnamon and cloves

Height: 3–4'

Spread: 4'

Blooms: summer to fall; repeat blooming

Hardiness zones: 2–9

Bees love this rose. If you want to attract bees to a sunny vegetable garden, then plant this rose nearby.

Fru Dagmar Hastrup is one of the most compact-growing rugosas, ideal for a smaller garden. It is sturdy and vigorous with a spreading habit and strong disease resistance. Pale, silvery pink, shallow-cupped flowers are followed by huge, dark red hips. Wrinkled leathery foliage covers the prickly gray canes.

- Fru Dagmar Hastrup is used widely in natural woodland settings, shrub borders, low ground-cover hedges or in front of larger-growing species roses or flowering shrubs.
- This low-maintenance rose tolerates a little shade to full exposure.
- The foliage changes from maroon to deep russet gold in fall. With its foliage and showy hips, this rose adds outstanding color to a fall setting when other plants are about to finish.
- This variety is highly resistant to disease but may experience dieback in harsh winters. It will re-shoot.
- Fru Dagmar Hastrup was originally released as a 1914 introduction from Denmark. It won the Royal Horticultural Society Award of Garden Merit in 1993.

Golden Wings

Since its 1956 introduction, Golden Wings has set the standard for single-flowered yellow shrub roses. It is a living memorial of its creator, Roy Shepherd, a famous rosarian who died in 1962. It bears delicately ruffled, soft yellow flowers that emerge long before almost any other rose and bloom continuously throughout the season. The cupped flowers consist of an average of five to seven petals that open into large saucers with prominent amber stamens. Each cluster is followed in fall by uniquely shaped green hips. It vigorously produces strong, prickly stems covered with clear, light green leaves.

Other names: none
Flower color: light yellow
Flower size: 3–4"
Scent: subtle, orange and honey
Height: 4–5'
Spread: 4'
Blooms: summer to fall; repeat blooming
Hardiness zones: 4–9

❀ Deadhead to extend the blooming season. It is best to prune Golden Wings back hard to reduce the possibility of straggly growth.

❀ This rose tolerates poor or less-fertile soils and partial shade. The foliage is impervious to disease unless under stress.

❀ Use this variety in mixed borders or hedges. It is considered one of the most valuable landscape roses available. It can provide structure within a wide border and is very effective as a specimen when left alone or planted en masse.

❀ The delicate flowers appear frail but can withstand harsh weather. Golden Wings has *Rosa spinosissima* parentage, which gives it more winter hardiness than you might expect in a yellow rose.

Graham Thomas

Other names:
English Yellow,
Graham Stuart Thomas

Flower color:
rich, pure yellow

Flower size: 4–5"

Scent: strong,
old-fashioned tea

Height: 3½–7'

Spread: 4–5'

Blooms: early summer
to fall; repeat blooming

Hardiness zones: 6–9

Graham Thomas was developed in 1983 by David Austin Roses Ltd. and was the first true yellow English rose. It was named after one of the most influential rosarians of our time. It bears beautiful apricot-pink buds that open into large golden yellow blooms. The double blooms carry up to 35 petals each and fade gracefully in time. The flowers remain cupped until the petals fall cleanly from the plant. This rose is very dense and upright in form, bearing an abundance of light green leaves.

✿ In warmer climates this extremely vigorous rose will reach greater heights if supported, developing into a pillar style or climbing rose. A light pruning will allow Graham Thomas to remain a little smaller if desired, but in cooler climates it usually grows a little smaller anyway.

✿ Deadheading may be required to extend the prolific bloom cycle. With protection, it is winter hardy to zones 4 and 5.

✿ Wet weather will not trouble this rose, but excessive heat causes reduced flowering and fading flower color.

✿ Long, flexible stems often flop under the weight of the beautiful but short-lived flowers.

✿ Graham Thomas received the Royal Horticultural Society Award of Garden Merit in 1993.

Hansa

Hansa, first introduced in 1905, is one of the most durable, long-lived and versatile roses. It's not unheard of to come across farmhouses that have been abandoned for decades and find Hansa specimens blooming. It bears deeply veined, leathery foliage on arching, thorny canes. Large, double, loose clusters of dark mauve blooms make this rose showy enough for mixed borders, beds and hedges or as a specimen. The uniquely colored blossoms are borne on a robust and reliable form. Spectacular foliage and large, orange-red hips follow in fall.

✿ Canes four years old and older may need to be pruned out to improve the vigorous flower production, which naturally declines with age.

✿ This rose thrives in silty clay to sandy soils, freezing weather, salt and wind. It tolerates hard pruning and poor conditions but dislikes alkaline soils.

✿ In milder climates the plant may become leggy, and the flower color may fade. Regular pruning can correct the leggy growth habit.

✿ Like most rugosas, Hansa is low maintenance and flowers profusely throughout the season.

Other names: Hansen's
Flower color: dark mauve
Flower size: 3"
Scent: strong, cloves
Height: 4–6'
Spread: 5–6'
Blooms: summer to fall; repeat blooming
Hardiness zones: 3–9

Hawkeye Belle

Other names: none
Flower color:
pale blush pink
Flower size: 4–4½"
Scent: intense, sweet
Height: 3½–5'
Spread: 3½–4'
Blooms: summer to fall;
repeat blooming
Hardiness zones: 4–9

*Dr. Buck named this
rose in honor of his
home state, Iowa,
known as 'The
Hawkeye State.'*

Hawkeye Belle is another of Dr. Griffith Buck's fine creations. The flowers emerge as plump, pointed buds flushed with pink atop tall, strong stems. The buds open to display high centers so tightly packed that they resemble coiled springs. The 35 to 40 petals of each bloom unfurl gradually to create overlapping layers, resulting in a charming effect when fully open. The blooms are known to become a touch darker over time, especially during cooler periods, as the pink in the center of each flower intensifies. If you didn't know better, you'd think that this rose was a hybrid tea, not a modern shrub.

✿ The foliage is tinted with copper hues when young but turns a rich dark green with a leathery texture as it matures.
✿ Hawkeye Belle blends beautifully into mixed borders where a naturally vigorous shrub of average growth is required.
✿ The petals do not fall cleanly on their own, resulting in a ragged appearance, so deadhead regularly until the end of summer.

Henry Hudson

Henry Hudson was introduced in 1976 and has lived up to its claims of being easy to maintain, hardy and resistant to powdery mildew and blackspot. This semi-dwarf, rounded shrub produces pink-tinged buds that open to white, semi-double, flat flowers that showcase the golden stamens. The flowers are reminiscent of double apple blossoms. It is known to bloom profusely from the moment a bud emerges in spring well into fall. Hips do not follow the spent flowers.

Other names: none
Flower color: white
Flower size: 3"
Scent: intense, cloves
Height: 24"–4'
Spread: 24"–4'
Blooms: spring to fall; repeat blooming
Hardiness zones: 2–9

✿ Henry Hudson has the dense, wrinkly, dark green leaves typical of its rugosa parentage. Rugosas have foliage that can become marked, mottled or burned if sprayed with pesticides.

✿ With its compact, thorny, impenetrable growth, this rose is suitable for use as a low hedge, barrier or groundcover or in a mixed bed or border. The stems spread by suckering.

✿ This rose tolerates a little more shade than other Explorer roses. The finished flowers don't fall cleanly from the plant for long periods, so deadhead to keep the plant tidy and to extend the bloom cycle. Pruning is necessary only to remove deadwood and old woody canes.

✿ Henry Hudson was the first European explorer to sail into Hudson Bay, in 1610. His name lives on not only in a rose, but also a bay, a river and a strait, none of which was discovered by him. Hudson died while trying to find the Northwest Passage. He, his son and seven of his crew were sent adrift by mutineers and were never seen again.

Henry Kelsey

Other names: none
Flower color: bright red with hints of purple
Flower size: 2½–3"
Scent: sharp and spicy
Height: 6–8'
Spread: 6'
Blooms: summer to fall; repeat blooming
Hardiness zones: 2–9

This rose was named after a British explorer who extended the trade routes of the Hudson's Bay Company.

Henry Kelsey is one of the more unusual Explorer roses. It is larger and can be trained as a climber or left as an arching, pendulous specimen. Intense red blossoms are borne in heavy clusters of 18 to 20 fully double cupped blooms with reflexed petals and bright gold stamens. The blossoms fade shortly before falling from the shrub. Thorny stems support glossy, dark foliage that is sometimes affected by blackspot but is highly resistant to powdery mildew and rust. It is ideal for just about any climate.

✿ Henry Kelsey takes a couple of years to reach its full potential, but it is well worth the wait. It will produce an abundance of lush growth among hundreds of blooms when given the chance. Henry Kelsey and varieties of Mockorange bloom in sync and set off one another's flowers.

✿ Henry Kelsey is most often trained as a climber, but if you want to use it as a shrub, prune hard after the flowering cycle is complete. Pruning may be necessary to remove the older canes and deadwood as well.

✿ During a severe winter with little or no snow, it may completely die back. It will produce new shoots and will bloom for a shorter time the following year.

Hope for Humanity

Hope for Humanity is a upright-growing rose with an open growth habit. Pointed buds emerge in mid-summer. The flowers open into double, cup-shaped, deep red flowers that resemble the blooms of high-centered hybrid teas. The flower color is even more intense and deeper than that of another red Parkland rose, Cuthbert Grant (p. 141). The stunning red flowers are borne on strong, moderately thorny canes and continue to produce over a period of 10 to 14 weeks. Two to 15 flowers can make up one single cluster. A small white spot is on the inner base of many of the petals, and the outer side of each petal has a white and yellow spot. The blooms have a subtle sweet fragrance.

Other names: none
Flower color: blood red
Flower size: 2–3"
Scent: light
Height: 3–4'
Spread: 3–4'
Blooms: mid-summer to fall; everblooming
Hardiness zones: 3–8

Introduced in 1995, Hope for Humanity was named in honor of the 100th anniversary of The Canadian Red Cross Society.

✿ Hope for Humanity is an everblooming rose, not a repeat bloomer. It doesn't send out just one short-lived flush of blooms but blooms continuously and profusely for months.

✿ This low-maintenance rose may require a little care to prevent blackspot but is highly resistant to mildew and rust.

✿ Pinch out the dominant center bud of each cluster so the outer buds can open without interference. Cut one spray of the long-lasting flower to create an instant bouquet.

J.P. Connell

This rose may require a little patience because it can take longer to establish than other Explorer varieties. One- to two-year-old plants may flower sparsely and sporadically, but after its first two years, this rose blooms profusely through most of the season. It bears high-centered, soft yellow flowers in early summer. The flowers resemble hybrid tea blossoms rather than the typical form of a hardier rose. Medium glossy foliage contrasts well with the flowers on almost thornless stems. The average-sized blooms are produced singly or in clusters of three to eight flowers, indicative of its floribunda parentage. The flower color fades to a creamy pale yellow just before the bloom is finished.

Other names: none
Flower color: creamy yellow
Flower size: 3–3¹/₂"
Scent: strong, tea
Height: 4–5'
Spread: 3–5'
Blooms: summer to fall; repeat blooming
Hardiness zones: 3–8a

J.P. Connell was developed in 1987 and is the only yellow-blooming rose of the Explorer series.

❀ This tough and versatile rose is used frequently in mixed beds and borders or as a specimen. It is highly resistant to powdery mildew but somewhat prone to blackspot.
❀ J.P. Connell blooms well on new growth. In warmer areas, this rose will experience little winter dieback, so it may be necessary to prune it back by at least half.
❀ The first rose in the Explorer Series that was not named after an explorer, this rose was named after a retired civil servant who had served as deputy minister of Agriculture Canada.

Jens Munk

The overall beauty and spicy fragrance of Jens Munk are its main attributes. It vigorously grows into a rounded, dense shrub. It has a sprawling and unshapely form when young but evens out with maturity. This rose is extremely tough, highly disease resistant and drought tolerant. It requires very little to no maintenance.

Other names: none
Flower color: medium pink with hints of lavender
Flower size: 3"
Scent: strong, sweet and spicy
Height: 5–6'
Spread: 5–6'
Blooms: summer to fall; repeat blooming
Hardiness zones: 3–9

❀ Jens Munk bears prickly stems and wrinkly foliage that changes into a beautiful yellowy orange in fall. Semi-double flowers are borne in pale pink clusters. Each petal is lightly streaked with white at the base and surrounds bright yellow stamens. The flowers' clear pink color is unusual for a rugosa. Bright red hips follow the flowers in fall.

❀ With its vast number of prickles, Jens Munk makes an impenetrable medium-sized hedge. It blends beautifully into mixed beds and borders or works well when left as a specimen.

❀ Although Jens Munk is typically resistant to disease, it has the foliage typical of rugosas. Do not spray the foliage with any pesticides or liquid fertilizers. If there is even a hint of powdery mildew, remove and destroy the infected foliage rather than spraying.

The person who told me that Jens Munk was thornless sure turned out to be wrong. After I pruned a group of these roses, it took days to remove the prickles from my fingers.
—Laura Peters

John Cabot

Other names: none
Flower color:
deep, vivid magenta
Flower size: 2–3"
Scent: mild, sweet
Height: 8–10'
Spread: 5–6'
Blooms: mid-summer
to fall; repeat blooming
Hardiness zones: 3–9

This rose was named after the first European since the Vikings to explore the mainland of North America and search for the Northwest Passage.

John Cabot was introduced in 1978 as the first climber in the Explorer Series. It is vigorous and tough, requiring little to no maintenance. It is considered one of the best of the series, exhibiting semi-double clusters of blooms that lose their intense color over time. The prominent yellow stamens stand out among the cupped petals and light green foliage. The flower color can range from deep pink to reddish purple. Clusters of flowers emerge in summer and then bloom again sporadically from late summer to early fall.

✿ This variety is best trained as a climber but can be pruned into a smaller specimen once it has finished flowering. Train the branches to climb on a decorative support such as a pergola, archway, trellis or obelisk.

✿ Pruning may be necessary to remove tip dieback in spring. Stems exposed during winter are vulnerable to seasonal damage, but pruning will help flowers develop on new shoots. This rose has good resistance to blackspot and powdery mildew.

✿ If the lower leaves turn yellow in summer, the rose isn't receiving enough water or the moisture level of the soil isn't consistent.

✿ John Cabot has a reliable reputation backed by a 1985 Certificate of Excellence from Britain's Royal National Rose Society.

John Davis

John Davis isn't just another pink rose. Its red buds open to large, double, pink flowers with a touch of creamy yellow at the base of each petal. The spice-scented clusters can consist of up to 17 flowers each. Long, graceful, arching red canes produce dark, glossy, tough foliage. This 1986 introduction has a trailing growth habit and is one of the longest blooming of the Explorer Series roses.

Other names: none
Flower color: medium pink
Flower size: 3–3½"
Scent: light, spicy
Height: 6–8'
Spread: 6'
Blooms: spring to fall; repeat blooming
Hardiness zones: 2b–9

✿ John Davis is ideal as a windbreak or specimen or in a mixed shrub border or an exposed area where nothing else thrives. It is most often trained as a climber, and few other climbing roses have all the positive qualities this rose possesses. It is striking when trained on a charming wooden fence or support.

✿ This hardy rose requires little to no maintenance, has healthy foliage and blooms profusely. It has a vigorous and healthy growth habit. Spring pruning is usually unnecessary because John Davis experiences so little winter dieback. Remove a few of the oldest canes, right from the base, on mature plants. This task can be done either in spring or in mid-summer, after the spring flush of bloom is complete.

This rose was named after a 16th-century explorer who wrote a book about his final voyage called the Traverse Book, *which became the model for present-day shipping log books.*

John Franklin

Other names: none
Flower color:
medium red
Flower size: 2½"
Scent: light, sweet
Height: 3–5'
Spread: 3–4'
Blooms: spring to fall;
everblooming
Hardiness zones: 3–9

John Franklin has a slightly different flowering habit than other Explorer roses. It is an everblooming rose, meaning that it blooms continuously from summer to fall, rather than repeat blooming. It bears tight, hybrid tea–like buds that open to semi-double flowers. The small, fringed, medium red flowers are borne in abundant, large clusters of 30 or more. The leaves are serrated and dark green with touches of burgundy around the edges.

✿ Its compact, bushy form makes this rose useful for hedging, borders, smaller gardens and any small areas that need a punch of color.
✿ This 1980 introduction was developed in Canada by Felicitas Svejda and bred from a cross between Lilli Marlene (a floribunda) and a hardy seedling that originated from Joanna Hill, Red Pinocchio and *Rosa spinosissima*.
✿ John Franklin is highly resistant to powdery mildew but is mildly susceptible to blackspot. It tolerates partial shade and requires very little maintenance. Prune out deadwood if winter dieback has occurred.

This rose was named after a well-known British naval officer and northern explorer remembered for his expeditions and for the highly publicized 12-year search for him and his lost ships in the mid-1800s.

Knock Out

This rose is simply one of the best new shrub roses to hit the market in years. It is considered to be virtually indestructible and was sure to become a favorite—and did it ever! Conard-Pyle has sold over 700,000 Knock Out roses in only two years, a great accomplishment for William Radler, the originator of this rose. An AARS winner in 2000, this rose is totally carefree and rarely without flowers. The single flowers are made up of 5 to 11 petals in small clusters atop truly disease-resistant foliage. Fall color is another showy feature of this rose as the semi-glossy, dark green leaves transform into shades of burgundy as the days grow colder.

Other names: Knockout
Flower color: deep but bright red-pink
Flower size: 3–3½"
Scent: moderate, tea
Height: 3'
Spread: 3'
Blooms: summer to fall; repeat blooming
Hardiness zones: 4–10

* Knock Out is just what its name suggests when planted en masse or as a specimen. Its rounded, well-behaved form is ideal for just about any garden setting.
* This rose responds best to light deadheading and pruning.
* The hotter the weather, the better Knock Out performs. The flower color tends to display more red in cooler weather, however.
* Orange-red hips emerge once the flowers are spent and last well into winter.
* If you've been afraid that roses need too much care, you'll appreciate the hardiness and disease resistance of this low-maintenance rose.

Martin Frobisher

Other names: none
Flower color: pale pink
Flower size: 2½–3"
Scent: strong and sweet
Height: 5–6'
Spread: 4–5'
Blooms: early summer to fall; repeat blooming
Hardiness zones: 2–9

Martin Frobisher was an Elizabethan seafaring explorer who discovered what is now known as Frobisher Bay on Baffin Island in 1576 as he was searching for the Northwest Passage.

Introduced in 1968, Martin Frobisher was the first rose to be introduced in the Canadian Explorer Series. It has the appearance of an old rose, bearing intensely fragrant, double, pale pink flowers that open from well-shaped buds. It is a vigorous, dense, compact, well-proportioned, pillar-shaped shrub. Dark red, smooth stems display wrinkly, grayish green leaves. This rose has some unique physical features—the older growth is covered in reddish brown bark, and the upper portions of the branches are spineless.

✿ Unlike most Explorer roses, hips do not form on this rose once the flowers are finished. The canes of the dormant rose are red, providing winter interest in the garden.

✿ Deadheading may be necessary to keep the plant tidy, since the flowers cling, rather than fall cleanly from the plant, especially in wet weather.

Molineux

M olineux is another beauty from David Austin Roses Ltd. Austin roses are primarily bred for fragrance and beauty, and this one is no exception. Introduced in 1994, this rose bears rich butter yellow blossoms with a faint undertone of pale orange. The blooms are borne both singly and in abundant clusters, and each blossom is made up of 110 to 120 petals that form into a shallow-cupped, full rosette. It flowers with exceptional freedom and continuity throughout the season. This variety grows into an upright and bushy form that supports the profusion of blooms.

Other names: none
Flower color:
butter yellow; orange undertones
Flower size: 3½–4"
Scent: musky tea
Height: 3–4'
Spread: 24–36"
Blooms: spring to fall; repeat blooming
Hardiness zones: 6–11

- Molineux is an excellent variety for beds, borders and hedges. It is an ideal substitution for Graham Thomas and Golden Celebration when a yellow rose that isn't too tall is desired.
- This rose has exceptional winter hardiness, unusual for a yellow rose. With winter protection, Molineux has been known to grow successfully in zones 4 and 5 throughout Michigan.
- Molineux won a Gold Medal, the President's Trophy for the Best New Rose of the Year and the Henry Edland Medal for the Best Scented Rose at the RNRS trials in the U.K.
- Molineux was named after the host field of the Wolverhampton Wanderers Football Club, which is located near the nurseries of David Austin Roses.

Morden Blush

Other names: Blush
Flower color: pale pink
Flower size: 2–3"
Scent: light, tea
Height: 24–36"
Spread: 24–36"
Blooms: late spring to fall; everblooming
Hardiness zones: 2b–9

Its pale pink, delicate blooms may lead you to believe that this rose is tender, but Morden Blush tolerates drought and extreme temperatures. It is heat and cold hardy, disease resistant and vigorous. It bears attractive buds that open flat into fully double sprays of rosette-shaped clusters. Each petal is infolded, forming into a muddled, button-shaped center. Cooler weather enhances the pale pink, while in hotter temperatures the color fades to ivory white. The matte green, semi-glossy foliage forms into a low-growing, bushy shrub and does not change color in fall. Once the flowers have finished for the season, hips follow.

❀ This Parkland Series rose was introduced in 1988. Morden Blush is the longest-blooming prairie-developed shrub rose to date. It was created by Collicutt & Marshall in Canada.

❀ Deadheading helps tidy the overall appearance of the plant during its bloom cycle. The flowers tend to look a little ragged as they come to an end.

❀ Morden Blush is mildly prone to powdery mildew and blackspot. Place it in a well-ventilated area, and water at the base of the plant in the morning.

❀ The blooms are frequently used for corsages and bouquets, and landscape uses include mass plantings, borders and mixed beds.

Morden Centennial

Morden Centennial was developed by H.H. Marshall for the Canadian Department of Agriculture and released in 1980 to correspond with the centennial of Morden, Manitoba. It was created to withstand severe winters with very little dieback. It bears clusters of double pink flowers that are always borne on new wood. Each flower consists of up to 40 to 50 petals in clusters of up to 15 flowers per stem. This rose can bloom so profusely that the beautiful flowers obscure the semi-glossy leaflets. It blooms from early summer until fall or hard frost, whichever comes first.

Other names: Centennial
Flower color: medium pink
Flower size: 2¾–3"
Scent: subtle
Height: 24"–4'
Spread: 3–4'
Blooms: early summer to fall; repeat blooming
Hardiness zones: 3–9

✿ Deadheading helps maintain a continuous bloom cycle. Remove the entire cluster once it is finished, rather than one flower at a time. The flowers should be left on the plant later in the season to allow hips to form. The hips provide stunning red color from fall well into winter.

✿ Because the petals fall cleanly from the plant, Morden Centennial is considered a self-cleaning plant. It is prone to disease, including powdery mildew and blackspot, when stressed.

✿ Prune the shrub back by one-third in spring to promote a bushier habit. Begin this process before the leaves unfurl.

✿ This Parkland rose is the perfect balance of beauty, vigor and strength. It was awarded the Outstanding Cultivar Award by the Canadian Society of Horticulture Science in 1996.

Morden Fireglow

Other names: Fireglow
Flower color: deep
scarlet red with orange
Flower size: 2–3"
Scent: light and mild
Height: 24"–4'
Spread: 24–36"
Blooms: early summer
to fall; repeat blooming
Hardiness zones: 2b–9

This Parkland Series rose bears flowers that are not quite red yet not quite orange—a color unlike that of any other hardy shrub rose. The formal flowers contrast beautifully with the dark, tough foliage. The upright form of Morden Fireglow is more like that of a hybrid tea than a modern shrub. The double blossoms form in loosely cupped sprays.

✿ This plant is considered self-cleaning because the petals fall cleanly from the plant once they've finished blooming.

✿ Morden Fireglow will stand out among a variety of sun-loving plants, making it ideal for mixed beds and borders. Cut the stems while the flowers are still buds to extend the longevity of the cut flowers in bouquets.

✿ Deadheading will increase the number of flowers. Stop deadheading in late summer to allow the plant to form hips and prepare for winter.

✿ Prune Morden Fireglow back by at least half in spring to encourage new growth and to keep it from becoming leggy. Remove a few of the oldest canes each year, right from the base of the plant.

The large globular hips remain on the plant well into the following spring.

Morden Ruby

The blooms of Morden Ruby have a unique blend of colors—not quite light pink and not quite dark pink, but a blend of dark and light flecks and tones. Some of the flowers change to solid colors or fade with age, but overall Morden Ruby flowers are notably different from other Parkland Series rose blooms. This rose bears strong stems that support shiny, dark green leaves. Clusters of double flowers open from oval, reddish buds in late spring. The flowers are very long lasting, suitable for cutting and arrangements.

Other names: Ruby
Flower color: mottled light and dark pink blend
Flower size: 3"
Scent: mild
Height: 3–4'
Spread: 4'
Blooms: spring to fall; repeat blooming
Hardiness zones: 2–9

✿ Morden Ruby has moderate to good disease resistance but is a little prone to blackspot in areas with humid summers. Take all appropriate precautions against blackspot.

✿ Morden Ruby is naturally vigorous and somewhat lanky. If you want a bushier plant, prune hard in early spring, before the plant fully leafs out, by removing the longest rangy canes to the ground and shortening the remaining canes by at least half.

✿ Morden Ruby is suitable for just about any garden setting including cottage gardens. It can be left as a beautiful specimen or mixed with a variety of blooming shrubs and perennials. Plant in large groups for a strong visual impact. It works well in more exposed areas where it could be forgotten from time to time.

Introduced in 1977, this rose is the sister of Adelaide Hoodless and was born as a solid-colored bud sport from a non solid-colored flower. A speckled sport has somehow gotten into commerce, which is often the Morden Ruby seen in your local garden center.

Morden Snowbeauty

Other names: Morden Snow Beauty, Snowbeauty
Flower color: white
Flower size: 3–4"
Scent: slight
Height: 24"–4'
Spread: 3–4'
Blooms: early summer to fall; repeat blooming
Hardiness zones: 2b–8

Morden Snowbeauty is the only white bloomer of the Parkland Series and one of the most recent series introductions, released in 1998. It bears rather large, semi-double clusters of flowers exposing bright yellow stamens. This low-spreading shrub is covered in shiny, dark green healthy foliage.

❀ This extremely hardy specimen, created by Davidson & Collicutt of Canada, bears a large quantity of blooms in early summer, with intermittent flowers thereafter. A heavy second flush can be encouraged by a little deadheading and regular fertilizing.

❀ A mass of white roses is strikingly beautiful. This variety is also ideal for borders or left as a prolific specimen.

❀ The foliage produced by Morden Snowbeauty is healthy, highly disease resistant and requires very little care or maintenance. This rose was selected by its breeders for its resistance to powdery mildew and blackspot.

Morden Sunrise

Morden Sunrise is an adorable semi-double rose. It was highly anticipated when it was introduced in 1999 and was very well received by the public. The first yellow variety in the Parkland Series, it has a clean and fresh look, with blooms in tones of apricot and yellow along with attractive, shiny, dark green leaves.

✿ With its compact size, erect stems, dense foliage and semi-double flowers, this rose is ideal for borders or mixed beds or as a specimen. Morden Sunrise is a colorful addition to just about any garden setting.

✿ Cooler temperatures cause the flower color to become more intense, while hotter weather results in paler, softer tones.

✿ Morden Sunrise has good early-season resistance to blackspot, powdery mildew and rust. The resistance dramatically decreases when the plant is in a damp location or humidity levels are higher. Powdery mildew problems can also be aggravated during times of drought, so water thoroughly when the need arises.

Other names: none
Flower color: apricot yellow
Flower size: 3–3½"
Scent: mild, citrus
Height: 24–36"
Spread: 24–30"
Blooms: summer to fall; repeat blooming
Hardiness zones: 3–8

This rose bred for harsh winters performs beautifully in areas with mild winters as well.

Penelope

P enelope bears coppery peach buds that open to semi-double flowers touched with soft pinkish white. The large flower clusters are borne on plum-colored stems. The semi-glossy foliage has hints of bronze and darkens with age, and the rose produces attractive orange hips. It is considered one of Reverend J.H. Pemberton's best hybrid musk roses.

Other names: none
Flower color: blush pink
Flower size: 2–3"
Scent: sweet musk
Height: 4–5'
Spread: 5'
Blooms: summer to fall; repeat blooming
Hardiness zones: 6–11

✿ This rose is excellent for informal hedges and mixed borders. It can be left as a graceful, spreading shrub or pruned into a more compact specimen. Its unique fragrance is reminiscent of musky paperwhites.

✿ Reasonably disease resistant, Penelope tolerates poor soil and partial shade. Remove spent blooms after the first flush to encourage repeat blooming.

✿ Introduced in 1924, Penelope has collected many honors and awards, including the National Rose Society Gold Medal of 1925 and the 1993 Royal Horticultural Society Award of Garden Merit.

✿ It can survive winters in zones 4 and 5 with protection.

Prairie Joy

Prairie Joy, introduced in 1990, was the first hedge rose to be released by the Morden Research Station. It bears fully double flowers in clusters of one to six blooms each. The pink blooms look old-fashioned, reminiscent of roses created hundreds of years ago. Each flower has at least 40 petals. The dark, healthy foliage is a complementary backdrop for the blossoms and has excellent resistance to disease.

❀ Prairie Joy best suits a casual cottage setting. The rounded, dense form is ideal for screening or hedging. Cut back to just above ground level each spring to create a low, dense hedge. This rose also works well with various flowering plants in mixed beds and borders.

❀ This rose blooms profusely in summer with a sparse repeat.

❀ Rosarians and gardeners alike consider this one of the most maintenance-free and rewarding roses. It has outstanding resistance to powdery mildew and blackspot.

Other names: none
Flower color: medium pink
Flower size: 3"
Scent: mild
Height: 3–5'
Spread: 3–5'
Blooms: summer; repeat blooming
Hardiness zone: 2–9

Rosa Zwerg

Pavement roses were created in Germany to use alongside busy roadways and are now being used in a similar way in North America. These roses can be used as groundcovers, foundation plantings, informal low hedges or in mixed beds and borders. They are hardy and tolerate intense heat, sunlight, drought and partial shade. All are fragrant and form decorative hips in fall.

Other names:
Rosazwerg, Dwf. Pavement, Dwarf Pavement

Flower color:
medium pink

Flower size: 2½–3"

Scent: intense

Height: 30–36"

Spread: 30–42"

Blooms: summer to fall; repeat blooming

Hardiness zones: 3–9

✿ Rosa Zwerg grows in a low, compact form. It bears semi-double, medium pink flowers that bloom repeatedly through summer. Deep, scarlet hips follow the flowers in fall and remain on the plant well into winter.

✿ The wrinkly textured, medium green foliage has a strong resistance to blackspot and mildew.

✿ Pruning and spraying are simply not required, because this rose can plainly take care of itself. Pavement roses are usually on their own rootstock, which only improves their hardiness.

✿ Deadhead regularly throughout the season, but stop deadheading five to six weeks before a hard fall frost to allow the shrub to set hips and prepare for winter.

By sending out side shoots, this rose can sometimes reach widths of 6'.

Roseraie de l'Haÿ

Roseraie de l'Haÿ looks like an elegant and compact version of Hansa, in form and bloom. The unforgettable scent carries on warm summer breezes. Considered one of the finest garden roses in its class, it is one of the most popular and widely grown rugosa roses. Its long, pointed buds open to large, double, rich magenta clusters. Unlike most rugosas, this variety rarely sets hips. The dense foliage is borne on heavily bristled, upright canes in a bushy form. Starting wrinkled and dark green, the foliage changes to a deep red in fall.

Other names: none
Flower color: rich magenta purple
Flower size: 4–4½"
Scent: cinnamon and cloves
Height: 4–5'
Spread: 5–6'
Blooms: summer to late fall; repeat blooming
Hardiness zones: 3–9

❀ This variety is weather and disease resistant, dense and vigorous. It is virtually maintenance free when planted in partial shade with good air circulation. Most rugosas boast of health, hardiness and an ability to tolerate neglect, and this rose is no exception.

❀ Attractive as a hedge or in mixed borders, this rose is often used in traditional garden settings, including cottage and English gardens.

❀ This rose is named in tribute to one of the best rose gardens in the world. The world's oldest existing garden devoted exclusively to roses, La Roseraie de l'Haÿ, in France, marked its centenary in 1994.

❀ Roseraie de l'Haÿ is thought to be a sport of an unidentified hybrid rugosa rose. The debate continues about its listed origin.

Rotes Meer

Rotes Meer bears showy clusters of fragrant semi-double flowers held in small trusses. The yellow stamens are especially prominent among the deep purple-red flowers and medium green, textured foliage. Dark red hips are produced after the flowering cycles, and the foliage slowly evolves into a blast of fall color. The hips continue to provide color to a winter landscape.

Other names: Purple Pavement, Rotesmeer, Rotsmere, Exception

Flower color: purple crimson

Flower size: 2½–3"

Scent: strong, cinnamon and cloves

Height: 3–4'

Spread: 3–4'

Blooms: summer to fall; repeat blooming

Hardiness zones: 3–9

❀ Rotes Meer is frequently used in massed bushy borders or as hedging or on its own as a specimen. It thrives in full sun to partial shade. It will continue to maintain itself in less sunlight, though it won't be as vigorous. This rose doesn't really require much maintenance, making it an ideal variety to display and enjoy.

❀ A Pavement Series introduction from 1986, Rotes Meer was developed by Baum in Germany. This hybrid rugosa rose is versatile, hardy, disease resistant and low maintenance.

❀ The petals fall cleanly from the shrub rather than remaining attached where they look less attractive. It is thus considered a self-cleaning rose.

Sally Holmes

Sally Holmes bears large trusses of single creamy white flowers lightly touched with peach. The flowers fade over time until they are almost pure white when fully open. The clusters are enormous, each stem carrying 50 or more blooms on graceful arching canes. Some claim that the clusters are too close together. Although the clusters may seem a little cluttered, they are stunning. Each flower is made up of five petals that open flat to expose prominent stamens. The flowers are complemented by large, semi-glossy, pointed leaves.

Other names: none
Flower color: creamy white with peach undertones
Flower size: 3½"
Scent: light, sweet
Height: 3–5'
Spread: 3–5'
Blooms: summer to fall; repeat blooming
Hardiness zones: 5–9

- ✿ It's easy to be impressed by the magnificent flowers, but the most beautiful feature of this rose is its balance—one feature isn't more prominent than another, and all the features work together, resulting in a beautiful package.
- ✿ The petals will fall cleanly from each stem, resulting in a well-formed hip.
- ✿ Deadhead early in the season to prolong the bloom cycle.
- ✿ This highly disease-resistant rose is easily trained as a climber along a fence or wall in warmer locations. It is effective as a specimen and blends well with various other flowering plants in mixed beds and borders.
- ✿ Although it was introduced fewer than 30 years ago, Sally Holmes has the classic look of hybrid musk roses developed in the early 20th century.

Schneekoppe

Other names:
Snow Pavement

Flower color: white;
tinged mauve pink

Flower size: 2½–3"

Scent: intense

Height: 3–4'

Spread: 3–4'

Blooms: summer to fall;
repeat blooming

Hardiness zones: 3–9

This 1986 introduction has some unusual characteristics compared to other pavement roses. The flower color, white tinged with tones of mauve and pink, is original. The large-petaled, double flowers open from long, pale pink buds. The bright green, textured foliage is very tough, healthy and disease resistant and moderately paler than that of other pavement roses.

❀ Orange hips are produced towards the latter part of summer into fall and remain on the plant until the following spring.

❀ This rose's low-growing, spreading, bushy habit makes it ideal for low hedging, in a border or as a specimen. In very rich soil, pruning may be needed to keep the plant compact and under control. Deadheading is unnecessary.

❀ This variety tolerates salt, extreme temperatures and poor soil. It is especially suited to locations near driveways, roads and sidewalks where salt may be applied in winter.

❀ As do all Pavement Series roses, Schneekoppe has superior resistance to disease, including blackspot and powdery mildew.

The flowers can appear glowing white at dusk, making this rose a very pretty addition to just about any garden setting.

The Fairy

The Fairy is popular with novice to experienced gardeners. The moderately thorny canes are hidden by glossy foliage that forms into a compact and mounding form. It bears dainty, baby pink rosettes that develop into large clusters perched atop the leaves.

Other names:
Fairy, Feerie
Flower color: soft pink
Flower size: 1–1½"
Scent: very little to light
Height: 24–36"
Spread: 24"–4'
Blooms: late summer to late fall; repeat blooming
Hardiness zones: 4–9

❀ This rose is ideal for a variety of landscape purposes. It can be planted in containers or as a groundcover or left to trail over a low wall or embankment. It is easily trained as a weeping standard and integrates nicely into mixed beds and borders. It packs a punch when planted en masse or as low hedging. It also makes a beautiful cut flower. Heavy spring pruning may be necessary to maintain The Fairy as a dwarf shrub. When left in its natural form, it grows into a delicate, spreading shrub.

❀ The Fairy is trouble free and highly resistant to disease, requiring very little care. It may, however, have problems with spider mites in hot, dry conditions.

❀ This rose blooms continually until fall frost.

❀ This highly successful rose is joined by a host of other roses with similar characteristics. Crystal Fairy is pure white, Lovely Fairy is dark pink and Fairy Queen is deep pink-red.

Thérèse Bugnet

Thérèse Bugnet is a little hesitant to bloom when young but it's well worth the wait. Once established, it will produce gray-green, rather smooth leaves on almost thornless canes. The stems are tipped with a profusion of ruffled, double, lilac pink blossoms that pale with age. After the flowers have all but finished, attractive fall color prevails with cherry red canes, dark orange hips and bronzed foliage.

Other names: Theresa Bugnet, Teresa Bugnet
Flower color: medium lilac pink
Flower size: 3–3½"
Scent: sweet cloves
Height: 5–6'
Spread: 4–5'
Blooms: summer to fall; repeat blooming
Hardiness zones: 2–9

✿ This exceptional variety tolerates cold and heat, wind and late frosts. One of the cold-hardiest roses in the world, this variety endures temperatures of −35° F. Thérèse Bugnet doesn't mind partial shade to full sun, alkaline, rocky, sandy or clay soils or neglect.

✿ Like other rugosas, Thérèse Bugnet resents being sprayed with fungicides. If powdery mildew occurs, prune out and destroy infected growth.

✿ Deadheading regularly and pruning after the first flowering cycle in early summer will prolong the bloom cycle. Otherwise the only pruning required would be to cut the magnificent flowers for arrangements.

✿ This variety was developed in Alberta by the late Georges Bugnet, who invested over 25 years creating this hybrid rugosa, which he then named after his daughter.

White Meidiland

The Meidiland Series includes two white roses. They are often confused, but they differ in subtle ways. White Meidiland does not grow as tall as its counterpart, Alba Meidiland, and bears larger flowers. The flowers are very double and made up of 40 petals each, overlapping to form a large, 4" wide blossom. The bloom period is also slightly different than that of the other white Meidiland rose, as this one bears flowers in prolific flushes from late spring to fall. White Meidiland is largely disease free, one of the reasons this rose is so ideally suited for use along roadways, borders and gardens that receive little care.

Other names:
Alba Meidiland,
Blanc Meillandecor
Flower color:
pure white
Flower size: 3–4"
Scent: sweet
Height: 18–24"
Spread: 4–5'
Blooms: summer to fall;
repeat blooming
Hardiness zones: 4–9

✿ The spreading growth and vigorous horizontal branching make this rose ideal for use as a groundcover, a use it was originally released for.
✿ White Meidiland does not drop its petals cleanly. It will require deadheading to keep it looking tidy.
✿ Marie-Louise Meilland developed White Meidiland in 1986 for Meilland Roses of France. It is officially registered with the ARS as MEIcoublan and should not be confused with Alba Meidiland, which is registered as MEIflopan.

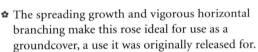

William Baffin

William Baffin is tall enough to be trained as a climber or pillar rose. It can be left in its natural form as a slightly arching specimen or trimmed into a taller hedge. Tough and versatile, hardy and vigorous, this rose meets all expectations. Its semi-double flowers are borne in clusters of 30 or more. Glossy, medium green foliage is vigorously produced in dense mounds.

Other names: none
Flower color: deep pink
Flower size: 2½–3"
Scent: little to none
Height: 8–10'
Spread: 5–8'
Blooms: summer to fall; repeat blooming
Hardiness zones: 2–9

✿ William Baffin is a truly impressive specimen. It is hardy enough to remain on a trellis, arbor or pergola in the coldest of winters, without pruning or any special protection. It can grow quite tall in milder climates.

✿ This rose was named after the famous explorer who in 1616 discovered Lancaster Sound when he was trying to find the Northwest Passage. Robert Bylot accompanied Baffin on this voyage, and they sailed farther north than any other explorer would for the next 236 years.

✿ William Baffin is highly disease resistant and requires very little to no maintenance. It is thought to be the best shrub or climbing rose for colder regions.

Winnipeg Parks

This rose used to be difficult to find, because it was so popular the rose growers couldn't grow plants fast enough to meet consumer demand. Thankfully it is now more readily available. The striking flower color is similar to that of Alexander Mackenzie (p. 131), though Winnipeg Parks has a slightly larger bloom. It bears pointed buds that open into velvety, cupped, double clusters of reddish pink, lightly scented blossoms. The striking color of the flowers contrasts well with the matte, medium green foliage. It quickly forms into a tight, dense, compact form and has the most attractive foliage of the Parkland roses.

Other names: none
Flower color:
deep, vivid reddish pink
Flower size: 2¾–3½"
Scent: slight
Height: 24–36"
Spread: 18–24"
Blooms: summer to fall; repeat blooming
Hardiness zones: 2–9

✿ In cooler weather the green leaves can be tinted with red.

✿ This variety is suitable for bedding, borders or as a specimen. Winnipeg Parks grows close to the ground, so it is ideal for the edges of mixed flower beds and containers.

✿ The disease resistance is good, and the foliage shouldn't require any special attention to prevent disease. Deadhead to encourage further blooming. Cut the flowers in the early stages; cut flowers are useful for arrangements, crafts or recipes.

✿ This 1990 introduction was named after the City of Winnipeg's Parks and Recreation Department in honor of its 1993 centennial.

GROUNDCOVER

These roses are not groundcovers in the true sense of the word but are a good choice for large areas that need color. Generally groundcover roses remain small and have a procumbent or spreading habit. They can be different kinds of roses but their growth habit makes them useful as groundcovers. The best groundcover roses grow wider than taller, repeat bloom throughout the summer without deadheading, are disease resistant and require minimal winter protection. Groundcover roses can reach heights of 3–4'. Their compact and floriferous growth habit provides a mass of dense foliage and color. Often groundcover roses send down roots where the canes touch the ground. Some hardy, low-growing hybrids have been developed recently that work very well as groundcovers. Smaller, hardy roses can also be mass planted to fill a large area with color.

Most groundcover roses benefit from a hard pruning in spring and extra mulching in late fall. Use once-a-year fertilizers in spring if the roses are planted in areas that are difficult to access.

Aspen

Other names: Gold Magic Carpet, Gwent, Sun Cover
Flower color: medium yellow
Flower size: 1–1½"
Scent: little to none
Height: 14–16"
Spread: 24–36"
Blooms: summer to fall; repeat blooming
Hardiness zones: 4–9

The growth habit of Aspen is dense enough to completely obscure the ground underneath the low, sprawling branches. This small modern shrub is about twice as wide as it is high. It resembles a naturally colorful outdoor carpet covered in yellow buds and semi-double, pastel yellow flowers. It is an ideal bushy, miniature shrub for planting en masse and perfect as a low-growing border. Aspen can also be used in hanging baskets. The effect is quite magical, as small clusters of colorful flowers cascade over the edge of the basket, creating a waterfall of blossoms.

✿ Unlike many yellow roses, Aspen is highly resistant to blackspot and has excellent winter hardiness.
✿ Aspen won the Belgium Certificate of Merit in 1992, the same year it was introduced by Poulsen Roser ApS in Denmark. Its official name is POUlurt.

Baby Blanket

Baby Blanket is a low-growing modern shrub rose that is trouble-free and constantly in bloom. It appears dainty but is rugged. Baby Blanket was a breakthrough in low-maintenance gardening when it was introduced in 1991 by Kordes Roses of Germany. It bears double, light pink flowers made up of 20 to 25 petals each. The flowers are borne in large clusters and are mildly fragrant. The delicate flowers stand above dark, glossy foliage that is tough as nails.

Other names: Oxfordshire, Sommermorgen, Summer Morning, Country Lass
Flower color: light pink
Flower size: 2–3"
Scent: slight
Height: 24–36"
Spread: 5'
Blooms: summer to fall; repeat blooming
Hardiness zones: 4–9

- Baby Blanket produces canes with an arching habit that allows it to be trained as a small rambling rose. Knee-deep mounds of foliage make this rose ideal as groundcover. It's also suitable when left as a specimen. It is also available as a short tree or standard rose for those areas that require a vertical lift, but in this form may require some winter protection.
- This rose requires very little care other than the basics. Baby Blanket is not only pretty but also practical in every sense.
- Plant Baby Blanket in front of taller Bonica (p. 135) for a striking combination.

Flower Carpet

Other names: Emera, Heidetraum, Emeura, Blooming Carpet, Emera Pavement, Pink Flower Carpet, Floral Carpet

Flower color: deep hot pink

Flower size: 2"

Scent: very little

Height: 24–32"

Spread: 3–3½'

Blooms: summer to early winter; repeat blooming

Hardiness zones: 5–9

Flower Carpet is very popular and easy to grow for either the beginner or the expert.

Flower Carpet was developed in 1991 and claimed to offer 'flowers for 10 months' and 'total disease resistance.' The claims proved a little too optimistic, but this modern shrub is beautiful and multifaceted. Vigorous, shiny, plentiful foliage complements the double, hot pink flowers with bright yellow stamens. The blooms are borne in large clusters, creating a dense, colorful carpet of flowers, hence the name.

✿ A characteristic of its rambler parentage is that the prolific flowering begins a little later than for most roses, and at times there are no blooms at all. A good early spring prune every year will restore the vigor of any Flower Carpet plant that has become too woody. Cut it down to 10–12" above ground at that time, removing any old wood.

✿ Deadheading isn't necessary—the petals fall cleanly from the plant while it continues to bloom.

✿ Flower Carpet can be used as a groundcover for a sunny location or as a low hedge. It can also be used in containers, mixed borders or beds.

✿ A new color of Flower Carpet has been introduced almost every year since its original release, including white and a variety of pink shades. Watch for Appleblossom, White, Pink, Red, Coral and Yellow, the color introduced in 2004.

Magic Meidiland

This shrub rose is not only beautiful but truly resistant to all forms of disease. Its low creeping habit, dense form and abundant blooms make this rose an ideal groundcover for slopes and banks or areas that require a physical barrier to keep foot traffic out. The semi-double flowers are borne in small clusters of three to seven flowers per stem. Dark lustrous foliage remains healthy and unscathed even on the hottest of days.

Other names:
Magic Meillandecor
Flower color: bright medium pink
Flower size: 1½–2"
Scent: spicy, freesia
Height: 18–24"
Spread: 5–6'
Blooms: late spring to fall; repeat blooming
Hardiness zones: 4–9

- Each small flower is made up of 17 to 25 petals that open flat, exposing bright yellow stamens. The flowers aren't affected by extreme weather. Deadheading will help prolong the bloom cycle during late summer lulls.
- This ground-hugging rose bears some prickles on lanky stems.
- If canes grow too close to a footpath, peg them down within the bed or border.

The beautiful pink blooms of this hardy groundcover will magically add color to your garden.

Red Ribbons

Other names:
Fiery Sunsation, Chilterns, Mainaufeuer, Island Fire, Roselina

Flower color:
bright, deep red

Flower size: 3"

Scent: mild

Height: 24"

Spread: 4–5'

Blooms: summer to fall; repeat blooming

Hardiness zones: 4–9

Red Ribbons is an ideal groundcover rose for difficult locations. Naturally vigorous, low spreading and with a dense growth habit, this rose works well cascading down embankments, growing up short pillars or planted en masse. It can also be used as a grafted standard or tree rose. The semi-double to double, dark red flowers stand out in any landscape setting. It is well recognized around the world for its hardiness, charm and versatility.

✿ Like so many roses bred by Kordes, Red Ribbons is winter hardy and has healthy foliage.

✿ Don't confuse Red Ribbons (KORtemma) with Red Ribbon (WILrib), a floribunda introduced in 1997 by J. Benjamin Williams. Both bear double, red flowers but along with their different parentage, breeder and country of origin, they have subtle differences in form as well.

✿ Red Ribbons is part of a collection of low groundcover roses called Rose Blanket Roses, introduced in the U.S. by Jackson & Perkins. Other members of this group include Baby Blanket, Electric Blanket and Magic Blanket.

Sea Foam

Sea Foam falls under several classifications. It is a modern shrub rose with a climbing or rambling habit, and it is often used as a groundcover rose. Abundant clusters of pale pink buds emerge in summer, a little later than other roses, opening to attractive pearly white blossoms. Sea Foam is rarely without its beautiful double, cupped flowers. The flowers are supported by moderately thorny canes clothed in dark, leathery foliage.

Other names: Seafoam
Flower color: white touched with pink
Flower size: 2–2½"
Scent: delicate tea
Height: 24–36"
Spread: 4–6'
Blooms: summer to fall; repeat blooming
Hardiness zones: 4–11

❀ The spreading habit causes it to grow out and downwards rather than up. It is easily trained as a groundcover rose trailing down an embankment or stone wall. It can also be trained as a short climber with adequate winter protection.

❀ The plant will root on its own wherever its flexible canes contact the ground. It is easily propagated by cuttings or by layering.

❀ Sea Foam prefers full sun but continues to thrive in partial shade. The pink tones will intensify in cooler settings or partial shade.

❀ This rose was developed by amateur hybridizer Ernest W. Schwartz in 1964. It shouldn't be confused with another rose called Seafoam, bred in 1919 by William Paul and said to be a seedling of Mermaid.

CLIMBERS & RAMBLERS

Climbing roses do not in fact climb. The canes must be trained and tied into place on some form of support. Climbers generally have long, stiff, arching canes ranging in length from 6 to 15'. The canes are productive for two to four years and often become thick and woody as they get older. Each year, some of the oldest canes should be removed from the base and new canes trained up a support to keep the rose young and productive.

Climbing roses come from various sources, and the hardiness of a variety depends on its parentage. For just about any climate or region, there is a climber, including climbing hybrid teas and climbing Explorer roses. Pruning practices can greatly influence the form of your climbing rose. Vigorous shrubs can be pruned to encourage climbing, and climbers can be pruned to resemble shrubs.

Hybrid teas, floribundas, grandifloras and other bush or shrub roses sometimes mutate to produce long, vigorous canes, referred to as sports. Climbing sports produce the same flower types and blooming habits of the roses they sported from. Some seedlings are grown and propagated as a source of climbers. The more recent introductions are less rampant than the older types and are repeat blooming. The canes terminate in an inflorescence, later flowering from laterals produced on the main canes.

Ramblers have longer flexible canes that can reach lengths of 20' or more. Rambler canes behave like raspberry canes in that new canes grow without flowering for their first season, and flowers are produced along the canes in the second season. When the flowering cycle is complete, the oldest canes should be pruned out. Ramblers need to be tied to a support when trained to grow in an upright direction. They can also be left to 'ramble' along the ground as a groundcover or trail down an embankment or stone wall.

Early climbers and ramblers arose from crossing hybrid teas and other classes mainly with *Rosa wichurana* and *Rosa multiflora*. They bloomed once a year and were often rampant

growers. *Rosa wichurana* is in the ancestry of many modern climbers, and there are still many non-repeating Wichurana climbers available in commerce.

Altissimo

American Pillar

Albéric Barbier

Other names: none

Flower color: cream with light yellow

Flower size: 3"

Scent: fruity apple, sweet

Height: 10–15'

Spread: 10–12'

Blooms: early to mid-summer; no repeat blooming

Hardiness zones: 5–10

Albéric Barbier was the first in a long line of prominent ramblers developed and released by Barbier et Compagnie of Orléans. It bears petite, creamy yellow buds that open to off white, large flowers in small clusters. It blooms profusely but has an unreliable repeat bloom cycle, so enjoy the flowers while they last. The flowers are supported by slender, flexible stems and nearly evergreen shiny, dark green foliage.

❀ Albéric Barbier is extremely vigorous and healthy. It tolerates poor soils and shade.

❀ This Wichurana rambler can climb up to 15' when trained so is ideal for twining up old trees, pergolas and arbors. It is not as good for climbing walls, because reduced air circulation around the plant encourages mildew problems. It is also useful as a groundcover.

❀ Albéric Barbier was honored 93 years after its introduction with the Royal Horticultural Society Award of Garden Merit in 1993.

Altissimo

Altissimo is Italian for 'in the highest.' It is an apt name for this large-flowered climber, as it grows high, is of high quality and is highly disease resistant. Large, matte, leathery, dark, serrated foliage complements the nearly flat, deeply colored flowers. The large blooms are borne on new and old growth. Altissimo is considered one of the best red climbers and one of the easiest climbers to grow. The single flowers almost obscure the plant throughout the season.

Other names:
Altus, Sublimely Single
Flower color: blood red
Flower size: 4–5"
Scent: slight, cloves
Height: 7–9'
Spread: 5–8'
Blooms: early summer; repeat blooming
Hardiness zones: 5–9

✿ Remove the spent blooms to encourage long-term, prolific blooming. The nearly rounded, blood red petals sometimes fall off soon after the single flowers have opened.
✿ When cut, the long-stemmed blooms keep well with unfading color and are useful in a variety of arrangements.
✿ This rose can be grown successfully as a large shrub if pruned hard and given room to fill out. If trained as a climber, it will require support on a pillar, pergola, veranda post or trellis. The stiff and sturdy stems create an upright, bushy and spreading form suitable for just about any garden setting. In a warm location it has been known to grow large enough to cover the side of a one-story building. In a cooler location, Altissimo doesn't grow as large.

George Delbard of Delbard-Chabert developed this stately climber in 1966 in France. Altissimo is a seedling of Tenor, a red climber created earlier by Delbard.

America

Other names: none
Flower color: deep salmon pink; lighter reverse
Flower size: 3½–4½"
Scent: intense, spicy
Height: 7–8'
Spread: 4–6'
Blooms: summer to fall; repeat blooming
Hardiness zones: 5–9

This large-flowered climber bears deep salmon pink flowers with a lighter reverse. Intensely spicy blossoms are borne singly and in clusters amid medium green, semi-glossy foliage. Famed hybridizer William A. Warriner of Jackson & Perkins created this rose in 1976. It was chosen as an AARS winner, one of very few climbers to receive such a prestigious distinction. It flowers freely throughout summer on old and new wood. The flowers are deeper and more vibrant immediately after opening but fade over time to a pale coral salmon. Each flower is very double, made up of 40 to 45 petals with a high center in a cupped form.

✿ This rose performs better as a climber in a protected location. In an exposed location, its canes will suffer winterkill and its height will therefore be limited. It can withstand zones 4 and 5 with winter protection.

✿ This rose is suitable for climbing walls, fences and pillars, and the blooms are excellent for cutting.

✿ America can tolerate being pruned to maintain a large, manageable shrub.

✿ Deadheading is recommended to boost repeat bloom cycles throughout the summer months until fall.

✿ This rose was introduced in the year of the bicentennial celebration of the United States, hence its name.

American Pillar

Despite its name, American Pillar is considered too aggressive to be a pillar rose and is better suited to climb up the side of a house, pergola, wire fence or lattice or to twine through an old, sturdy tree. It bears large clusters of small, deep pink flowers with prominent yellow stamens. Elongated, thick, arching stems support long-lasting blooms that fade from deep to light pink with age. The blooms have a tendency to be mottled by rain. Bright red oval hips and bronze fall foliage follow the summer flowers.

Other names: none
Flower color: bright carmine pink; white centers
Flower size: 2–3"
Scent: light to none
Height: 10–15'
Spread: 10–12'
Blooms: mid-summer; no repeat blooming
Hardiness zones: 4–9

❀ This rose has more impact if it is allowed to grow to its mature height rather than being pruned into a smaller shrub. Once established, it requires little attention.
❀ American Pillar tolerates partial shade and poor soil but resents hot, dry weather.
❀ Relatively disease free, it is somewhat prone to powdery mildew in locations with poor air circulation.
❀ Though this rose begins to bloom a little later than most ramblers, the flowers last a very long time. The flowers are perfect for cutting and simple arrangements.

Aunt Ruth

Other names: none
Flower color: pink blend with a white eye
Flower size: 3–3½"
Scent: slight, sweet
Height: 7–8'
Spread: 4–6'
Blooms: summer to fall; repeat blooming
Hardiness zones: 5–10

This rose was bred in Cleveland, Ohio, by Paul E. Jerabek, who hybridized over 30 roses in his lengthy and distinguished rose-breeding career. This climber bears large semi-double flowers of approximately 14 petals each. The petals, edged with different shades of pink, meet in the center to form a white eye. The flowers are sweetly scented and borne in clusters of varying sizes. The long canes have few prickles and grow into a spreading and bushy form. This rose received a Bronze Certificate from the ARS trial grounds competition in 1998 after years of testing.

✿ In Michigan, Aunt Ruth is a great climber to train laterally along a fence. In the south, it grows taller and can cover an arbor or pergola.

✿ Deadhead to improve the bloom production of this cheerful climber.

✿ The canes may be damaged by severe winter weather, but Aunt Ruth grows quickly and blooms well even on new growth. It can be overwintered successfully with protection.

✿ This rose was selected and named by the nieces and nephews of Ruth Esler, a distinguished rosarian who enjoyed a long career of service to numerous gardening organizations in her home state of Michigan.

Awakening

Awakening was resurrected after an interesting journey from Czechoslovakia in 1988. Former president of the RNRS, Dick Balfour, traveled to Blatna where he noticed a rose called Probuzeni that resembled the rambler New Dawn. It displayed only one subtle difference: each bloom had twice the usual number of petals. He returned to the U.K. with wood from the rose so Peter Beales could propagate it. The resulting rose was later introduced by Hortico Inc. in Canada. Almost five years later it was reintroduced as Awakening.

Other names:
Probuzeni, Probuzini
Flower color: light pink
Flower size: 1½–2¾"
Scent: moderately sweet
Height: 8–10'
Spread: 8'
Blooms: summer to fall; repeat blooming
Hardiness zones: 4–9

* Awakening bears beautiful quartered blooms that emit a moderately sweet fragrance. Each flower has a muddled center packed with petals. The charming flowers sit above light-colored glossy foliage.
* Compared to other climbers, Awakening bears its flowers for an extended period of time.
* It is easily adapted for training on just about anything including arbors, trellises, fences and obelisks.
* This fully double sport of New Dawn was originally introduced as Probuzeni in Blatna, Czechoslovakia, in 1935.

Blaze Improved

Other names:
Demokracie, Blaze Superior, Imperial Blaze, New Blaze

Flower color: pure red

Flower size: 2–3"

Scent: light, fruity

Height: 8–10'

Spread: 6–8'

Blooms: spring to fall; repeat blooming

Hardiness zones: 4–10

Blaze Improved was bred in Czechoslovakia and introduced by Jackson & Perkins in 1950. As popular now as it was then, it bears abundant clusters of pure red, fully double blossoms that emit a lovely light and fruity scent. The cupped flowers are made up of 20 to 25 petals each. Widely used as a climber throughout Michigan, Blaze Improved has largely replaced the original Blaze, which has little to no repeat bloom. Blaze Improved reliably blooms in the heat of summer when most roses are resting.

✿ Blaze Improved blooms most profusely when it is trained horizontally along a fence. It produces a profusion of lateral side shoots, each of which ends in a flower cluster.

✿ This rose blooms on old and new wood and tolerates salt.

This winter-hardy rose is easy to grow and resistant to disease.

City of York

City of York, developed during World War II and named after a city in Pennsylvania, well deserves the accolades and honors it has received, including the ARS National Gold Medal Certificate in 1950. It bears large clusters of creamy white, semi-double, saucer-shaped flowers surrounding bright yellow stamens. The rich flowers emerge from the tips of long, arching, pliable canes clothed in glossy, deep green foliage. Large hips follow the flowers, so this rose is attractive well into winter.

✿ Because the growth habit of this rose is more like that of a rambler than a climber, it is best for growing up pergolas, trellises and pillars instead of walls or flat surfaces.

✿ It is relatively disease and maintenance free, easy to grow, extremely vigorous and produces a large crop of hips well into fall. Provide City of York and most other climbing roses with adequate air circulation to discourage potential disease.

✿ City of York tolerates full sun, but in semi-shade it thrives and the flowers remain on the plant with very little discoloration.

Other names:
Direktör Benschop

Flower color:
creamy white

Flower size: 3–3½"

Scent: strong, citrus

Height: 10–12'

Spread: 8–10'

Blooms: early summer; no repeat blooming

Hardiness zones: 5–9

City of York is capable of covering a large pergola in white blossoms.

Clair Matin

Clair Matin was the result of a complicated series of crosses. Classed as a cluster or large-flowered climber, this rose bears sweetbriar-scented blossoms in cotton candy pink. The flowers are borne in huge panicles of 30 to 40 small flowers. Each flower consists of 15 petals that open quickly, displaying showy stamens. Very few hips are produced, leading to what seems to be continuous blooming. Dark, leathery foliage complements the semi-double, cupped to flat blossoms in round clusters.

Other names:
Grimpant Clair Matin

Flower color: medium pink; hints of coral

Flower size: 2–3"

Scent: sweetbriar

Height: 7–8'

Spread: 4–6'

Blooms: summer to fall; repeat blooming

Hardiness zones: 4–9

❀ Upright and well branched in form and vigorous in habit, Clair Matin is suitable as a pillar rose or grown on a tripod or obelisk. It would also nicely accent the back of a large border.

❀ The long, arching panicles of flowers are ideal for decorations and arrangements.

❀ Clair Matin means 'morning light' in French.

Clair Matin was introduced in 1960 by well-known hybridizer Marie-Louise Meilland from Meilland Roses in France.

Constance Spry

Constance Spry was created in 1961 and named after the famous floral arranger, author and collector of old garden roses from the 1950s to 1960s. It was the first English rose that David Austin created. It bears extremely large, cupped, fully double, soft pink flowers. The showy blooms blend well with the plentiful, semi-glossy, coarse, grayish green leaves. This rose bears one large profusion of blossoms, with no repeat, so you must appreciate the strongly fragrant flowers while they are in bloom.

Other names:
Constanze Spry
Flower color: soft pink
Flower size: 4–5"
Scent: strong, myrrh
Height: 10–12'
Spread: 5–8'
Blooms: early summer; no repeat blooming
Hardiness zones: 4b–9

✿ This rose blooms with or without care or attention. It prefers moderately fertile soil and cooler climates but tolerates light shade, long hot summers and little care. It is highly disease resistant.

✿ Once the flowers are finished, a light pruning may be needed to keep the plant from growing too large.

✿ Ideal for climbing walls, heavy lattices or pergolas, this rose can also be used at the back of a mixed border as a large shrub or specimen. Support of some kind is necessary to reinforce the vigorous, sprawling, arching stems.

Dortmund

F ew roses are rated as highly and respected as much as Dortmund, which has many excellent qualities. It grows tall and upright but dense in form. It bears large, single, deep red flowers with a glowing central white eye and bright yellow stamens. The single flowers have an average of five to seven petals. Dark glossy foliage complements the rich flower color. The foliage alone makes Dortmund worth having in the garden.

Other names: none
Flower color:
red with a white eye
Flower size: 3–4"
Scent: light apple, old rose
Height: 8–12'
Spread: 6–8'
Blooms: spring to fall; repeat blooming
Hardiness zones: 4b–9

✿ Dortmund is a little slow to bloom in spring, but once it begins to take off the results are worth the wait. It tolerates light, dappled shade and poorer soil and is highly disease resistant.

✿ This rose can grow large enough to cover one side of a small building. To create a medium-sized shrub useful for hedging or as a specimen, prune to control the size. As a climber it can be trained up a pillar, veranda post, wall or trellis.

✿ To encourage blooming, deadhead heavily and frequently. Discontinue deadheading at least five weeks before first frost to allow the plant to form a large crop of bright red hips in fall.

Dublin Bay

Dublin Bay is one of the best red-bloomed climbers available and is especially successful in southern Michigan, where it bears visually stunning blossoms throughout the season. The first flush of blooms can last six weeks or more. It has a reliable growth habit and weatherproof flowers and is low maintenance and highly disease resistant. Large oval buds emerge in spring on new and old wood and open to well-shaped, double blooms. The moderately thorny stems support dark green, shiny foliage.

Other names: Grandhotel
Flower color: bright red
Flower size: 4¹/₂"
Scent: mildly fruity
Height: 7–10'
Spread: 5–7'
Blooms: summer to fall; repeat blooming
Hardiness zones: 4–11

❀ Deadhead to encourage repeat blooming.
❀ Dublin Bay fans out well on low fences and trellises. It is very attractive climbing up tripods, pillars, pergolas or arches. It can be pruned into an informal hedge.
❀ This rose prefers full sun and moist, well-drained soil. It holds up well in cold or hot conditions but should not be planted in windy locations.
❀ Dublin Bay was bred by Sam McGredy IV of New Zealand. Its coloration and structure derive from Altissimo, and its free-flowering nature from its other parent, Bantry Bay. It was introduced in 1975.
❀ Dublin Bay won the Royal Horticultural Society Award of Garden Merit in 1993 and continues to win blue ribbons at many local Michigan rose shows.

The rich, long-lasting flowers hold their color well even when cut for crafts or arrangements.

Fourth of July

Other names:
Crazy for You, Hanabi

Flower color: velvety scarlet red with white stripes

Flower size: 2–3"

Scent: sweet, apple

Height: 8–10'

Spread: 3–6'

Blooms: spring to fall; repeat blooming

Hardiness zones: 4–9

Fourth of July was the first climbing rose to be named an All-America Rose Selections winner in over 20 years. It received this prestigious honor in 1999, the year it was introduced by hybridizer Tom Carruth of Weeks Roses. This colorful climber has also received accolades in the U.K., including the Breeder's Choice Award. Known as Crazy for You in England, this rose was named in the U.S. to celebrate America's independence. Often trained on fences, arbors and trellises, this climber bears large sprays of velvety, semi-double blooms, each made up of 10 to 16 ruffled petals. The blooms are different from one another, displaying varied combinations of stripes and speckles. Bright yellow centers surround the prominent cluster of stamens in each bloom.

❀ Fourth of July is best grown in moderately moist, slightly acidic, well-drained soil. It tolerates partial shade but thrives in full sun.

❀ This rose will remain smaller in locations with colder winters and shorter seasons. With training it could be grown as a shrub rather than a climber.

❀ The deep green foliage provides a dramatic background for the blooms during the long blooming season. The foliage is unaffected by disease and continues to look fresh and crisp.

❀ Fourth of July always seems to be covered with a profusion of blooms on Independence Day.

Handel

Handel is one of the loveliest climbing roses available. It is stunning in full bloom, displaying a profusion of semi-double, white and creamy-centered blossoms edged in deep pink. The slender buds open to loosely double, wavy flowers in mid-summer and bloom less frequently as fall approaches. The glossy, dark foliage is only mildly affected by blackspot, and the flowers can withstand a rainfall without any damage. It begins to develop slowly but gradually increases in vigor and performance as it ages.

✿ This rose is a strong grower, and the upright, stiff stems are best growing on a fence, wall, arbor or pergola. Handel can be trained as a shrub with moderate pruning. The pruning will not affect the bloom cycles, as this rose bears flowers on new and old wood.

✿ The mid-season blooms sometimes look ragged, but a little deadheading will take care of that and will also encourage further flowering in larger quantities.

✿ The young flowers are neatly formed and high centered, reminiscent of hybrid tea blooms, and then open cupped in wide clusters. These blooms look best when grown in a cooler location or during cooler periods.

Other names:
Haendel, Händel

Flower color: creamy white; deep pink edges

Flower size: 3½"

Scent: light honey

Height: 8–10'

Spread: 4–8'

Blooms: summer to fall; repeat blooming

Hardiness zones: 5–9

Handel has received many awards including the Portland Gold Medal in 1975.

Jeanne Lajoie

Other names: none
Flower color: medium pink
Flower size: 1"
Scent: slight, tea
Height: 8–12'
Spread: 5–8'
Blooms: summer to fall; repeat blooming
Hardiness zones: 4–11

J eanne Lajoie is a climbing miniature that will easily fill out a trellis or a freestanding pillar or obelisk. It is a hybrid rather than a naturally occurring mutation. Few match its sheer production of miniature blooms, hardiness and healthy foliage. It appears to be in bloom all summer and well into fall.

✿ A staggering number of non-fading florets with good form and substance make Jeanne Lajoie one of the best climbers available.

✿ This rose is an excellent choice for a location where a dramatic vertical display is desired.

✿ The disease resistance for this rose is very reliable, but there is a slight tendency for blackspot. If blackspot is caught early and treated, Jeanne Lajoie recovers quickly and easily.

✿ A bit slow to establish, Jeanne Lajoie will begin to bloom prolifically by its third season.

✿ The tall canes can be easily trained to assume a lateral horizontal position to optimize bloom production along the cane.

✿ Only two years after its introduction Jeanne Lajoie received the ARS Award of Excellence for Miniature Roses in 1977. It was developed by hybridizer E.P. Sima of Seattle, Washington.

Laura Ford

Laura Ford is a simple yet elegant yellow rose. The burgundy buds and stems contrast beautifully with the lemony blossoms that in turn showcase amber stamens. It is resistant to disease, easy to maintain and grow, produces weatherproof blooms and is a good example of a modern miniature climber. What more could you ask? The soft yellow blooms touched with pale pink form into semi-double, dense clusters that vary in shades with age. Shiny, small, medium green leaves complement the flowers on a tall, upright, well-branched framework.

* This rose is suitable as a climber on low walls, pillars, fences or trellises. It is ideal as a specimen for average garden settings.
* No pruning or deadheading is required, and large hips set well into fall, which is unusual for a miniature rose. Deadheading will encourage a lengthy flush of blooms.
* This fragrant variety was named after a well-known English artist. It received the Royal National Rose Society Certificate of Merit in 1988 and the Royal Horticultural Society Award of Garden Merit in 1993.

Other names: Normandie, King Tut

Flower color: yellow; pale pink edges; amber stamens

Flower size: 1¾–2"

Scent: moderate, sweet and fruity

Height: 6–7'

Spread: 4'

Blooms: spring to fall; repeat blooming

Hardiness zones: 5–9

Laura Ford doesn't require any special conditions or care. It is a relatively hardy miniature climber, ideal for any gardener or rose aficionado.

New Dawn

New Dawn is one of the all-time favorite climbing varieties among gardeners and rosarians. Dr. William Van Fleet of the U.S. originally introduced the hybrid seedling in 1910. In the 1930s, a repeat-blooming sport was introduced as The New Dawn. During the 1997 Triennial Convention in Benelux, members of the World Federation of Rose Societies elected New Dawn into the Hall of Fame. It was celebrated as the first patented plant in the world.

Other names:
Everblooming Dr. W. Van Fleet, The New Dawn

Flower color:
pale pearl pink

Flower size: 3–3½"

Scent: sweet and fresh apples

Height: 10–15'

Spread: 10–15'

Blooms: early summer to fall; repeat blooming

Hardiness zones: 4–9

❀ New Dawn is known for its soft pink clusters of double flowers that fade from a cameo pink to a more pinkish white. The blossoms, which feature bright yellow stamens, are borne both in small clusters and singly. It bears plentiful shiny foliage on upright arching canes. The canes have sturdy, hooked thorns.

❀ Considered one of the easiest climbers to grow, this rose is suitable for pergolas, walls, fences, arches or pillars. It can be pruned as a hedge or shrub and is also a good rose for exhibition.

❀ New Dawn is on of the most reliable large-growing climbers for Michigan.

Polka

This rose has style. Though it was introduced by Meilland Roses in the 1990s, Polka resembles an old-fashioned rose. It bears very large, double blooms in shades of pale peachy salmon. Each flower is made up of 30 to 35 petals that open wide to form flat blossoms in small clusters. The flowers tend to fade a little over time to a pale apricot. Thorny, upright canes grow into a shrubby form covered in semi-glossy, medium green foliage. Its naturally vigorous growth habit is not rampant or overpowering. It is ideal for climbing pillars, walls or fences where a shorter than average climber is required.

Other names: Lord Byron, Polka 91, Scented Dawn, Twilight Glow

Flower color: pale coppery salmon

Flower size: 4½–5"

Scent: moderate, spicy

Height: 10–12'

Spread: 6–8'

Blooms: summer to fall; repeat blooming

Hardiness zones: 4–9

* Polka is very resistant to disease and requires little care.
* This large-flowered modern climbing rose is part of the Romantica Climber Series of roses, which also includes Guy de Maupassant (p. 238).
* Polka's old-fashioned fragrance is reminiscent of days gone by.

Russelliana

Other names: Russell's Cottage Rose, Old Spanish Rose, Scarlet Grevillei, Souvenir de la Bataille de Marengo

Flower color: magenta red

Flower size: 2–2½"

Scent: moderate, damask

Height: 10–15'

Spread: 5–10'

Blooms: late spring to mid-summer; no repeat blooming

Hardiness zones: 5–9

Russelliana was once used as a rootstock for other roses. This might explain why specimens are often found at abandoned home sites and cemeteries.

Russelliana is a very old rose, dating from before 1837. During its long history, it has acquired a number of other names and fallen into different classes, and its place of origin, breeder and parentage are no longer clear. It is, however, a worthy contender for Michigan gardens. Russelliana grows into a large mounding shrub with long, arching canes that are covered with distinctively large, deeply veined, blue-green foliage edged with just a touch of red. Each double flower is made up of at least 50 petals, arranged in a quartered form that slightly obscures the central green button eye. The flowers are borne in clusters of five to seven and open flat. The bright magenta red flowers will fade over time to a beautiful shade of mauve and are followed by reddish orange hips in fall.

✿ Bristles cover the sepals at each flower's base.
✿ Russelliana tolerates partial shade and poor soil.
✿ Its overall size makes this rose ideal for climbing through old, established trees or on pillars, arbors or even small buildings. This naturally vigorous rose can also be trained as a large mounding shrub or a moderate climber.
✿ It is only somewhat susceptible to powdery mildew and may drop a leaf or two in extremely hot weather.

Veilchenblau

V eilchenblau is German for 'violet-blue,' a reference to the color of the blossoms. The flowers are not a true blue but appear more blue when grown in partial shade. The color is further enhanced as the blooms fade with age and take on a gray-blue cast.

❁ Veilchenblau is a small-flowered rambler with loose clusters of semi-double, violet blooms with white streaks. The flowers have a subtle fruity scent and are complemented by fine, sharply pointed, glossy, medium green leaves on arching, almost thornless canes.

❁ This rose is generally disease resistant but can suffer from blackspot and powdery mildew when planted where air circulation is poor.

❁ This variety was introduced in 1909. It is the best known of the three violet purple multiflora ramblers, which include Rose Marie Viaud and Violette. It has continued to be popular and won the Royal Horticultural Society Award of Garden Merit in 1993.

❁ This vigorous rose is most attractive when twining through an old, sturdy tree in an informal setting.

Other names:
Blue Rambler, Violet Blue, Blue Rosalie

Flower color:
soft reddish violet

Flower size: 1–1½"

Scent: light green apple

Height: 10–12'

Spread: 8–12'

Blooms: spring;
no repeat blooming

Hardiness zones: 4–9

This rose is considered to be the best purple rambler and remains the standard for judging so-called 'blue' roses.

HYBRID TEA

The first hybrid teas were bred around 1867, a turning point for roses. Hybrid teas are the dominant roses in the cut-flower industry. They are upright bushes with strong prickly canes and usually have one flower per cane. The flowers in this class bloom continually throughout the growing season until a hard fall frost. The flowers are large, double blooms with high, pointed centers and an extensive color range with all colors except for blue, black and green. Some varieties are intensely fragrant.

Hybrid teas need winter protection throughout Michigan and are somewhat susceptible to blackspot. Use hybrid teas in a formal rose garden or cut-flower garden, in the border or as a specimen. Hybrid teas can also be grown in containers although they will require further care and protection to get them successfully through winter.

Chicago Peace

Chicago Peace is a sport of the Peace rose and has the overall appearance of its parent but in a more spectacular color range. The yellow-based petals are touched with deep pink, copper and soft orange. This rose bears large, colorful, evenly spaced flowers atop dark, leathery foliage on moderately thorny, sturdy branches.

Other names: none
Flower color: yellow, pink and apricot blend
Flower size: 4½–6"
Scent: mild, fruity
Height: 3–4½'
Spread: 3–4'
Blooms: summer to fall; repeat blooming
Hardiness zones: 7–9

Chicago Peace can survive winters in zones 5 and 6 in Michigan with sufficient protection.

✿ Each flower is made up of 45 to 60 petals. The flower color fades with age to a softer palette yet remains stunning until the petals fall freely to the ground.

✿ Upright and vigorous, Chicago Peace is resistant to all common rose diseases except blackspot. Take all necessary precautions to prevent the onset of blackspot.

✿ Prune each spring to reshape the shrub. Follow the technique used for pruning floribundas— prune the shrub down to the best five to seven buds on the best five to seven canes before the bud breaks.

✿ This rose was discovered as a sport by a gardener named Johnston in Chicago, Illinois. It was entered into cultivation and introduced to the public for sale by the Conard-Pyle Company in 1962.

Dainty Bess

Dainty Bess, named after the hybridizer's wife, is still as popular and beautiful as when it was introduced in 1925. Its single, ruffled, light pink flowers make it one of the most unusual hybrid tea varieties available. Most roses have yellow stamens, and only 10 percent of roses have burgundy stamens. Dainty Bess is one of these rarities. The flowers are produced either singly or in clusters on sturdy canes. When Dainty Bess is in flower, it truly is one of the most beautiful roses you could ever imagine.

Other names:
The Artistic Rose
Flower color: pale pink
Flower size: 3½–4"
Scent: light tea, spicy
Height: 3–4'
Spread: 24–36"
Blooms: summer to fall; repeat blooming
Hardiness zones: 6–9

* This rose isn't ideal for cutting, as the flowers are short-lived and the plant is so compact.
* The blossoms of this variety close at night, which is very unusual for roses.
* Dainty Bess can survive winters in zones 4 and 5 with sufficient protection.
* Among other awards, Dainty Bess received the 1925 Royal National Rose Society Gold Medal.

Double Delight

Other names: none
Flower color: cream; carmine red edges
Flower size: 5–5½"
Scent: strong, sweet with hint of spice
Height: 3–4'
Spread: 24–36"
Blooms: summer to fall; repeat blooming
Hardiness zones: 6–9

Double Delight is aptly named, as it delights with its strong, sweet fragrance as well as its unique flower color. The only drawback is the plant will very likely experience powdery mildew or blackspot or both. But don't let that stop you, because it is one of the most popular roses available and worth growing for the fragrance alone! The fully double, high-centered flowers open cream with red edges and gradually darken to solid red. The color prompted the French to name this variety *La Rose de Rouge á Lévres*, 'The Lipstick Rose.'

❀ The unique color makes this beauty a delight to place in a bed or border. Its compact size makes it suitable for containers, where it can be easily monitored for disease. It is ideal as a specimen, left to its own devices to display its special qualities.

❀ This 1977 AARS winner is suitable for a warm, dry location. Rain doesn't seem to affect the blooms, but cool, wet weather can promote powdery mildew. Blackspot can also be a problem, so monitor the rose closely for any signs of disease.

❀ Double Delight has a tendency for blooms to form 'split centers,' with the petals swirling to two points. This will not adversely affect the overall appearance of this famous rose, however. The blooms are ideal for cutting as the flowers last and last.

❀ No two flowers are alike. Heat intensifies the flower color while in cooler, shadier locations the color becomes more subtle. The award-winning fragrance is unaffected by temperature, light or age.

Electron

Electron is a compact, tidy rose bearing leathery foliage and large, high-centered, fully double flowers. The blooms hold color well but are a little slow to open. Each flower is made up of an average of 30 to 40 velvety petals. Electron has a classic hybrid tea form, excellent for competition and exhibiting. It is known for its rich fragrance and vibrant fuchsia pink color.

✿ The average rose gardener will appreciate this rose, which requires very little maintenance and is moderately disease resistant. The glowing reddish pink blooms can be seen from a distance and withstand just about any type of weather. Electron can survive winters in zones 5 and 6 with adequate protection.

✿ This rose requires more moderate temperatures, so plant it away from surfaces that could reflect heat.

✿ Electron was named an All-America Rose Selections winner in 1973. In 1998, the Montréal Botanical Garden conducted a survey of its roses' resistance to blackspot, powdery mildew and rust. Electron was one of the outstanding varieties, with a zero- to five-percent infection rate.

Other names:
Mullard Jubilee
Flower color: deep pink
Flower size: 4–5"
Scent: sweet and strong
Height: 3–4½'
Spread: 3–4'
Blooms: summer to fall; repeat blooming
Hardiness zones: 7–10

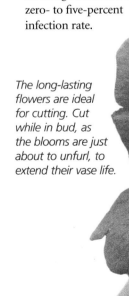

The long-lasting flowers are ideal for cutting. Cut while in bud, as the blooms are just about to unfurl, to extend their vase life.

Elina

Other names:
Elena, Peaudouce

Flower color: ivory white; yellow centers

Flower size: 4–5¹/₂"

Scent: very light

Height: 3–4¹/₂'

Spread: 30"–3¹/₂'

Blooms: summer to fall; repeat blooming

Hardiness zones: 7–9

This rose used to be known as Peaudouce, French for 'soft skin.' The name was changed after a brand of infant diapers of the same name was introduced.

Elina is one of the best of its color and class. It is the perfect rose for the beginner to use as an exhibition variety, and in just about any garden setting it provides a stunning display. The long stems are great for cutting. Slightly delayed flowering extends the season with color. The large, dark, glossy leaves are slightly tinted red, a color that contrasts beautifully with the white, evenly petaled, double, high-centered blooms.

- While many light-colored blooms get mottled or spotty after rain, the flowers of this variety stand up well to rain.
- In 1987, Elina was named the Anerkannte Deutsche Rose and received the New Zealand (Gold Star) Gold Medal; in 1994 it was awarded the James Mason Gold Medal.
- It boasts outstanding vigor, form and resistance to disease. It can withstand winters in zones 5 and 6 with sufficient protection.

Folklore

Folklore produces classically formed blossoms atop extremely strong growth, almost reaching climbing proportions with stems up to 3' in length. Multifaceted and multipurpose, this rose is ideal for a number of locations, including the back of borders or climbing a small tree, obelisk, trellis or arbor. It could also be left as a specimen, tall hedge or thorny barrier. It bears long, pointed buds that open into intensely fragrant flowers well into fall. Each flower displays exhibition form, bearing petals with substance and vigor in salmon orange with a lighter reverse. The double flowers are made up of 45 to 50 petals each and hold their shape remarkably well.

Other names: none
Flower color: salmon orange with lighter reverse
Flower size: 4½–5"
Scent: intense
Height: 5–6'
Spread: 3½–4'
Blooms: summer to fall; repeat blooming
Hardiness zones: 6–9

✿ The flowers are sometimes reluctant to open in cool weather. Folklore is most active on warm, sunny days.

✿ The flowers last for a long time, especially when cut and placed into arrangements. To extend the vase life even more, cut the stems when the flowers are about to open.

✿ Folklore blooms a little later than most hybrid teas but is well worth the wait. It is also hardy to zones 4 and 5 with sufficient winter protection.

✿ Kordes Roses of Germany introduced Folklore in 1977.

Folklore is a favorite and consistent winner for rose exhibitors in the northern U.S.

Honor

Other names:
Honour, Michèle Torr
Flower color: soft white
Flower size: 4–5"
Scent: light
Height: 4–4½'
Spread: 3–4'
Blooms: summer to fall; repeat blooming
Hardiness zones: 7–9

Honor was introduced in 1980 as an All-America Rose Selection along with two other roses, Love (p. 251) and Cherish. Honor has been a popular exhibition rose since its introduction and still wins awards at local rose shows. This rose has a tall, upright and vigorous growth habit and bears satiny white buds that open to large white blossoms with golden stamens. The flowers bloom in clusters or singly on long, moderately thorny canes and are suitable for cutting and arrangements. Each flower has 25 to 30 clear, velvety petals.

✿ As with many white hybrid teas, Honor is tender throughout Michigan, so winter protection will be necessary, especially in zones 5 and 6.

✿ This rose produces long, strong stems ideal for cutting. To extend the vase life of the flowers, cut when the blooms are in bud.

✿ Honor is perfectly suited to mixed borders and beds and works well as a stunning specimen. White-flowered roses stand out among just about any color grouping, especially when planted in large groups.

✿ You don't have to be a rose aficionado to grow this variety, as it is highly disease resistant and easy to maintain.

Ingrid Bergman

Ingrid Bergman is considered one of the best red-flowering hybrid teas for cutting. The blooms are long-lasting, both on the plant and as cut flowers. It is also extremely easy to grow. It is valued as one of the most dependable dark red garden roses available. The flowers are borne in clear red with no blue tones, and the velvety petals hold their color very well. Long stems bear semi-glossy, deep green foliage.

Other names: none
Flower color: crimson red
Flower size: 4½"
Scent: moderate, sweet
Height: 30"–3½'
Spread: 24–36"
Blooms: summer to fall; repeat blooming
Hardiness zones: 7–9

- This hybrid tea is perfect for containers or borders. It can be grown in zones 5 and 6 but would require adequate winter protection, especially if in a standard form.
- Generally very disease resistant, this rose is somewhat prone to blackspot.
- This rose has done extremely well in worldwide rose trials, proving over and over again that it would be an ideal addition to just about any garden setting. Similar to other Poulsen-bred roses, Ingrid Bergman is adaptable and versatile. It is as popular now as it was in the year of its introduction, 1984.

Developed in Denmark and named after the Hollywood actress, Ingrid Bergman was one of the most highly acclaimed roses of the 1980s. In 2000 it was chosen as the World's Favorite Rose by the World Federation of Rose Societies.

Kordes' Perfecta

Other names: Kordes Perfecta, Perfecta
Flower color: pale creamy pink; red edges
Flower size: 4½–5"
Scent: intense, orris root and raspberry
Height: 4–5'
Spread: 3–5'
Blooms: summer to fall; repeat blooming
Hardiness zones: 6–10

Kordes' Perfecta has stood the test of time since it was introduced in 1957. It has won a number of awards, including the RNRS Gold Medal in 1957 and the Portland Gold Medal in 1958. It grows into an upright, well-branched form with thorny canes and glossy, healthy, leathery foliage. Urn-shaped buds emerge in early summer and open into double, high-centered, loose-petaled blossoms. Each flower has 65 to 70 pale creamy pink petals with varied degrees of red on the petal edges. Bred by Kordes Roses in Germany, Kordes' Perfecta is a distinctive hybrid tea that has endured for more than four decades. Once you try it you'll understand why it's been such an overwhelming success.

- Kordes' Perfecta is disease resistant and tolerates poor soil and a touch of shade.
- The color of the large, shapely blooms is especially striking during the cooler days of fall.
- This rose tolerates cold winters better than most hybrid teas. It can survive in zones 4 and 5 with sufficient winter protection.
- The name of this rose refers to its breeder, its overall performance and its popularity.

Liebeszauber

Liebeszauber is a vigorous rose with an upright growth habit. The foliage emerges red in early spring and matures to a deep, dark green. The pure dark red blossoms are loosely cupped, wavy petaled and sweetly fragrant.

❀ The strong stems are suitable for cutting or training. This rose would be ideal for exhibiting at your local rose show or for display planting in a mixed border. It is best planted at the back of borders because it is so vigorous—the occasional shoot reaches heights of $6^1/_2$' by fall if left intact.

❀ This hybrid tea blooms like a floribunda, bearing its flowers singly and in clusters, and the blooms stand up well in the rain. It can tolerate winters in zones 5 and 6 with sufficient protection.

❀ Liebeszauber has a tendency to send up spindly canes occasionally, but these are easily removed with a quick snip. A more manageable, balanced bush can be trained by pinching out the side buds. This rose requires a hard prune each year.

❀ The name of this rose is German for 'love's magic.'

Other names:
Crimson Spire
Flower color:
rich dark red
Flower size: 5–6"
Scent: very sweet
Height: 4–5'
Spread: $3^1/_2$–4'
Blooms: summer to fall; repeat blooming
Hardiness zones: 7–9

Marijke Koopman

Other names: none
Flower color: medium pink
Flower size: 4–5"
Scent: moderate
Height: 4–5'
Spread: 3–4'
Blooms: summer to fall; repeat blooming
Hardiness zones: 6–9

This rose was named in memory of the daughter of a friend of Gareth Fryer.

Marijke Koopman is a shapely rose in two-tone, satiny pink, the perfect specimen for a water-color portrait. It blooms a little later than most in its class but continues to bloom profusely all season long. Its best asset is the enormous quantity of flowers it produces. Another unique feature of this classic, high-centered hybrid tea is its high degree of resistance to spotting from rain. The flowers are borne three to five to a cluster, and each flower is made up of 25 petals. Red prickles cover the upright canes, including the new strong canes produced each year.

✿ Best grown in cooler climates and only a little prone to powdery mildew, this rose can successfully grow in zones 4 and 5 with winter protection.
✿ This hybrid tea produces armloads of shapely flowers for cutting. It is an excellent rose for both exhibition and garden use.
✿ Marijke Koopman received the Hague Gold Medal in 1978, about the same time it was introduced into commerce by its breeder, Gareth Fryer of Fryer Roses in England.

Miss All-American Beauty

M iss All-American Beauty is all that it describes— a beauty offering strength and versatility. Its best feature is the consistent, lasting flower color. The flowers can hold the same unfading hot pink tone from the bud stage until the petals drop. The vivid flower color is easily maintained in the hottest conditions but is most intense in the cool days of fall. The buds emerge singly or in clusters and open to classic high-centered, cupped, fully double flowers with muddled centers. The large, leathery foliage provides a dramatic contrast to the flowers.

Other names:
Maria Callas
Flower color:
deep dark pink
Flower size: 4–6"
Scent: peppery and sweet
Height: 3–4½'
Spread: 30"–3½'
Blooms: summer to fall; repeat blooming
Hardiness zones: 7–10

✿ Almost every bud eye can produce a newly emerging, long-stemmed rose, ideal for cutting and blending into various arrangements. It is easy to remove the few thorns on the medium-length stems—use your thumb to gently push the thorns to the side, popping them off the stem cleanly, without injury.

✿ Miss All-American Beauty is stunning when allowed enough room to mature. It is suitable for bedding and in the middle of borders.

✿ This rose was an AARS winner in 1968 and honors Maria Callas, an American-born prima donna famed for her lyric soprano and fiery temperament.

Mister Lincoln

Other names:
Mr. A. Lincoln, Mr. Lincoln, President Lincoln
Flower color: dark red
Flower size: 4–5½"
Scent: damask, intense
Height: 4–5'
Spread: 30"–3½'
Blooms: summer to fall; repeat blooming
Hardiness zones: 7–9

The blooms of Mister Lincoln are among the darkest red of any red rose. It was introduced by Herbert C. Swim and O.L. Weeks in 1964 and boasts immense, velvety, deep red flowers with a scent reminiscent of damask roses. It has been one of the most popular hybrid tea roses in its color class or category since its release. The urn-shaped buds open very quickly in late spring or early summer. Up to 8 to 10 flowers are borne at the tip of each long stem. The fully double flowers first emerge cupped, resulting in a flat, classic high-centered form. Each flower consists of 30 to 40 petals, displaying the characteristics of its parents, Chrysler Imperial and Charles Mallerin. The flowers' beauty is enhanced by dark, semi-glossy, leathery foliage.

✿ Mister Lincoln is at its most beautiful when the flowers completely unfurl, exposing the bright yellow stamens.

✿ This tough, dependable rose is one of the hardiest hybrid teas but still requires winter protection in zones 5 and 6.

✿ This rose prefers hot, dry conditions. The flowers and foliage won't burn in the hot sun as easily as other red roses will. The deep red flower color will eventually fade to magenta.

✿ Use Mister Lincoln as a specimen in a garden or at the back of a rose bed or border. It was an AARS winner in 1965.

✿ The leaves are sometimes marred by blackspot. Remove the infected leaves and this vigorous plant will quickly grow new ones.

Olympiad

With Olympiad, the breeder hoped to create a rose whose intense red tone would resist discoloration. Mr. McGredy was successful in his attempts, releasing this suitable contender in 1984 and naming it for the Los Angeles Olympics of the same year. It bears abundant clusters of brilliant, large, double flowers. The flowers are most often borne singly, with an average of 35 petals each in a high-centered form. Occasionally the blooms are borne in irregular clusters of three to four. It vigorously produces large, semi-glossy foliage in an upright but compact form.

Other names: Olympia, Olympiode
Flower color: medium red
Flower size: 4–5"
Scent: light fruity tea
Height: 4–5'
Spread: 24–36"
Blooms: summer to fall; repeat blooming
Hardiness zones: 7–9

- ✿ In cooler weather the flowers can grow even larger. Rain can't harm the thick petals, and the color remains intense from the moment the flowers open until they fall to the ground. Deadheading may be necessary to maintain a prolific, lengthened bloom cycle.
- ✿ This 1984 AARS winner works well as a bedding plant or a specimen. It is an excellent cut flower as well, with a vase life of six to seven days.
- ✿ Olympiad is generally resistant to disease except for blackspot, to which it is highly vulnerable when planted in poor soil. It's not fond of continuous humid weather. It performs best in conditions usually conducive to a rose's success. If planted in less than ideal conditions it will quickly rebel and may even die within a few seasons. It can survive in zones 5 and 6 with sufficient winter protection.
- ✿ Medal winners at the L.A. Olympics were each presented with one Olympiad rose.

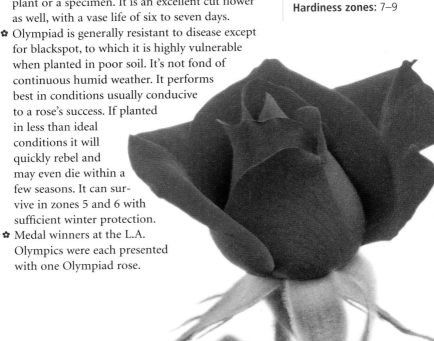

Pascali

Other names:
Blanche Pasca
Flower color:
soft creamy white
Flower size: 3½–4½"
Scent: fresh and sweet
Height: 3½–4½'
Spread: 30"–3½'
Blooms: early summer to fall; repeat blooming
Hardiness zones: 7–9

Pascali was designated World's Favorite Rose in 1991. Its urn-shaped double flowers with tightly spiraled centers are borne one to a stem and consist of 30 petals each. The flowers emerge on the tips of long, straight stems. The exceptionally long-lasting flowers are suitable for cutting, but make sure to cut the blooms when in bud.

✿ The moderately thorny canes are produced in an open and upright growth habit, which makes this rose ideal for bedding and borders. The dark, leathery, semi-glossy foliage tends to be rather sparse.

✿ Pascali prefers cooler conditions. It thrives in open sunny sites with adequate air circulation. To prevent burning and sun scald, do not plant it in extremely hot areas. It is hardy to zones 5 and 6 with adequate winter protection.

✿ This rose is mildly prone to blackspot. Avoid wetting the foliage, and water only at the plant's base, not from overhead.

✿ Prune this rose as you would a floribunda (see Pruning in the introduction).

✿ Since it was introduced by Louis & Victor Lens of Belgium in 1963, Pascali has won many awards, including the Golden Rose of The Hague and the NRS Certificate of Merit, both in 1963, the AARS Award in 1969 and the Portland Gold Medal in 1967.

Peace

Peace has been referred to as the Rose of the Century, which is a lot to live up to, but this rose is more than capable. It is very easy to grow and one of the most famous roses ever produced. It has won many awards including the All-America Rose Selection in 1946. It is an upright grower with moderately thorny canes and large, glossy foliage. Even out of bloom, this shrub looks great. The yellow can become pale if the location is too hot, while the pink intensifies in heat.

Other names: Gloria Dei, Mme A. Meilland, Gioia, Beke, Fredsrosen
Flower color: soft yellow; baby pink edges
Flower size: 5$^1\!/_2$–6"
Scent: mild, fruity
Height: 4$^1\!/_2$–6'
Spread: 3–3$^1\!/_2$'
Blooms: summer to fall; repeat blooming
Hardiness zones: 7–9

❀ Peace is an ideal cut flower. It is suitable for rose beds, hedges and borders. It is considered one of the best varieties to grow as a standard. It is a little resentful of hard pruning but fares well with moderate pruning.

❀ Peace requires sufficient winter protection to survive in zones 5 and 6.

❀ The overall health of this rose has been compromised over time because it has been cloned millions of times since its introduction in 1945. Peace has a moderate level of disease resistance but is prone to blackspot in cooler climates.

❀ In 1976 Peace became the first rose to be selected World's Favorite Rose by the World Federation of Rose Societies.

This rose was originally named after the breeder's mother, Claudia, but was renamed in the United States to celebrate the end of World War II and to promote world peace.

Princesse de Monaco

Princesse de Monaco is known by many names, but no matter what it's called, this rose is something to behold, a wonderful representation of the graceful figure it was named after. It bears high-centered, double flowers. Each flower is made up of 35 overlapping petals in creamy white tones touched with soft pink edges. It is popular in rose shows or professional competitions, suitable for any level of rose gardening experience. Dark glossy leaves complement the exquisite form and scent.

Other names: Princesse Grace, Princesse Grace de Monaco, Grace Kelly, Princess of Monaco, Preference

Flower color: ivory blend; pink edges

Flower size: 5–5½"

Scent: strong, fruity

Height: 24"–4'

Spread: 24"–3½'

Blooms: summer to fall; repeat blooming

Hardiness zones: 7–9

✿ In 1998, it was tested at the Montréal Botanic Garden for blackspot, powdery mildew and rust. It came through successfully, rarely experiencing problems with these diseases that typically affect other hybrid teas.

✿ Its upright growth habit makes this rose perfect for cottage and English gardens, beds and borders or planted in large groups for impact.

✿ This rose can survive zones 5 and 6 with adequate winter protection.

✿ Very few roses equal the graceful beauty of Princesse de Monaco, the second of two roses from Meilland Roses in France named after Princess Grace. The first, Grace de Monaco, was created by Francis Meilland in 1955. Princesse de Monaco was created by Marie-Louisette, Francis Meilland's widow, and introduced in 1982.

Rosemary Harkness

Rosemary Harkness is often the first hybrid tea to bloom in late spring or early summer. It bears delicate apricot- and pink-edged flowers followed by abundant glossy, dark green foliage. The marbled flower color is a stunning, eye-catching combination of tones and shades.

❀ This variety requires very fertile soil. Amend soil as necessary with organic matter to improve its nutrient content, texture, water retention and drainage. With sufficient winter protection this rose can survive in zones 5 and 6.

❀ This vigorous, spreading variety is ideal as a garden feature or specimen. It also blends easily into a mixed bed or border, but leave enough space for it to reach its mature size.

❀ Rosemary Harkness was raised in England by Harkness in 1985. It was named after the niece of the late Jack Harkness, former rose breeder of Harkness Roses.

Other names: none
Flower color: apricot yellow; salmon pink edges
Flower size: 4"
Scent: sweet like passionfruit
Height: 2½–3'
Spread: 30"
Blooms: late spring to fall; repeat blooming
Hardiness zones: 7–9

FLORIBUNDA

Floribundas are free-blooming bushes that were produced by crossing hybrid teas with polyanthas. They have the same color range of the hybrid teas but are smaller and somewhat hardier. The clusters or sprays of small flowers bloom abundantly throughout the growing season, often smothering the foliage with blossoms. They often lack the fine flower form of the hybrid teas, but continued hybridization is improving the flower form. Use a floribunda in a bed or border, as a specimen, in a container or as a hedge.

Polyanthas, produced from crossing *Rosa multiflora* with *Rosa chinensis*, are the forerunners to the floribundas. Polyanthas are compact, free-branching bushes with sparsely prickly stems. They are hardier than floribundas.

Polyantha is Latin for 'many flowers,' and these roses do flower profusely in clusters. There are few polyantha varieties left in commerce as they have been superseded by the floribundas.

Apricot Nectar

Other names: none
Flower color: golden apricot with a hint of pink
Flower size: 3–4"
Scent: fruity
Height: 24–36"
Spread: 24–36"
Blooms: summer to fall; repeat blooming
Hardiness zones: 6–9

Apricot Nectar has been a big hit ever since it was introduced over 35 years ago, and was an AARS winner in 1966. One of the smallest floribunda roses, it vigorously grows into a bushy and dense form tipped with flowers as large as those of most hybrid teas. Fruity scented, cupped blossoms emerge in summer in shades of peach or golden apricot with a hint of pink. The flowers, made up of 35 to 40 petals each, are borne on small trusses atop dark green, glossy foliage.

❀ Apricot Nectar is a great cut flower. For a long vase life, cut the flowers when they are in bud, shortly before they are to open.
❀ This rose becomes less prolific during cloudy, cool conditions.
❀ Apricot Nectar is one of the toughest floribunda roses. It is highly resistant to disease, insects, heat and humidity. It is relatively winter hardy, which is unusual in an apricot rose. It grows successfully in zones 4 and 5 with winter protection.
❀ This rose was hybridized by Eugene Boerner, 'Papa Floribunda,' of Jackson & Perkins in 1965.

Betty Boop

This vibrant white-and-red floribunda was named after the famous cartoon character of the 1930s because of its perky nature and bright coloration. Bred by Tom Carruth of Weeks Roses, this recent introduction was named an AARS winner in 1999. This fragrant rose is almost always in bloom, bearing flowers from spring to fall frost. Each flower consists of 6 to 12 petals borne in clusters of three to five flowers per spray. It is a naturally rounded plant with a shrub-like density and a slight spreading habit.

Other names:
Centenary of Federation
Flower color: white; yellow centers; red edges
Flower size: 4"
Scent: moderate, fruity
Height: 3–5'
Spread: 3–4'
Blooms: spring to fall; repeat blooming
Hardiness zones: 5–10

✿ Betty Boop tolerates light shade, is highly disease resistant and is hardy to zone 4 with adequate winter protection.

✿ It re-blooms quickly without deadheading or shaping. It is known to be a consistent grower in most climates.

✿ The flowers remain crisp for a long time although the colors tend to fade a little.

✿ Its rounded shrub form and flowers from top to bottom make Betty Boop an ideal landscape plant. It is also suitable as a hedge or foundation plant or as part of a mixed bed or border, a cottage garden or a mass planting.

Betty Prior

Other names: none
Flower color: medium carmine pink
Flower size: 3–3½"
Scent: little to none
Height: 4–5'
Spread: 3–4'
Blooms: summer to fall; repeat blooming
Hardiness zones: 4–9

Betty Prior is a cluster-flowered floribunda that bears five-petaled pink blooms. Though not particularly unique in color, form or fragrance, this rose is one that any gardener can grow in any location, and it flowers throughout the season with minimal care. The lightly scented flowers are charming and look old fashioned. Clusters of single cupped or saucer-like flowers are borne amid disease-free foliage. This rose has an upright, bushy form and a vigorous nature.

- This rose tolerates extreme heat, cold, poor soil and neglect. It is particularly popular in the north because it is hardy and is rarely without flowers.
- If you have the space, consider mass planting Betty Prior, as it is simply breathtaking in this form. It is also an excellent choice for a low hedge.
- This rose is often used as a garden and parks rose because it is dependable, long-lived and hardy. These favorable qualities have enabled it to survive as a widely grown rose where most of its contemporaries have long since vanished.
- Hybridized by D. Prior and Son, near Colchester in Essex, this rose was named after a member of the Prior family.

Cuyahoga

C uyahoga is part of a newer series of floribundas called The National Parks Rose Collection, which includes Grand Canyon, Redwood, Shenandoah and Yellowstone, all named after well-known American national parks. Cuyahoga is a healthy and hardy floribunda that blooms abundantly and repeats frequently throughout most of the growing season. The double, hot pink flowers are the perfect complement to the rich foliage. This rose has already won more than 15 awards and certificates in International Rose Trials since it was introduced in 1996.

Other names: Jasper, Berleburg, Bewitched, Memory Lane, Castle
Flower color: hot pink
Flower size: 3–4"
Scent: sweet
Height: 24–36"
Spread: 24–30"
Blooms: spring to fall; repeat blooming
Hardiness zones: 5–10

✿ Cuyahoga has very good to excellent disease resistance and requires only minimal care. It is a suitable rose for any level of gardening expertise. It is hardy in zone 4 with adequate winter protection.
✿ Cuyahoga Valley National Park is in Ohio, between Cleveland and Akron. Poulsen Roser ApS in Denmark created this rose in partnership with the National Park Foundation in the U.S. to raise awareness and funds for the preservation of the parks.

This rose is ideal for use in containers, mixed beds and borders. It also works well in a traditional cottage setting or in a smaller modern garden.

Easy Going

Easy Going is a sport of Livin' Easy (p. 241), an orange floribunda, and has all the fine attributes of its parent. It is known for its reliable vigor, attractive foliage and long-lasting, colorful blossoms. It bears cupped blooms of 30 to 40 petals each. The flowers are produced in large clusters atop a rounded growth habit. The glossy foliage contrasts well with the bright blooms and is especially resistant to blackspot and other typical rose problems. This vigorous rose is easy to maintain.

Other names: none

Flower color:
medium yellow

Flower size: 2½–3"

Scent: pleasant and fruity

Height: 3–3½'

Spread: 24–30"

Blooms: summer to fall; repeat blooming

Hardiness zones: 5–9

✿ Easy Going is most effective in group plantings. The golden flowers stand out in a formal border. It is also a great cut flower.

✿ Easy Going was introduced by Harkness of the U.K. in 1996.

✿ The sturdy canes are often quite thick and are able to support the large clusters of long-lasting blooms.

Europeana

Europeana, a superb red rose with unfading color, is one of the most popular roses of its class and color for exhibition purposes and is wonderful in the garden as well. It blooms so profusely that the top of the plant is almost completely obscured by crimson red blossoms. The semi-double blooms consist of 25 to 30 petals each. They open to cupped, rosette-shaped blooms that are produced in well-spaced, large clusters of up to 30 flowers per cluster. The young foliage emerges burgundy red and matures over time to a leathery dark bronze. It forms into a compact bush of medium height, with an upright and vigorous growth habit.

Other names: none
Flower color: dark crimson red
Flower size: 3–3½"
Scent: very slight
Height: 24–36"
Spread: 30–36"
Blooms: summer to fall; repeat blooming
Hardiness zones: 6–9

✿ This red floribunda not only tolerates intense heat but actually thrives in heat, and the blooms maintain their vivid red even in the hottest of flowerbeds. It is cold hardy to zone 5 with adequate winter protection.

✿ This 1968 AARS winner is stunning when planted en masse or in borders. It blends well with lighter-colored flowers, especially flowers in shades of cream and white.

✿ This rose is mildly prone to powdery mildew and can defoliate due to blackspot in humid areas, but preventive measures are easy and effective. Water at the plant's base early in the morning and provide adequate air circulation. Overall this is a relatively disease-free rose.

✿ The large, heavy trusses of blooms are sometimes inclined to bow down to the ground in wet or windy weather.

Guy de Maupassant

Other names: LaRose
Flower color:
light carmine pink
Flower size: 3–4"
Scent: tart and spicy, apple
Height: 3–4'
Spread: 3'
Blooms: summer to fall; repeat blooming
Hardiness zones: 5–9

Individual flowers from each cluster are ideal to cut for small arrangements and crafts.

This floribunda is marketed as part of the Romantica Series by its creator, Meilland Roses of France. Introduced in 1994, this rose bears old-fashioned blooms with a modern flair. Naturally vigorous, prickly canes support large, dark, glossy foliage in an upright and bushy form. Carmine pink globular buds open into double, quartered blossoms that are borne in small clusters. Each flower consists of over 100 infolded petals. The blossoms are especially dazzling in the low light of dusk. This is only one of many Romantica roses available that resemble roses from days gone by but inhabit the disease resistance, fragrance, upright habit, repeat flowering and beauty of a modern variety.

✿ Guy de Maupassant will provide color well into fall when planted in a bed or border behind slightly lower-growing roses or perennials.
✿ This rose was named after the famed French author Guy de Maupassant (1850–93), who wrote over 300 short stories, 6 novels, 3 travel books and 1 volume of verse.
✿ Romantica roses are a collection of floribundas, hybrid teas, shrub roses and climbers named after poets, artists, musicians, writers and composers. All are fragrant and have large, full blooms. They are disease resistant and fairly winter hardy to zones 4 and 5 with protection.

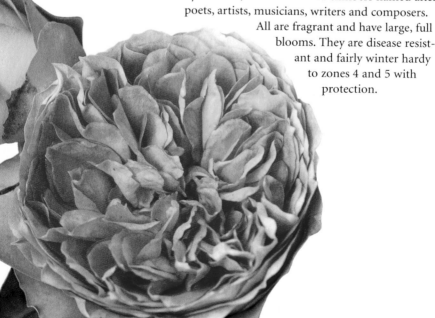

Iceberg

Over 40 years have passed since Reimer Kordes introduced this exceptional rose into commerce, and it has stood the test of time. The shapely, rain-resistant blooms last a long time and are ideal for cutting or left on the plant to adorn a special place in the garden. The buds emerge with a touch of pink and open into well-formed, dainty, white, semi-double flowers. Each flower is made up of 30 to 35 petals in clusters of up to 15 flowers. It can survive zones 4 and 5 with sufficient winter protection.

Other names: Fée des Neiges, Schneewittchen
Flower color: white
Flower size: 3–4"
Scent: strong, sweet
Height: 3–4'
Spread: 3–4'
Blooms: early to mid-season; repeat blooming
Hardiness zones: 6–9

✿ The blooms tend to be flushed with pink when the nights are cold and damp, especially in early spring and fall. If dew or a raindrop remains on a petal in the morning, it may also activate the color change and turn the part of the petal that it touched pink.

✿ This sweetly fragrant rose is ideal used in mixed beds or borders, planted in large groups or left alone as a specimen.

✿ Iceberg was voted World's Favorite Rose in 1983 by the World Federation of Rose Societies.

✿ The lull between bloom cycles for this rose is very short, so it appears to be in bloom continually.

Lavaglut

Other names:
Lavaglo, Lavaglow

Flower color: dark red

Flower size: 3"

Scent: light tea

Height: 3–3¹/₂'

Spread: 24–36"

Blooms: summer to fall; repeat blooming

Hardiness zones: 6–9

Lavaglut is sometimes confused with Intrigue, a rose bred in 1982 by Warriner that bears dark reddish purple flowers. Lavaglut is not always as readily available as the later-bred Intrigue, but it is well worth a search as it possesses great floribunda qualities.

Lavaglut was developed in 1978 by Kordes. It bears camellia-like red flowers that are so dark they almost appear black. An average of 20 to 25 petals make up each velvety blossom. The evenly spaced clusters are well maintained through summer and fall. Glossy, purplish green leaves complement the ruffled, velvety flowers that last and last. With its huge clusters of blooms, it often wins in the 'Best Floribunda Spray' category at local Michigan rose shows.

* Its balanced growth habit makes this an outstanding bedding variety. Other uses include mixed borders or hedging.
* Protection from blackspot may be required where damp weather is common. It can tolerate winters in zones 4 and 5 with sufficient protection.
* Dark red roses can often suffer scorch in heat and wind, but the blooms of Lavaglut do not suffer in hot sun, wind or rain.
* This rose was awarded the Royal National Rose Society Trial Ground Certificate in 1980.

Livin' Easy

People love a rose that's rarely out of bloom, and this is one such rose. Livin' Easy produces well-formed buds followed by glowing blooms that retain their color very well. This rose is dense and spreading in form. Its glossy and healthy foliage is a solid base to the fully open flowers with their showy yellow stamens. It is ideal in beds or planted en masse. It makes a beautiful cut flower or exhibition rose.

- ✿ Livin' Easy won the RNRS Gold Medal in 1990 and was an All-America Rose Selections winner in 1996.
- ✿ Livin' Easy lives up to its name. The beautiful glossy foliage is highly disease resistant.
- ✿ This is one of the healthiest roses ever grown at Great Lakes Roses in Belleville, MI.

Other names: Fellowship
Flower color:
fiery apricot orange blend
Flower size: 3–3½"
Scent: fruity and sweet
Height: 3–4'
Spread: 3'
Blooms: summer to fall; repeat blooming
Hardiness zones: 5–9

Nearly Wild

Other names: none
Flower color: medium pink with a white eye
Flower size: 2–2½"
Scent: sweet, apple
Height: 24–36"
Spread: 24–36"
Blooms: spring to fall; repeat blooming
Hardiness zones: 4–10

Nearly Wild is one of the hardiest floribunda roses and one of the first to bloom in the spring. Though it looks wild, its growth habit is quite tame. It bears small, long, pointed buds that open into single, medium pink blossoms with a central white eye. The moderately sweet, apple-scented blossoms are made up of five petals each, resulting in a simple yet classic form. The flowers are borne in clusters on long straight stems atop a bushy form. Nearly Wild blooms prolifically, and the flowers almost totally obscure the foliage underneath.

✿ Nearly Wild is a little prone to blackspot but otherwise resistant to most disease. Take the necessary precautions to prevent blackspot.
✿ The plant is nicely rounded and dense, making it ideal as a short hedge.
✿ This rose was hybridized by H.C. Brownell in 1941. If introduced today, this tough little rose would probably be sold as a shrub rose.

Pensioner's Voice

This rose is a little underused in the home gardener's landscape but attracts a lot of attention wherever it's grown. It bears long-arching stems tipped with well-spaced flower clusters. The flowers are large for a floribunda, and their form and substance are reminiscent of hybrid tea blooms. The petals reflex as the flowers open into the high-centered, cupped form. The flowers are apricot, often flushed with orangy red towards the edges of each petal.

Other names:
Michelle Wright
Flower color: apricot
Flower size: 2½–3"
Scent: fruity
Height: 36"
Spread: 24–36"
Blooms: summer to fall; repeat blooming
Hardiness zones: 6–9

✿ Pensioner's Voice is quick to repeat its bloom cycle, so it is useful as a cut flower in dry or fresh arrangements.

✿ This rose is highly disease resistant and extremely vigorous. It won the National Rose Society Trial Ground Certificate in 1989. The neatly formed flowers may be overwhelmed by younger shoots. Prune as you would any floribunda (see Pruning in the book's introduction.)

✿ Pensioner's Voice is most effective in mass plantings or along the back of mixed borders—shorter plants in front will disguise its irregular, delicate growth habit. This rose is fantastic in beds in just about any setting.

Pensioner's Voice is also available as a standard, through specialty rose catalogs by mail order or via the Internet.

Playboy

Other names: Cheerio
Flower color: yellowy orange; scarlet edges
Flower size: 3½"
Scent: light apple
Height: 3–4'
Spread: 24–36"
Blooms: summer to fall; repeat blooming
Hardiness zones: 6–9

When arranged with the right combination of flowers, Playboy packs a lot of punch as a cut flower.

Playboy has been widely used in warmer climates because the intense flower color is enhanced by hot weather. Wavy-petaled flowers appear almost single, opening from clusters of pointed buds. Each blossom displays dazzling tones of yellow blended with shades of apricot and reveals beautiful bright yellow stamens. Moderately thorny canes support an abundance of dark, glossy leaves. Each slightly cupped, semi-double flower consists of 7 to 10 petals, resulting in a typical floribunda form.

✿ This rose truly lives up to its name, as it is smooth and charming in nature and appearance.
✿ Playboy is great for hedges, mixed beds and borders but is best suited to a location that's begging for bright colors. This vigorous, compact yet slightly upright rose lends a brilliant impact to any garden. It can survive in zone 5 with sufficient winter protection.
✿ It was introduced in 1976 by Cocker's Roses in Scotland and won the Portland Gold Medal in 1989, one of many honors it has received throughout the years.

Sun Flare

S un Flare is an abundant-flowering floribunda and recipient of the prestigious AARS designation, the 1981 Gold Medal in Portland and the 1983 Gold Medal in Japan. It bears long, pointed buds that open into flat, double blooms in small to medium-sized, well-spaced clusters of 3 to 15 flowers each. Each blossom is made up of 20 to 30 medium yellow, ruffled or wavy petals surrounding bright and attractive stamens. Reddish prickles cover the shorter canes, which are slightly obscured by small, glossy foliage. Overall, it grows into a low, mounded form with compact growth and loads of bright, colorful flowers.

✿ Sun Flare is highly resistant to disease and requires little care or maintenance.

✿ This rose is fun to grow as a standard or tree rose. It may require a little more care in this form but it's well worth the effort for those hard-to-fill vertical spaces.

✿ The flower color will remain true without fading over time or in the hot sun.

Other names: Sunflare
Flower color:
medium yellow
Flower size: 2–3"
Scent: subtle, licorice
Height: 3–4'
Spread: 24–36"
Blooms: spring to fall;
repeat blooming
Hardiness zones: 6–9

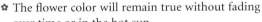

Tabris

Other names:
Raspberry Ice,
Hannah Gordon, Nicole
Flower color: creamy
white; magenta red edges
Flower size: 3"
Scent: light and sweet
Height: 3–4'
Spread: 30–36"
Blooms: spring to fall;
repeat blooming
Hardiness zones: 6–9

*Tabris is frequently used
around the world in
rose competitions, from
community contests to
international shows.*

Tabris blooms prolifically in its first year. By the second year, the flower production plateaus but the blooms maintain themselves for longer periods. Showy blooms top glossy, dark green foliage. Sprays of cupped, double flowers consist of 35 petals each. The foliage grows in plentiful mounds, a little open in habit and spreading in nature.

✿ This rose can be used in containers, cutting gardens, beds and borders. With its spreading thorny canes and growth habit, it can also work as a great barrier rose.

✿ This rose is a little prone to blackspot but otherwise is very weather resistant. A warmer location helps prevent the disease and intensifies the flower color. It is hardy to zone 5 with winter protection.

✿ Some people think that this is the same rose as Hannah Gordon and Nicole and that, though they have different registered names, all three were bred by the same breeder. The three appear to be almost identical, with subtle differences noticed only by keen eyes. Regardless of the confusion, if you find a specimen by any of these names, the overall coloration, growth habit and fragrance will be the same.

Westerland

The fresh-scented, double, bright orange-apricot flowers of Westerland are borne in clusters and have ruffled petals and serrated or scalloped edges. The reverse side of each petal is a sunny shade of yellow, creating a soft blend of warm colors throughout summer. The semi-glossy, dark green foliage is generally disease resistant but can suffer blackspot where air circulation is poor. The oldest canes should be pruned out every year to encourage new, dense growth and prolonged blooming.

Other names: none
Flower color: blend of bright apricot orange and yellow
Flower size: 3–3¹/₂"
Scent: fruity and spicy
Height: 6–8'
Spread: 4–6'
Blooms: summer to fall; repeat blooming
Hardiness zones: 5–9

✿ Sturdy, stiff, moderately thorny canes allow this variety to climb pillars, pergolas and veranda posts. Pruned into a shrub form, it is ideal at the back of a mixed border.

✿ Westerland is hardy to zone 4 with adequate winter protection.

✿ Widely grown since its 1969 introduction, this rose has received a number of awards including the Anerkannte Deutsche Rose in 1974 and the RHS Award of Garden Merit in 1993.

✿ Autumn Sunset is a sport of Westerland that bears yellow-apricot blooms. It is equally fragrant and requires as little care as its parent.

GRANDIFLORA

The grandiflora class was created in 1954 to accommodate a new rose—Queen Elizabeth (p. 252)—which didn't easily fit into any other existing class. This class arose from crossing hybrid teas and floribundas.

There is some controversy about this cluster-flowered class. The grandiflora class is recognized as a distinct class only in North America; elsewhere in the world these varieties are grouped with other large-flowered roses such as hybrid teas or floribundas. They are tall, upright, vigorous growers with several small stems arising from the main canes. Each cane has flowers growing singly or in small clusters, with each stem long enough for cutting. The flowers are similar to, but usually smaller than, hybrid teas and are borne in larger quantities. Some varieties are hard to distinguish from hybrid teas. Use grandifloras in the same way as hybrid teas, but prune them like floribundas. The disease-resistance and winter hardiness of grandifloras is similar to that of hybrid teas.

Earth Song

Other names: none
Flower color: deep pink; pale pink edges
Flower size: 4–4½"
Scent: moderate, sweet honey
Height: 4'
Spread: 3'
Blooms: summer to fall; repeat blooming
Hardiness zones: 4–9

After working with roses for over 35 years, Dr. Buck developed an allergy to roses.

Earth Song was created by none other than Dr. Griffith Buck, a well-known hybridizer, horticulturist and researcher. He spent a significant part of his career at Iowa State University developing hardy, disease-free roses now known as the Buck Collection. At the time of his research, the idea that a rose could be hardy and disease resistant was radical. The rose test fields at ISU were tilled under shortly after his retirement, but thankfully this rose was saved. It bears long pointed buds that open into double, high-pointed blossoms. Each sweetly scented flower consists of an average of 25 to 30 petals in a cupped form, borne both singly and in magnificent clusters of 5 to 10. Contrasting dark, glossy foliage tipped with young coppery growth blends beautifully with the deep pink blossoms with pale pink edges. Earth Song is a naturally vigorous rose that grows into a bushy and upright form. Each cane is covered in red-brown, awl-like thorns.

✿ Earth Song is highly resistant to both blackspot and powdery mildew.
✿ Dr. Buck's roses are also known for their scent, and this one is no exception. For a fragrant bouquet, cut the stems in bud when they're just about to open.

Love

This rose was part of a group of roses introduced in 1980 by Warriner of the U.S. It was released along with Honor (p. 218) and Cherish, and all three won the All-America Rose Selections designation. Some classify Love as a hybrid tea while others consider it a grandiflora. Either way, it is one of the most stunning roses ever developed. The rounded buds open slowly into tightly packed, high-centered, double blooms. The reverse of the petals is bright silvery white and is well displayed when the blooms first begin to unfurl. The brightness eventually disappears as the cupped form takes shape. The thorny stems bear sparse foliage.

Other names: none
Flower color: deep crimson pink with silvery white reverse
Flower size: 3½"
Scent: light and spicy
Height: 3–5'
Spread: 30–36"
Blooms: spring to fall; repeat blooming
Hardiness zones: 5–10

- Love has a stocky form borne from moderately vigorous branches. It tends to spread over time, but not in an aggressive manner. The foliage is moderately resistant to disease but mildly susceptible to blackspot.
- During a rainfall, the weight of the blooms will sometimes cause the stems to bow down to the ground. The flowers are easily spotted by rain.
- Dark pink and silver bicolored roses are rare, but this particular variety is certainly the best of the few. It received the Portland Gold Medal in 1980.
- The elegant stems and long-lasting blooms make Love ideal for cutting.

Queen Elizabeth

Other names:
The Queen Elizabeth Rose,
Queen of England, The
Queen Elizabeth

Flower color:
soft pearly pink

Flower size: 3½–4"

Scent: light tea

Height: 4½–6'

Spread: 30–36"

Blooms: summer to fall;
repeat blooming

Hardiness zones: 6–9

This rose was introduced in 1954, an important year for roses. Queen Elizabeth was so unusual that the grandiflora classification had to be created just to accommodate it. It is one of the most widely grown and best loved roses and has received many honors, including being named an AARS winner in 1955 and World's Favorite Rose in 1979. It bears large, double, high-centered, medium pink flowers singly or in clusters. Each flower consists of 35 to 40 petals in a cupped form. The dark, glossy foliage is highly resistant to disease.

❀ This trouble-free rose is ideal for hedging and at the back of borders and planters. It thrives in the worst conditions. It can endure extreme heat and humidity or a bout with insects with very little assistance.

❀ Prune it back quite hard each spring to rejuvenate it and allow the shrub to become more compact and dense. Then the flowers will bloom at eye level so you can enjoy them. Another option is to remove the older canes to the crown, leaving the younger shoots to flourish. This grandiflora can survive winters in zone 5 with adequate protection.

Long, sturdy stems make it easy to cut and display the infinitely rewarding blooms.

Tournament of Roses

Tournament of Roses is one of those roses that fit into a variety of classifications. It is considered a grandiflora in North America but a hybrid tea elsewhere. The double, high-centered flowers have an excellent continuity of bloom throughout summer into fall. Three to six flowers form a symmetrical cluster. Each flower has 35 to 40 petals, and the petals are varying shades of pink.

✿ This 1989 AARS winner is easy to grow and almost always in bloom.
✿ Tournament of Roses blends easily into mixed beds and borders and is a good variety for hedging and group plantings. It is one of the best grandifloras for display and exhibition. The flower color is particularly spectacular in warm weather.

Other names:
Berkeley, Poesie
Flower color:
medium coral pink
Flower size: 3½–4"
Scent: mild and spicy
Height: 36"
Spread: 30–36"
Blooms: summer to fall; repeat blooming
Hardiness zones: 5–9

The name refers to the annual rose parade held in Pasadena, California. This rose was released to the public for sale on the occasion of the parade's centenary.

MINIATURE

Miniature roses are small, sparsely prickly and usually grown on their own roots. Miniatures were very popular in the early 19th century when the first miniatures, cultivars of *Rosa chinensis* 'Minima,' were produced in abundance. Their popularity waned with the introduction of the polyantha roses. Interest in miniatures was rekindled when Dr. Roulet found a China rose growing in a window box in a Swiss village in the early 20th century. This small rose was called Rouletii. Many miniature varieties were bred from Rouletii.

Most modern miniature roses were developed from the breeding program of Ralph Moore in California. Some newer varieties arise from other than miniature parents. These popular roses look like their bigger relatives—the hybrid teas and floribundas—but they are smaller, usually less than 18" tall. They bear tiny flowers and foliage.

Miniature roses are ideal for edging beds and borders, for raised beds, planters or rock gardens or for use indoors as houseplants. Climbing and trailing miniatures are also available, a result of crossing miniatures with *Rosa wichurana*. Patio roses, another type of miniature rose, are slightly larger than miniatures and resemble floribundas. Another type has been introduced that bears flowers slightly larger than miniatures but smaller than floribundas. They are called mini-flora.

Miniatures bloom best on new growth, so they benefit from a hard spring pruning to force new growth and to keep them petite. They are heavy feeders and thrive with applications of dilute liquid fertilizer every two or three weeks from early May through August.

Glowing Amber

Other names: none
Flower color: scarlet red; yellow reverse
Flower size: 2–2½"
Scent: mild
Height: 1½–2½'
Spread: 1–2'
Bloom period: summer to fall; repeat blooming
Hardiness zones: 5–9

The blossoms are resistant to rain and extreme weather and can tolerate dappled shade. Glowing Amber is highly disease resistant.

I n its short life, Glowing Amber has won a number of awards from around the globe. This is a remarkable feat on the part of George Mander, who developed this miniature beauty in 1996. The classic hybrid tea–formed blossoms are velvety red with a vibrant yellow reverse. The balanced flowers are made up of 26 to 40 petals each, often emerging one flower to a stem. The dark, glossy foliage beautifully complements the brightly colored flowers.

❀ This upright, prolific bloomer has straight stems long enough for cutting. The fiery shades look great in fresh arrangements with a variety of perennials and annuals.

❀ Glowing Amber is easy to grow and has enormous exhibition potential; in fact, it is ranked as one of the top 10 miniature roses for exhibition purposes. It is also ideal as a garden rose for a number of traditional or contemporary settings.

❀ George Mander is one of North America's leading amateur rose hybridizers. Known within rose circles throughout the world, he continues to create new crosses in his home in British Columbia, Canada.

Gourmet Popcorn

Gourmet Popcorn is a sport of Popcorn and has similar characteristics but a few unique traits as well. It bears cascading clusters of rounded, white, semi-double flowers with short stems. Each flower consists of 6 to 14 petals and is borne in large clusters of 30 to 60 flowers. The flowers are complemented by deep green, lush foliage. Gourmet Popcorn vigorously forms into a compact, cushion-like, rounded shrub. It really is more of a small shrub than a miniature rose.

Other names: Summer Snow

Flower color: white

Flower size: ¾"

Scent: mild, honey

Height: 18–24"

Spread: 24"

Blooms: summer to fall; repeat blooming

Hardiness zones: 5–10

❀ This rose is stunning planted en masse or in pots, containers, hanging baskets or any small spaces that need a boost. Gourmet Popcorn emits a distinctive honey scent. Plant this rose where the fragrance can be best enjoyed—alongside pathways, under windows or next to a garden bench.

❀ It is highly resistant to disease and virtually maintenance free. It can withstand winters in zone 4 with adequate protection.

❀ In warmer regions, Gourmet Popcorn can grow up to twice its typical height, creating a stunning specimen bearing hundreds of flowers at a time.

Introduced in the U.S. in 1988 by Luis Desamero, this rose won the RNRS Trial Ground Certificate in 1995.

Green Ice

Other names: none
Flower color: white, hints of chartreuse
Flower size: 1¼"
Scent: slight
Height: 12–18"
Spread: 16–20"
Blooms: mid-season; repeat blooming
Hardiness zones: 5–11

The blooms' color intensity is greatly affected by light levels. The flowers have a deeper green tone in partial shade and fade to white with a hint of green in full sun.

The unique flower color of Green Ice is its most outstanding characteristic. Pinkish buds emerge in spring and open to double, white blooms touched with a hint of pink. The flowers then change to a light chartreuse green as they age. Green Ice is a dwarf, vigorous, low-growing shrub with a spreading form. It can be trained as a tiny climber in the right location. Glossy, dark green foliage is produced on short, lax stems. It bears hundreds of flowers during the first bloom cycle.

✿ Green Ice is ideal for cascading over rock walls and embankments. It is suitable for hanging baskets, edging or borders and blends nicely in larger garden settings. Some people think it resembles an old garden rose, displaying double, pompom-like blooms.

✿ Green Ice is generally disease resistant but requires good air circulation and regular feeding to prevent powdery mildew. It is hardy to zone 4 with sufficient winter protection.

✿ This variety was introduced in 1971 by Ralph Moore of the U.S.

Hot Tamale

Hot Tamale bears extraordinary flowers that transform from one color to another. When they first emerge, the flowers are a striking yellow-orange blend. Over time a vibrant pink slightly obscures the yellow coloring until finally the three colors merge, resulting in an electric glow unlike any other rose color. This rose frequently wins show after show with its exhibition form and unique color. The flower color lasts and lasts against the dark, semi-glossy foliage.

Other names: Sunbird
Flower color: yellow, pink and orange blend
Flower size: 1½–2"
Scent: slight, sweet
Height: 18–22"
Spread: 24–28"
Blooms: summer to fall; repeat blooming
Hardiness zones: 5–11

❧ This tiny rose has a bushy and compact form. The stout canes are covered with dense, healthy foliage and few prickles. It can survive in zone 4 with adequate winter protection.

❧ Hot Tamale is a little flower factory, producing wave after wave of blooms when planted in full sun with routine fertilizing and ample water.

❧ Hot Tamale was bred by Dr. Keith W. Zary of the U.S. in 1993. The year following its introduction it won the ARS Award of Excellence, an honor reserved for the best.

With its bright colors, Hot Tamale is a great choice for containers on porches or patios.

Minnie Pearl

Other names: none
Flower color: light pink with a yellow base
Flower size: 1–1½"
Scent: slight
Height: 14–20"
Spread: 14–20"
Blooms: mid-season; repeat blooming
Hardiness zones: 5–10

This rose can survive winters in zone 4 with adequate protection.

The character of Minnie Pearl on the long-running television program *Hee Haw* was dubbed the 'Queen of Country Comedy,' famous for her trademark 'Howdy!' Sarah Cannon, the actress who played Minnie, spoke of her alter ego and the connection to her fans when she said, 'The price tag on my hat seems to be symbolic of all human frailty. There's old Minnie standing on stage in her best dress, telling everybody how proud she is to be there, and she's forgotten to take the $1.98 price tag off her hat.' A beautiful and lasting tribute to the character, this rose has country appeal, with soft pink tones touched with darker pink hues and a soft yellow base.

✿ The long, elegant buds unfurl evenly from a high center. The flowers, made up of at least 35 petals each and reminiscent of tiny hybrid tea blossoms, are produced among semi-glossy, small foliage in a rounded form.

✿ The flower color tends to darken in hot sun.

✿ Minnie Pearl bears enough flowers to cut for arrangements. The blooms are easily spotted by rain—deadhead consistently so the damaged flowers are readily replaced.

✿ Minnie Pearl vigorously produces exhibition-quality blooms. It is an upright and well-shaped bush suitable for any garden setting. It looks adorable along the front of borders and beds in a country garden setting. It is also effective grouped in containers.

Rise 'n' Shine

Rise 'n' Shine has been a favorite of gardeners for over 25 years, and for good reason. As a yellow rose, this one is hard to beat. It bears uniquely formed quill-like petals, with about 30 or 40 petals per flower. The flowers exhibit hybrid tea form in rosette clusters. Deadheading is a must to encourage a continuous flush of flowers throughout summer.

Other names: Golden Sunblaze

Flower color: brilliant yellow

Flower size: 1½–1¾"

Scent: slight, fruity

Height: 16–20"

Spread: 12–14"

Blooms: summer to fall; repeat blooming

Hardiness zones: 5–10

❀ Though generally resistant to disease, Rise 'n' Shine is a little prone to blackspot and powdery mildew. Plant it in a sunny location with good air circulation. This mini tolerates extreme heat and is great for cutting. It can also be grown successfully in zone 4 with sufficient winter protection.

❀ Rise 'n' Shine is well suited to beds, borders, edgings and container plantings. It is also a popular show variety.

❀ This rose is one of the finest yellow miniatures and outstanding in its color class. It has received honors such as the ARS Award of Excellence in 1978, and it was one of the first inductees to the Miniature Rose Hall of Fame when it was inducted in 1999.

❀ It was hybridized by Ralph S. Moore of the U.S., who is known as the greatest miniature rose breeder to date.

Resources

Gardens To Visit

Cooley Gardens
225 W. Main Street at Townsend
Lansing, MI
517-483-4332
www.cooleygardens.org

Dow Gardens
1809 Eastman Ave. at the corner of
Eastman Ave. and West St. Andrews
Road
Midland, MI
800-362-4874
www.dowgardens.org

Ella W. Sharp Park
3225 Fourth Street
Jackson, MI
517-788-4343

Edsel and Eleanor Ford House
1100 Lake Shore Road
Grosse Pointe Shores, MI
313-884-5977
www.fordhouse.org

Matthaei Botanical Gardens
University of Michigan
1800 North Dixboro Road
Ann Arbor, MI
734-998-7061
www.lsa.umich.edu/mbg

The Gardens at Meadow Brook Hall
Meadow Brook Hall, Oakland
University
Rochester, MI
248-370-3140
www3.oakland.edu

Michigan State University
Horticultural Demonstration Gardens
Wilson Road and Bogue Street
East Lansing, MI
517-353-4800 or 517-355-0348
www.hrt.msu.edu/garden.htm

MSU Tollgate Center
28115 Meadowbrook Rd.
Novi, MI
248-347-3860
www.msue.msu.edu/reg_se/tollgate.html

Frederik Meijer Gardens
1000 East Beltline NE
Grand Rapids, MI
888-957-1580
www.meijergardens.org/generalinfo.htm

Anderson Enrichment Center
Lucille E. Anderson Memorial Garden
120 Ezra Rust Dr.
Saginaw, MI
517-759-1362
http://mentasm.mentasm.com/~mra
miga/aec/about.html

Grand Hotel (checked)
Mackinac Island, MI
906-847-3331
www.grandhotel.com/

Rose Societies and Clubs

American Rose Society (ARS)
To find your local rose society ARS
affiliate, contact:
8877 Jefferson Paige Road
Shreveport, LA 71119
318-938-5402
www.arg.org

Cherry Capitol Rose Society
Traverse City, MI
231-223-7856
email: <kschmid@pentel.net>

Detroit Rose Society
Detroit, MI
586-268-5194
email: <rosered251@coslink.net>
www.personal.umich.edu/~sue/drs/DR
S.htm

Grand Valley Rose Society
Grand Rapids, MI
616-532-6354
email: <harlan_kay@yahoo.com
http://pws.chartermi.net/~hmrankin/>

Greater Lansing Rose Society
PO Box 32011
Lansing, MI 48909-3011
517-484-0021
email: <GLRS2003@yahoo.com>
www.geocities.com/glrs2003/

Grosse Pointe Rose Society
Grosse Point Park, MI
586-778-4832

Huron Valley Rose Society
Ann Arbor, MI
734-996-3892
email: <a2pammie@comcast.net>

Jackson Rose and Garden Society
Marshall, MI
616-781-5336
email: <vannerie@yahoo.com>

Kalamazoo Rose Society
Kalamazoo, MI
616-381-4310

Master Gardener Program
Michigan State University
422 Plant & Soil Sciences Bldg
East Lansing, MI 488224
517-353-3774
http://www.msue.msu.edu/master
gardener/

Metropolitan Rose Society
Grosse Pointe, MI
313-886-5698
email: <twkressbach@aol.com>

Mid-Michigan Rose Society
Piconning, MI
517-879-2173

Northeastern Michigan Rosarians
Linwood, MI
989-697-5377
email: <sunsilk@qix.net>

Roses-West Rose Society
Novi, MI
734-459-4085
email:
<jamessockolosky@ameritech.net>
www.angelfire.com/me4/roses_west

Saginaw Rose and Garden Club
Saginaw, MI
989-754-7274

Thumb Rose Society
Bad Axe, MI
989-269-7154
email: <choltrop144@hotmail.com>

Garden Centers and Suppliers
Bordine Nursery
For information regarding their four
locations in Metro Detroit:
www.bordines.com/contact_us.html

English Gardens
For information regarding their five
locations in Metro Detroit:
www.EnglishGardens.com

Telly's Greenhouse
3301 John R Road
Troy, MI
248-689-8735
www.tellysgreenhouse.perennials.com

Ray Wiegand's Nursery
47625 Romeo Plank Rd.
Macomb Township, MI
586-286-3655
www.wiegandsnursery.com

Great Lakes Roses
49875 Willow Road
Belleville, MI
734-461-1230
www.greatlakesroses.com

Michigan Miniature Roses
45951 Hull Road
Belleville, MI
734-699-6698
www.michiganminiroses.com

Wildtype
900 North Every Road
Mason, MI
517-244-1140
www.wildtypeplants.com

Pine Hill Nursery
Information regarding both locations,
including Pine Hill North and Village
Gardens:
231-599-2824 or 231-941-1808
www.PineHill-Nursery.com

Ludema's Flower & Produce
3408 Eastern Ave. SE
Grand Rapids, MI
616-452-2961

Manitou Gardens
12086 S. West Bay Shore Dr.
Traverse City, MI
231-947-5639

Soil Testing

Michigan State University
Soil and Plant Nutrient Laboratory
A81 Plant and Soil Sciences Building
East Lansing, MI
517-355-0211
www.css.msu.edu/SoilTesting/

To locate your county's MSU
Extension office for over 80 counties,
contact:
517-355-2308
www.msue.msu.edu/msue/ctyentpg/
or
www.msue.msu.edu/msue/ctyentpg/
ctyunits.html

Websites

www.ag.iastate.edu/centers/cad/
    rose1.html
www.davidaustinroses.com
www.everyrose.com
www.fryers-roses.co.uk
www.heirloomroses.com
www.helpmefind.com/Roses
www.JacksonandPerkins.com
www.kedemroses.com
www.pickeringnurseries.com
www.rogersroses.com
www.rosefile.com
www.rosemania.com
www.starroses.com
www.weeksroses.com

Forums

www.gardenweb.com
www.icangarden.com
www.northerngardening.com
www.rosarian.com

Books

Abler, Elizabeth. 2003. *Secrets of the Miniature Rose.* Taylor Trade Publishing, Maryland.

Agriculture and Agri-Food Canada. 2000. *Winter-hardy Roses.* Revised Edition. Agriculture and Agri-Food Canada, Saint-Jean-sur-Richelieu.

Botanica's Roses. 2000. Foreword by William A. Grant. Laurel Glen Publishing, San Diego.

Brown, Deni. 1996. *Eyewitness Garden Handbook: Roses.* DK Publishing, New York.

Browne, Jim et al. 1995. *The American Garden Guides: Rose Gardening.* Pantheon Books, New York.

Cairnes, Tommy. 2002. *Ortho's All About the Easiest Roses to Grow.* Meredith Books, Des Moines.

Druitt, Liz. 1996. *The Organic Rose Garden.* Taylor Publishing Co., Dallas.

Harrap, David. 1993. *Roses for Northern Gardeners.* Lone Pine Publishing, Edmonton.

Hole, Lois and Jill Fallis. 1997. *Lois Hole's Rose Favorites.* Lone Pine Publishing, Edmonton.

Krüssmann, Gerd. 1981. *The Complete Book of Roses.* Timber Press, Portland.

MacOboy, Stirling. 1993. *The Ultimate Rose Book.* Henry N. Abrams Inc., New York.

Martin, Clair G. 1999. *100 Old Roses for the American Garden.* Workman Publishing, New York.

Moody, Mary. 1992. *The Illustrated Encyclopedia of Roses.* Timber Press, Portland.

Olson, Jerry and John Whitman. 1998. *Growing Roses in Cold Climates.* Contemporary Books, Lincolnwood.

Ondra, Nancy J. 2002. *Taylor's Guide to Roses.* Revised Edition. Houghton Mifflin Co., Boston/New York.

Osborne, Robert and Beth Powning. 1995. *Hardy Roses: An Organic Guide to Growing Frost and Disease Resistant Varieties.* Storey Books, North Adams, Massachusetts.

Phillips, Roger and Martyn Rix. 1988. *The Random House Book of Roses.* Random House, New York.

Quest-Ritson, Charles. 2003. *Climbing Roses of the World.* Timber Press, Portland.

Verrier, Suzanne. 1999. *Rosa Gallica.* Firefly Books, New York.

Verrier, Suzanne. 1999. *Rosa Rugosa.* Firefly Books, New York.

Zuzek, Kathy et al. 1995. *Roses for the North.* University of Minnesota, St. Paul.

Glossary

acid soil: soil with a pH lower than 7.0

alkaline soil: soil with a pH higher than 7.0

bud union: the junction on a stem where a bud of one plant has been grafted to the stock of another

button eye (button center): the round center in a double rose blossom, composed of stamens that have turned into petals; these petals are tightly packed and cannot unfold, resulting in a button-like appearance

cane: a woody, often flexible stem, usually arising from the base of the plant

cultivar: a cultivated (bred) plant variety with one or more distinct differences from the parent species; e.g., in flower color or disease resistance

deadhead: to remove spent flowers to maintain a neat appearance and encourage a longer blooming period

desiccation: loss of moisture through foliage

double flower: a flower with an unusually large number of petals, often caused by mutation of the stamens into petals

forma (f.): a naturally occurring variant that retains most of the characteristics of the species but differs naturally in some way, such as plant size or leaf color; below the level of variety in biological classification

genus: category of biological classification between the species and family levels; e.g., the genus *Rosa*

grafting: method of propagating a tree or shrub by joining a bud or cutting of a desired plant with the rootstock of another plant; the tissues grow together and top growth develops in the form of the more desirable plant

hardpan: a layer of compacted subsoil that often prevents the penetration of water or of shrub or tree roots; hardpan can occur naturally or be caused by repeated cultivation by mechanical means

hardy: capable of surviving unfavorable conditions, such as cold weather

hip: the often colorful fruit of a rose, containing the seeds

hybrid: a plant resulting from cross-breeding between varieties, species or genera; the hybrid will not breed true (yield identifical offspring) when crossed with itself

inflorescence: a shoot bearing more than one flower and usually clusters of flowers

lateral (lateral bud): bud produced in the junction between the stem and a leaf

muddled: a flower with petals that are disorganized, not forming a pattern

neutral soil: soil with a pH of 7.0

pH: a measure of acidity or alkalinity (the lower the pH, the higher the acidity); the pH of soil influences availability of nutrients for plants

pesticide: a general term for any compound used to kill insects, mites, weeds, fungi, bacteria or other pests

pith: the spongy central tissue of a stem

quilled: the narrow, tubular shape of petals or florets of some flowers

remontant: able to bloom again one or more times during a growing season

rhizome: a root-like stem that grows horizontally underground and from which shoots and true roots emerge

rootball: the root mass and surrounding soil of a container-grown plant or a plant dug out of the ground

rootstock: the root system and lower portion of a woody plant (the stock) onto which another plant can be grafted; a vertical rhizome

runner: a modified, creeping stem that runs along the ground, forming roots and new shoots at the joints or tip

self-seeding: reproducing by means of seeds without human assistance, so that new plants constantly replace those that die

semi-double flower: a flower with petals in two or three rings

semi-hardy: a plant capable of surviving the climatic conditions of a given region if protected

sepals: leaf-like structures that protect the flower bud and surround the petals in the opened flower

single flower: a flower with a single ring of petals

species: the original plant from which cultivars are derived; the fundamental unit of biological classification, indicated by a two-part scientific name; e.g., *Rosa glauca* (*glauca* is the specific epithet)

sport: an atypical plant or flower that arises through mutation; some sports are horticulturally desirable and propagated as new cultivars

subspecies (subsp.): a naturally occurring, regional form of a species, often isolated from other subspecies but still potentially interfertile with them

sucker: a cane that sprouts from the roots or from below the bud union, therefore originating from the rootstock and different from the grafted plant

tender: incapable of surviving the climatic conditions of a given region; requiring protection from frost or cold

terminal bud: a bud formed at the tip of a stem or branch

variety (var.): a naturally occurring variant of a species; below the level of subspecies in biological classification

Index

A

Abraham. *See* Abraham Darby
Abraham Darby, 130
Alba Meidiland. *See* White Meidiland
Albéric Barbier, 190
Alex Mackenzie. *See* Alexander
    Mackenzie
Alexander Mackenzie, 131
Altissimo, 191
Altus. *See* Altissimo
A. Mackenzie. *See* Alexander
    Mackenzie
America, 192
American Pillar, 193
Apothecary's Rose. See *Rosa gallica
    officinalis*
Apricot Nectar, 232
Apricot Parfait. *See* Evelyn
Aspen, 182
Aunt Honey, 132
Aunt Ruth, 194
Awakening, 195

B

Baby Blanket, 183
Ballerina, 133
Belle Courtisanne. *See* Königin von
    Dänemark
Belle Dijonnaise. *See* Zéphirine
    Drouhin
Berkeley. *See* Tournament of Roses
Berleburg. *See* Cuyahoga
Betty Boop, 233
Betty Prior, 234
Bewitched. *See* Cuyahoga
Bingo Meidiland. *See* Carefree Delight
Bingo Meillandecor. *See* Carefree
    Delight
Bizarre Triomphant. *See* Charles de Mills
Blanc de Coubert. *See* Blanc Double
    de Coubert
Blanc Double de Coubert, 134
Blanc Meillandecor. *See* White
    Meidiland
Blanche Double de Coubert. *See* Blanc
    Double de Coubert

Blanche Pasca. *See* Pascali
Blaze Improved, 196
Blaze Superior. *See* Blaze Improved
Blooming Carpet. *See* Flower Carpet
Blue Rambler. *See* Veilchenblau
Blue Rosalie. *See* Veilchenblau
Blush. *See* Morden Blush
Bonica, 135
    '82. *See* Bonica
    Meidiland. *See* Bonica
Buffalo Gal, 136

C

Cardinal de Richelieu, 106
Cardinal Richelieu. *See* Cardinal de
    Richelieu
Carefree Delight, 137
Carefree Wonder, 138
Carefully Wonder. *See* Carefree
    Wonder
Castle. *See* Cuyahoga
Centenary of Federation. *See* Betty
    Boop
Centennial. *See* Morden Centennial
Champlain, 139
Charles Albanel, 140
Charles Bonnet. *See* Zéphirine
    Drouhin
Charles de Mills, 107
Charles Mills. *See* Charles de Mills
Cheerio. *See* Playboy
Chicago Peace, 212
Chilterns. *See* Red Ribbons
City of York, 197
Clair Matin, 198
Constance Spry, 199
Constanze Spry. *See*
    Constance Spry
Country Darby. *See* Abraham
    Darby
Country Lass. *See* Baby Blanket
Crazy for You. *See* Fourth of July
Crimson Spire. *See* Liebeszauber
Cuthbert Grant, 141
Cuyahoga, 235

D

Dainty Bess, 213
Demokracie. *See* Blaze Improved
Demon. *See* Bonica
Direktör Benschop. *See* City of York
Distant Drums, 142
Dortmund, 200
Double Delight, 214
Double French Rose. See *Rosa gallica officinalis*
Double Tuscany. *See* Tuscany Superb
Double Velvet. *See* Tuscany Superb
Dublin Bay, 201
Duchesse d'Istrie. *See* William Lobb
Dwarf Pavement. *See* Rosa Zwerg
Dwf. Pavement. *See* Rosa Zwerg
Dynastie. *See* Carefree Wonder

E

Earth Song, 250
Easy Going, 236
Eglantine. *See* Eglantyne
Eglantine. See *Rosa eglanteria*
Eglantyne, 143
    Jebb. *See* Eglantyne
Electron, 215
Elena. *See* Elina
Elina, 216
Emera. *See* Flower Carpet
    Pavement. *See* Flower Carpet
Emeura. *See* Flower Carpet
English Yellow. *See* Graham Thomas
Everblooming Dr. W. Van Fleet. *See* New Dawn
Europeana, 237
Evelyn, 144
Evermore. *See* Carefree Delight
Exception. *See* Rotes Meer

F

Fairy. *See* The Fairy
Fantin-Latour, 108
Fée des Neiges. *See* Iceberg
Feerie. *See* The Fairy
Fellowship. *See* Livin' Easy
Fiery Sunsation. *See* Red Ribbons
Fireglow. *See* Morden Fireglow
F.J. Grootendorst, 145
Floral Carpet. *See* Flower Carpet

Flower Carpet, 184
Folklore, 217
Fourth of July, 202
Foxi. *See* Buffalo Gal
    Pavement. *See* Buffalo Gal
Foxy Pavement. *See* Buffalo Gal
Frau Dagmar Hartopp. *See* Fru Dagmar Hastrup
Frau Dagmar Hastrup. *See* Fru Dagmar Hastrup
Fredsrosen. *See* Peace
Fru Dagmar Hastrup, 146

G

Gioia. *See* Peace
Gloria Dei. *See* Peace
Glowing Amber, 256
Gold Magic Carpet. *See* Aspen
Golden Sunblaze. *See* Rise 'n' Shine
Golden Wings, 147
Gourmet Popcorn, 257
Grace Kelly. *See* Princesse de Monaco
Graham Stuart Thomas. *See* Graham Thomas
Graham Thomas, 148
Grandhotel. *See* Dublin Bay
Green Ice, 258
Grimpant Clair Matin. *See* Clair Matin
Grootendorst Red. *See* F.J. Grootendorst
Grootendorst. *See* F.J. Grootendorst
Gul e Rescht. *See* Rose de Rescht
Guy de Maupassant, 238
Gwent. *See* Aspen

H

Hanabi. *See* Fourth of July
Handel, 203
Hannah Gordon. *See* Tabris
Hansa, 149
Hansen's. *See* Hansa
Harisonii. *See* Harison's Yellow
Harison's Yellow, 109
Hawkeye Belle, 150
Hébé's Lip, 110
Heidetraum. *See* Flower Carpet
Hénri Martin, 111
Henry Hudson, 151
Henry Kelsey, 152
Honor, 218

Hope for Humanity, 153
Hot Tamale, 259

I

Iceberg, 239
Imperial Blaze. *See* Blaze Improved
Ingegnoli Prediletta. *See* Zéphirine
    Drouhin
Ingrid Bergman, 219
Island Fire. *See* Red Ribbons

J

Jacques Cartier, 112
Jasper. *See* Cuyahoga
Jeanne Lajoie, 204
Jens Munk, 155
John Cabot, 156
John Davis, 157
John Franklin, 158
J.P. Connell, 154

K

King Tut. *See* Laura Ford
Knock Out, 159
Knockout. *See* Knock Out
Königin von Dänemarck. *See* Königin
    von Dänemark
Königin von Dänemark, 113
Kordes' Perfecta, 220

L

LaRose. *See* Guy de Maupassant
Laura Ford, 205
Lavaglut, 240
Le Bienheureaux de la Salle. *See* Mme.
    Isaac Pereire
Liebeszauber, 221
Livin' Easy, 241
Louise Odier, 114
Lord Byron. *See* Polka
Love, 251

M

Madame Hardy, 115
Magic Meidiland, 185
Magic Meillandecor. *See* Magic
    Meidiland

Mainaufeuer. *See* Red Ribbons
Marchesa Boccella. *See* Jacques Cartier
Margined Hip. *See* Hébé's Lip
Maria Callas. *See* Miss All-American
    Beauty
Marijke Koopman, 222
Marquise Boccella. *See* Jacques Cartier
Marquise Boçella. *See* Jacques Cartier
Martin Frobisher, 160
Memory Lane. *See* Cuyahoga
Michèle Torr. *See* Honor
Michelle Wright. *See* Pensioner's Voice
Minnie Pearl, 260
Miss All-American Beauty, 223
Mister Lincoln, 224
Mme A. Meilland. *See* Peace
Mme. de Stella. *See* Louise Odier
Mme. Gustave Bonnet. *See* Zéphirine
    Drouhin
Mme. Hardy. *See* Madame Hardy
Mme. Isaac Pereire, 116
Molineux, 161
Morden
    Blush, 162
    Centennial, 163
    Fireglow, 164
    Ruby, 165
    Snow Beauty. *See* Morden
        Snowbeauty
    Snowbeauty, 166
    Sunrise, 167
Mullard Jubilee. *See* Electron

N

Nearly Wild, 242
Nelkenrose. *See* F.J. Grootendorst
New Blaze. *See* Blaze Improved
New Dawn, 206
Nicole. *See* Tabris
Normandie. *See* Laura Ford

O

Officinalis. See *Rosa gallica officinalis*
Old Red Moss. *See* Hénri Martin
Old Spanish Rose. *See* Russelliana
Old Velvet Moss. *See* William Lobb
Olympia. *See* Olympiad
Olympiad, 225
Olympiode. *See* Olympiad
Oxfordshire. *See* Baby Blanket

P

Pascali, 226
Peace, 227
Peaudouce. *See* Elina
Penelope, 168
Pensioner's Voice, 243
Perfecta. *See* Kordes' Perfecta
Pink Flower Carpet. *See* Flower
  Carpet
Pioneer Rose. *See* Harison's Yellow
Playboy, 244
Poesie. *See* Tournament of Roses
Polka, 207
  91. *See* Polka
Prairie Joy, 169
Preference. *See* Princesse de Monaco
President Lincoln. *See* Mister Lincoln
Princess of Monaco. *See* Princesse de
  Monaco
Princesse de Monaco, 228
Princesse Grace. *See* Princesse de
  Monaco
Princesse Grace de Monaco. *See*
  Princesse de Monaco
Probuzeni. *See* Awakening
Probuzini. *See* Awakening
Pterancantha. See *Rosa sericea
  pteracantha*
Purple Pavement. *See* Rotes Meer

Q

Queen Elizabeth, 252
Queen of Beauty and Fragrance. *See*
  Souvenir de la Malmaison
Queen of Denmark. *See* Königin von
  Dänemark
Queen of the Violets. *See* Reine des
  Violettes

R

Raspberry Ice. *See* Tabris
Red Moss. *See* Hénri Martin
Red Ribbons, 186
Red Rose of Lancaster. See *Rosa gallica
  officinalis*
Red-leafed Rose. See *Rosa glauca*
Reine Blanche. *See* Hébé's Lip
Reine des Violettes, 117

Reine du Dänemark. *See* Königin von
  Dänemark
Rise 'n' Shine, 261
Rosa
  x *centifolia provincialis*. See *Rosa
    gallica officinalis*
  damascene rubrotincta. See Hébé's
    Lip
  eglanteria, 98
  ferruginea. See *Rosa glauca*
  foetida harisonii. *See* Harison's Yellow
  gallica
    maxima. See *Rosa gallica
      officinalis*
    officinalis, 118
    plena. See *Rosa gallica
      officinalis*
    rosa mundi 'Weston.' See *Rosa
      gallica versicolor*
    'Variegata.' See *Rosa gallica
      versicolor*
    variegata 'Thory.' See *Rosa
      gallica versicolor*
    versicolor, 119
      'Linnaeus.' See *Rosa gallica
        versicolor*
      'Versicolor.' 119 See *Rosa gallica
        versicolor*
  glauca, 99
  x *harisonii*. *See* Harison's Yellow
  x *harisonii* 'Harison's Yellow.' *See*
    Harison's Yellow
  x *harisonii* 'Yellow Rose of Texas.'
    See Harison's Yellow
  lutea hoggii. *See* Harison's Yellow
  officinalis. See *Rosa gallica officinalis*
  omeiensis pteracantha. See *Rosa
    sericea pteracantha*
  omiensis var. *sericea*. See *Rosa
    sericea pteracantha*
  palustris, 100
  provincialis. See *Rosa gallica
    officinalis*
  x *rosa mundi*. See *Rosa gallica
    versicolor*
  rubiginosa. See *Rosa eglanteria*
  rubrifolia. See *Rosa glauca*
  sericea pteracantha, 101
  suavifolia. See *Rosa eglanteria*
  walpoleana. See *Rosa eglanteria*
Rosa Mundi. See *Rosa gallica versicolor*
Rosa Zwerg, 170

Rosamund's Rose. See *Rosa gallica versicolor*
Rosazwerg. *See* Rosa Zwerg
Rose de Rescht, 120
Rose of the World. See *Rosa gallica versicolor*
Rose van Sian. *See* Cardinal de Richelieu
Roselina. *See* Red Ribbons
Rosemary Harkness, 229
Roseraie de l'Haÿ, 171
Rotes Meer, 172
Rotesmeer. *See* Rotes Meer
Rotsmere. *See* Rotes Meer
Rubrotincta. *See* Hébé's Lip
Ruby. *See* Morden Ruby
Russelliana, 208
Russell's Cottage Rose. *See* Russelliana

S

Sally Holmes, 173
Scarlet Grevillei. *See* Russelliana
Scented Dawn. *See* Polka
Schneekoppe, 174
Schneewittchen. *See* Iceberg
Sea Foam, 187
Seafoam. *See* Sea Foam
Shakespeare's Eglantine. See *Rosa eglanteria*
Shakespeare's Rose. See *Rosa eglanteria*
Snow Pavement. *See* Schneekoppe
Snowbeauty. *See* Morden Snowbeauty
Sommermorgen. *See* Baby Blanket
Souv. de la Malmaison. *See* Souvenir de la Malmaison
Souvenir de la Bataille de Marengo. *See* Russelliana
Souvenir de la Malmaison, 121
Stanwell Perpetual, 122
Sublimely Single. *See* Altissimo
Summer Morning. *See* Baby Blanket
Summer Snow. *See* Gourmet Popcorn
Sun Cover. *See* Aspen
Sun Flare, 245
Sunbird. *See* Hot Tamale
Superb Tuscan. *See* Tuscany Superb
Superb Tuscany. *See* Tuscany Superb
Swamp Rose. See *Rosa palustris*
Sweet Briar Rose. See *Rosa eglanteria*
Sweetbriar. See *Rosa eglanteria*

T

Tabris, 246
Teresa Bugnet. *See* Thérèse Bugnet
The Apothecary's Rose of Provins. See *Rosa gallica officinalis*
The Artistic Rose. *See* Dainty Bess
The Fairy, 175
Theresa Bugnet. *See* Thérèse Bugnet
Thérèse Bugnet, 176
Tournament of Roses, 253
Tuscany Superb, 123
Tuscany Supreme. *See* Tuscany Superb
Twilight Glow. *See* Polka

V, W, Z

Veilchenblau, 209
Violet Blue. *See* Veilchenblau
Westerland, 247
White Meidiland, 177
William Baffin, 178
William Lobb, 124
Wingthorn Rose. See *Rosa sericea pteracantha*
Winnipeg Parks, 179
Zéphirine Drouhin, 125